TRANSFORMED BY ADOPTION

THE SPIRITUAL LIFE OF A NORMAL CHRISTIAN

Romans 6:1 – 8:17

David A. Christensen

Thanks to Beth Montgomery who patiently endured, and helped improve, all those manuscript drafts.

Thanks to Tom Hasbrouck who helped me format and edit the final manuscript for publication.

Names have been changed to protect the identities of people and some stories are composite accounts drawn from similar events with various people, places and times.

ISBN – 10: 1497507359
ISBN – 13: 978-1497507357

To my parents, Jack and Edna Christensen, whose legacy of faithful service and passion for the Lord has shaped my life. Thank you, Mom and Dad.

CONTENTS

PROLOGUE
MY STORY

I was nearing the completion of my seminary years when I had one of those "Aha" moments in my spiritual life. I was preparing for an exam in a Greek Exegesis of Romans course making certain that I could parse all the verbs and explain all the syntactical constructions of Romans 6-8. My wife was working her shift as a nurse at the local hospital so I was alone in our mobile home for the evening. My Greek New Testament, class lecture notes, papers and books were spread out all around me in our living room. I was concentrating on memorizing all the exegetical arguments for the various positions scholars had taken over the years regarding the interpretations of the controversial section of Romans 7:14-25. Several hours passed as I committed the arguments to memory and began to focus on Romans 8. It was as if a light bulb turned on in my brain. I saw clearly what the text was telling me about my own spiritual struggles over the years. I stopped studying and began worshiping. I put down my notes and my books and for the next hour or so I prayed, laughed, and sang songs to the Lord. Nobody else was around. It was just me ... and very unlike me! I was, and I suppose still am, very focused on the task at hand. I sought to achieve top grades and rarely lost focus on what I needed to do to earn those grades in seminary. Suddenly it did not matter. Something far more vital was taking place in my spiritual life – a moment that would change my understanding of the Christian life and pastoral ministry. Perhaps for others it would not seem so important but for me, at that time, it was a significant change in thinking. To understand my moment of enlightenment you must hear a bit of my story because this book rises out of that experience.

MY EARLY YEARS IN PAKISTAN

I grew up in Pakistan, the son of missionary parents, Jack and Edna Christensen. I doubt if I have personally known anyone whose passion for God's Word and God's world was stronger than my parents. They set a godly example for me to follow. My mother grew up in northern Maine, where she was raised by a single mom because her father was an alcoholic. She left home in 1949 to travel south by train to Providence Bible Institute in Rhode Island because she felt God's hand on her life. Dad grew up in the farm country of Long Island, New York, the son of immigrant parents from Norway. He too felt God's hand on his life and traveled north to Providence; where they met. Together they followed God's call to seminary in Indiana and on to missionary work in Pakistan. I was three years old and my younger brother was one when the four of us boarded a cargo ship named the S.S. Steel Traveler in New York City and set sail on May 13, 1957, for a month long voyage to Karachi, Pakistan.[1]

When I was 6 years old, I remained behind to attend Murree Christian School in the Himalayan Mountains 7,000 feet above sea level as my parents returned to the Sindh region of Pakistan 600 miles away. Murree Christian School was formed in 1957 as a cooperative venture serving several missions. The school began at Sandes Home, a large sprawling wooden structure that had once been a rest home for British soldiers. The students would travel south by "train party" in December for the winter break, and return, in March to start school again. It was here at MCS that the twin streams of spiritual formation began to shape my life. Legalistic discipline and Keswick teaching would frame my spiritual growth over the years. The legalism of boarding school was mild compared to many mission schools of this era, more of an undercurrent moving in my life. The

---

[1] Edna Christensen, His Hand on Us, self published book.

Higher Life teaching was far more influential during these boarding school years. These two streams of thinking would continue influencing me until my "aha" moment in seminary many years later.

The boarding school was based upon the British educational system, complete with afternoon tea and cookies. The school applied a discipline to my life with a firm hand intended to build character and motivate achievement. I have often said to those who asked what it was like to live in a boarding school that it was the type of environment that either would make you or break you. I think it made me into a person of strong will and character, and moved me to be very achievement focused in life. Studies have demonstrated that students who grew up in the British boarding school culture often became high achievers. My first year in boarding school, I had a housemother who was a rigid disciplinarian. She believed that it was her job to instill toughness in her little 6-year-old charges, and she did not spare the rod for fear of spoiling the child. If she caught us crying for any reason she administered a spanking to drive out the crying. We slept in an open ward with half a dozen bunk beds, and she would make her rounds checking on us. I remember often crying myself to sleep under my pillow so that she would not hear me and spank me. I learned very early not to show weakness and to exercise will power to control life in order to succeed in school.

America in the 1960s was a foreign country to me. I enjoyed glimpses of it at best. Our school would travel down from the mountains to a community called Mangla Dam. Mangla Dam was an American construction site with a secure community for its employees. It was a "little America" in an Islamic world. Our high school basketball team played them and the trip was an all school event. We marveled at what we saw inside "little America." There were movie theaters, swimming pools, air conditioned bowling alleys and suburban American houses. We could watch television in the bowling alley, buy soft drinks and eat hot dogs. This was not our world. My heroes growing up were not the superheroes of television or movies. My heroes were not the sports stars and famous singers of American culture. I knew nothing of that world because we did not have access to television or radio. My world was a world where we went hiking in the mountains and camping on the Indus River. My world was a Christian cocoon set within a world antagonistic to Christianity. My heroes were the Pakistani Christians who suffered much for their faith, and the missionaries who brought the message to them. I was an avid reader and the school library was well stocked with missionary biographies. When I wasn't reading the "Hardy Boys" I was reading the stories of Hudson Taylor, William Carey and Adoniram Judson. These giants of the faith were my childhood heroes.

The Higher Life Movement of the early 20th century spawned a powerful drive for missions around the world. Many of the missionaries in Pakistan had learned their faith through the Bible Schools and Bible Conferences that spread rapidly across both England and America. These Bible Schools and Conferences were noted for Keswick teaching, so named for the little town in England where the Higher Life Movement began. The emphasis was on absolute surrender and total consecration to God so that the Holy Spirit would fill our lives and empower us to reach the world for Christ. This spiritual dynamic produced a powerful movement for God in the 20th century, and from it came many of the hymns we still sing and books we still read in established churches today. The expectation that Christians could live on a higher plane of spiritual life pervaded the movement and produced some of the most effective missionaries in history. This was no morbid, dour faith, but an exhilarating, joyous spirit. I never knew my parents, or any of the other missionaries, to ever express any regret at the sacrifices they made to serve in Pakistan – and those sacrifices were real, as were the tears they must have experienced but did not show.

The boarding school closed down in the winter because of heavy snow in the Himalayas, and in the summer our parents would come up to the hill country to get away from the heat. We would live at home and commute to school during the summer months. Those were wonderful days of childhood happiness. Our mission families lived in Alpine Lodge, a large wooden building with 8 apartments, along with another nearby building housing 4 apartments, so we children never lacked for friends. The mothers with the children stayed out of the intense desert heat all summer, but the fathers would travel back to the Sindh Desert for ministry, returning for periods of rest in the hill country. On Sunday evenings we would gather on the large upper porch of Alpine Lodge for a "singspiration," and oh how the missionaries could sing! Every day at supper time the family next door would sing a hymn before eating and sometimes we would join them in song since the walls were paper thin. The hymns of Fanny Crosby, Philip Bliss and Frances Havergal filled my childhood with visions of emptying my life of self and being filled for God's service. Everyone would laugh together as one of the missionaries would tell stories of her pet flea named "Herman" doing somersaults and "loop de loops" until he landed in someone's hair only to discover it was not her "Herman." We knew the punch line and still laughed because she could tell it with such delightful expressions. These were hardly dour faced Christians doing their duty. They were people living on a higher plane of spiritual experience, seen from my childhood perspective.[2]

MY TEEN YEARS IN AMERICA

I loved life in Pakistan. I hated life in America. The only time I ever saw my parents openly shed tears of regret was when the doctor told them they could not return to Pakistan. My mother had become very ill during our last year in Pakistan, and she came home to recover her health. As we neared our time to return, with everything packed and ready to go, she had a relapse. The doctors said she could not return and the sense of loss was palpable. We all knew it. It was like we had died to the life God had called us to, and a time of mourning took place for them and for me. I did not want to

---

[2] To read a wonderful account of these years see Pauline Brown, Jars of Clay: Ordinary Christians on an extraordinary mission in southern Pakistan, Doorlight Publications, 2006.

stay in America. I did not fit in with the other teens, even the Christian teens. I felt like a misfit - out of place and alone in a world I didn't understand.

The fundamentalist churches in America were steeped in legalism as they fought back against the encroaching world around them. This was America in the late 1960s, recovering from a decade of social revolution, and the Christians were fighting back with rules to protect against worldliness. My father took a pastorate in Maine and I remember those days for the rules I had to live by to look spiritual to the congregation he served. This is not to deny that there were many godly people in church. There were many Christians who richly blessed my life and the church grew and prospered but, for me, legalism shaped my life as I tried to be the good Christian that I thought I ought to be. I imposed the discipline of mandatory morning and evening devotions on myself. If I missed either morning or evening devotions I felt that God would not bless my day. I was not a good Christian.

Long hair for me was out in a day when long hair on men was in. I could not watch television on Sunday, but I could listen to football games on the radio in my room. I became a New York Giants fan because they had a good radio network in Maine, and Fran Tarkenton, their Hall of Fame quarterback, became my hero. I was not allowed to play baseball or football in our backyard on Sunday, out of concern that church members might see me and consider us worldly. Going to the movies, playing cards and certainly dancing were out of the question in those days. Good Christian young people, especially pastor's kids, did not participate in such worldly activities. My dad was not a legalist by nature. He was simply accommodating our family life to the expectations of the church. When we were away at our log cabin on East Grand Lake he would gladly throw a baseball or football with me on Sunday but not at home where someone might see us. At camp we swam, and took the boat out on Sunday with no problem but not around church people. We had to live by the expectations of others. I developed a performance mentality for my Christian life during these years. I

6

must look right and act right if I wanted to be considered holy. Holiness had a look.

The Higher Life Movement remained a strong undercurrent to the legalism that governed my spiritual life. Speakers at youth rallies and snow camps regularly challenged us to totally surrender our lives to Christ. We were called to "let go and let God" so that we might live a victorious Christian life. Stop striving and start resting in Him. If we failed it was because of a lack of faith in the power of the Holy Spirit to counteract our sin nature. As a result, I was constantly dedicating and re-dedicating my life to Christ during those years. Our church youth group spent a week at the very remote Allagash Bible Camp in far northern Maine. It was always a highlight of the summer, especially when a skunk took up residence under our cabin and we didn't have to pass cabin inspection the rest of the week! I can remember one year consecrating my life once again, along with two of my best friends. We were determined to change the world for Christ but they both soon went back to their wayward ways, and I was holy on the outside while struggling on the inside.

MY COLLEGE YEARS

I enrolled at Philadelphia College of Bible in center city Philadelphia. PCB gave me an excellent Bible education, for which I am grateful, but the same two streams of spiritual thinking continued to shape my life. Legalism was strong. Rules and regulations governed our spiritual lives even as we sometimes chafed under those rules. Hair must be off the ears and off the collar. Many of us grew our hair as long as we could and would push it behind our ears while on campus, pulling it back out when we left the college. One year I arrived for the start of the semester with my hair pushed behind my ears. The staff member registering me took one look and told me I couldn't have my room key until I cut my hair. I went to a bathroom with my luggage, took out a pair of paper scissors, and hacked off my hair. We had to sign a code of conduct that governed not only life on campus but life off campus even on our breaks. We could not play cards or go to the movies even when away from school We could play cards if it was a "Rook" deck so "Rook" became our favorite game and we could play any card game we wanted with a "Rook" deck. Movies were not allowed, and I had to get special permission from the Dean of Students to be a counselor at a Billy Graham movie because it was held in a movie theater. We had to fill out our Christian service forms each semester and we had to verify that we had witnessed to 15 people. I can remember finding drunks on the street to whom I could witness during the final week of the semester, just to get my quota. I always felt like a hypocrite doing it, but it had to be done or I couldn't fill my quota.

PCB, like most Bible Schools, had strong historical ties to the Higher Life Movement. Charles G. Trumbull initiated an American Keswick conference in Keswick, New Jersey in 1923. Trumbull was a personal disciple of C. I. Scofield, one of the founding fathers of Philadelphia College of Bible. Trumbull called himself "Timothy" to Scofield as his "Paul." Trumbull's close associate, Robert McQuilkin, founded Columbia Bible School.[3] Keswick teachers spoke often in our chapels challenging us to empty ourselves of fleshly motives to serve Christ in the fullness of the Spirit. Higher Life teachers often dismissed critics of the movement as people who just wanted to justify a shallow, worldly faith. This reinforced the notion that the higher life was the better life – a sort of pride masquerading as humility. I also learned through these teachers that I could do the right things and perform well in my Christian service, but I might be doing all those good things in the flesh. This led to deep introspection to examine my motives so that whatever I did was in the Spirit and not in the flesh, even if it was good. Guilt was always there even if I did well, because I might have done well in the flesh. We were often warned that the flesh is so subtle that we might not see our fleshly motives until it was too late.

---

[3] George M. Marsden, Fundamentalism and American Culture: The Shaping of Twentieth-Century Evangelicalism, 1870-1925, Oxford University Press, 1980, p. 96.

I lived a life of spiritual duty punctuated by moments of spiritual high. I traveled for a year with a singing group called "The Crusader Men." There were five men in the group (including me), and they all participated in my wedding the following year. I was not a gifted singer but I could preach, so I was one of the two men designated to preach. We toured several states for 8 weeks that summer, giving concerts almost every night in churches and Bible conference centers. The two of us took turns preaching. I began to notice that the results were much better when he preached than when I preached, and this bothered me. I prided myself on being a good preacher even if I wasn't the best singer and I became jealous of his success. Night after night he would preach and people would respond to the invitation. Night after night I would preach and nobody raised their hands. We arrived early one afternoon to set up for a concert. I was in a foul mood about it all and left the church for a walk while they set up the equipment. It was very hot that afternoon and I finally found a small shade tree in the middle of a field. I sat down to sulk like Jonah! I wrestled with God about the lack of results and my attitude eventually surrendering my will once again to Him. I went back in and told the other men that I was preaching that night, and preach I did. When I gave the invitation hands shot up all over the congregation in that rural church. I looked around and my fellow teammates all had their hands up too! They knew my struggle and knew that I had resolved it with God. It was a spiritual high for me but I soon felt guilty all over again. Did I do it in the flesh? How could you tell if it was the Spirit or the Flesh? The only way I could tell was to assume that the results validated my spirituality, sadly leading to an even greater performance mentality.

MY SEMINARY YEARS

The twin streams of legalism and higher life merged into one river of performance Christianity. By now I knew that legalism never produced holiness in anyone. Artificial markers of worldliness made little sense. Christians disagreed over many of these artificial standards and I knew godly people on both sides of many of the markers that had defined my background. I didn't have to subscribe to such codes for my spiritual life. Whether I did or did not do certain activities those practices could not make me holy or unholy. I also knew that the Higher Life emphases were flawed. I had studied enough history to know that my childhood heroes of holiness were giants with clay feet. They too struggled with sin and failure just like me. The vestiges of the Higher Life Movement were all around me in seminary. The Winona Lake Conference had been at the forefront of the movement for many years. I worked in the maintenance crew for the conference grounds one summer and knew the history. We graduated from seminary in the Billy Sunday Tabernacle, where many a speaker had called people to victorious living in years past. The crowds that once thronged the grounds of Winona Lake had dwindled to small gatherings of Christians meeting for the purpose of encouragement and instruction.

All that remained of those streams of spiritual life was a common river of performance. I was focused on achievement. I needed to do well – to perform well – because this validated my spiritual life. And I did well. I achieved top grades, winning awards for excellence. These affirmed my spiritual life for me. I was determined to control sin through how I lived, not by legalism but by willing myself to holiness. I was determined to be obedient, to work hard and to succeed as a Christian through my own efforts at living right. Outwardly, I certainly achieved my goal. I was a successful Christian. Inwardly, I was often frustrated at my inability to control my sinful tendencies. I did not experience God's grace as much as I felt a sense of duty and obligation to serve God's calling. I had arrived at an uneasy state of spiritual life until that day in Merrywood Trailer Park, studying for my Greek exam on Romans 6-8.

SUMMARY

I realized that Romans 7 was a normal but frustrating part of the Christian life. Whenever a Christian tries to be holy by will power he will end up in frustration, yet we often fall into that very trap. I was trying to "will" myself to holiness through my performance in life and, as a result, I was not experiencing God's grace. Paul was explaining what happens to all of us in our normal Christian lives any time we try to be holy by our performance and not by His grace. Willing ourselves to holiness never works to control sin. Yet we often try anyway, as he did in his life.

Romans 7 is not a stage we grow out of as Christians but a description of our lives whenever we stop depending on the power of the Spirit to control the flesh. Romans 8 is not a new stage of the Christian life that we can attain by an act of absolute surrender. The greatest giants of the faith lived in both Romans 7 and Romans 8 throughout their lives. We do not arrive at a victorious life – a higher life in the Spirit – and leave Romans 7 and the frustrations of our struggle with sin behind. Romans 8 is a description of the same battle within but from a different perspective. These two chapters are two perspectives on our spiritual lives. It is like standing on a mountain and looking one direction and seeing the darkness and looking the other direction and seeing the dawn. Romans 7 is the dark side of the mountain, and Romans 8 is the dawn side.

The Father has adopted me into His family. He wanted me. He chose me. I belong to Him. The Father does not condemn me even when I fail (8:1). He has given me the spirit of adoption (8:15) so I can cry out to Him in my frustrations (7:24) and He will rescue me. I do not have to perform to be approved. I do not have to achieve to be accepted. He loves me even when I disappoint Him and He will not disown me even when I fail Him.

I am gradually being transformed as I learn my Father's values and learn to walk in His Spirit's ways. I can learn to walk in the habits of the Spirit and not the habits of the flesh. His power can help me control the flesh as I choose to follow Him daily in learning new habits of holiness and killing the old habits of sinfulness. As I do this I will progressively grow in grace. The normal Christian life is a progressive process of growth by the power of the Spirit whereby I participate in gradually transforming the habits of the flesh to the habits of the Spirit until I reach heaven. This truth is both liberating and challenging at the same time. It is liberating to realize that I don't have to live by my performance. I no longer have to be perfect to be approved. It is challenging to realize that I must choose to walk daily in the Spirit. My choices in life are essential to my growth in holiness as I learn to live in His family.

SECTION ONE:

Thinking Straight About Who We Are

1
GETTING OUR DUCKS IN A ROW

Pornography – It is Joe's Achilles heel. Joe is a Christian husband and father. He came to Christ as a child and has grown up in the church. He is well respected and active in his church, serving on several boards and committees as well as helping in the men's ministry. But Joe struggles with pornography – not all the time, of course. He may go months, even a year between episodes. Yet he falls back into the sin and goes through the guilt and shame all over again. Joe knows that God is holy and calls him to live a holy life. He wants to live up to His calling in Christ. What should Joe do? How does he achieve holiness anyway?

Option #1: Joe can accept the fact that he will never be holy this side of heaven. He is saved by God's grace. The blood of Christ covers his sins and he is forgiven even for the sins he will commit in the future. God's grace has made him perfect. He just needs to claim that grace by faith and be freed from his guilt. The sin is dealt with and he can move on with his spiritual life. Christians sin. God forgives. Sin is normal and grace is the answer. He needs to fall back on God's grace whenever he falls away from God's grace. Holiness is an ideal beyond our reach. Everybody sins. Sin is no big deal.

Option #2: Joe can determine to lead a more disciplined life. He will set up rules to govern his life so that he avoids the problem situations and controls the sinful propensities of his body. If he spends an hour every day in prayer and Bible study God will help him avoid the sin. He will set up rules that will help him with his self-discipline. He will not allow himself to be on the computer at home by himself. He must attend church every week and participate in their community group religiously. He can live a holy life if he simply tries harder and is more disciplined. His performance determines his holiness. Joe is frustrated but even more determined. If he works harder he can be the person God wants him to be.

Option #3: Joe needs to consecrate his life to God. He has trusted Christ as His Savior but He has not surrendered his life to Christ as Lord. He needs to go through a crisis experience whereby he comes to consecrate himself fully to the Lord. He must seek a special empowerment from the Holy Spirit to live a deeper, more holy life. As his conversion experience brought him to Christ, this consecration experience will set him on a higher level in Christ if he has enough faith. By faith in the power of the Holy Spirit to change him forever he can live a life free from any known sin. If Joe just had more faith he could live a holy life. The reason he is not holy is that he has not absolutely surrendered himself to God.

Option #4: Joe needs to remember that the Holy Spirit energized his life at conversion and he already has the power to turn away from sin because of the Holy Spirit working in him. God has given him everything he needs to live a holy life and he needs to learn to appropriate that power in his daily experience. He will never be perfect short of heaven but he can live progressively more holy as he lives consistently in the power of the Holy Spirit. He needs to develop this power through his daily practice in life, just as an athlete exercises the muscles God gave him. His holiness is not dependent on the power of his will but on the power of the Holy Spirit in his daily life. Joe will not lower the bar of expectations nor make excuses for his failures but he will see change in his life by God's power at work in him. The victorious Christian life is not a once for all event but a life-long process of growth.[1]

Joe wants to live a normal Christian life. Not average! Joe knows what average is. He sees average in himself and many others in the church. Joe wants a normal Christian life. He isn't aspiring to be a spiritual giant like the Apostle Paul but he doesn't want to be a spiritual pygmy either. So …

WHAT IS A NORMAL CHRISTIAN LIFE?

Normal is not average. Suppose I am teaching a class with 10 students. They take a test and I average the test. The average score is 50. Some scored 20 and some scored 80 but the average is flunking. This is the average but it is not the norm. If the average was 100 it would not be the norm either.   The norm is the score that corresponds to whatever was established as the standard for passing the class. Normal is whatever corresponds to a standard or pattern. Normal is what demonstrates a rule or norm. Normal is normative. Normal is a passing grade so that the student gets credit for the class. What is normative for the Christian life? God sets the standard and a normative Christian corresponds to that standard. Jesus said, "You are to be perfect, as your heavenly father is perfect" (Mt. 5:48). Is this the norm? No. Perfection is like everybody getting 100 on the test. God knows we will not achieve perfection and tells us we won't in Scripture (Romans 3:10-11). No one is perfect. No one scores 100. It is impossible. God grants forgiveness by His grace because no one is righteous. I know that is true for conversion but it is just as true for my sanctification. Perfection is not the norm for the Christian life because we will never achieve it this side of heaven. Perfectionism will rob a Christian of any joy in life by setting the norm so high that

---

[1] For an explanation of the various views of sanctification see: <u>Christian Spirituality: Five Views of Sanctification</u>, edited by Donald Alexander, InterVarsity Press, 1988; and <u>Five Views on Sanctification</u> edited by Stanley Gundry, Zondervan, 1987.

he will always be frustrated. Even in our Christian lives we must regularly confess our sins and seek His forgiveness and cleansing whenever we fall short of perfection (1 John 1:9). So what are the norms that God calls Christians to live? What is a passing grade for our spiritual lives? How do we know when we are being spiritually successful?

God sets high standards for us. We see several descriptions in the New Testament regarding the characteristics a Christian should exhibit. At the very least these should form the goals for a normal Christian life. Paul writes in Ephesians that we should "walk no longer just as the Gentiles walk, in the futility of their mind" (Eph. 4:17). Instead, Paul says, if we have been taught the truth in Christ we should "lay aside the old self, which is being corrupted in accordance with the lusts of deceit, and … put on the new self, which in the likeness of God has been created in righteousness and holiness of truth." He goes on to charge us not to lie or let our anger control us and we are not to let "any unwholesome word" come out of our mouths. We are to avoid bitterness and anger, slander and malice and we are to be kind, tender and forgiving (Eph. 4:24-32). This process of putting off and putting on surely describes the normal Christian life. Paul expresses similar descriptions in Galatians 5, where we are exhorted to "walk in the Spirit" so we "will not carry out the desire of the flesh" (Gal. 5:16). Paul sets the Spirit and the flesh in opposition to one another, and states that the works of the flesh are not to characterize the Christian. The works of the flesh include "immorality, impurity, sensuality, idolatry, sorcery, enmities, strife, jealousy, outbursts of anger, disputes, dissensions, factions, envying, drunkenness, carousing and things like these" (Gal. 5:19-21). Obviously, these works are not what the normal Christian life is all about. Instead we should exhibit the fruit of the Spirit which is "love, joy, peace, patience, kindness, goodness, faithfulness, gentleness, self control," because all those in Jesus have "crucified the flesh with its passions and desires" (Gal. 5:22-24). Paul strikes these same chords in Romans 6-8, the subject of this book.

Normal corresponds to reality. Normal cannot be perfection or else there would be no normal Christians. The reality of the Christian life is that we are constantly at war, striving for holiness while battling with the flesh. It is a "Holy War." The normal Christian strives to reach the goals God has established, while wrestling with his disposition toward sin. This "Holy War" continues until the "upward call of God in Christ Jesus" (Phil. 3:14), which Paul confesses is the conclusion to a life-long struggle. "Not that I have already obtained it or have already become perfect, but I press on so that I may lay hold of that for which also I was laid hold of by Christ Jesus" (Phil.3:12). Paul graphically describes this battle in Romans 7:23. "I see a different law in the members of my body, waging war against the law of my mind, and making me a prisoner of the law of sin which is in my members." (cf. Rom. 7:8,11) Peter writes, "Beloved, I urge you as aliens and strangers to abstain from fleshly lusts which wage war against the soul" (1 Peter 2:11). Normal Christianity is not a battle between two natures, the old nature and the new nature. It is a life-long holy war between the flesh and the Spirit inside the new person in Christ. The Holy Spirit gives us the power to wage this holy war with the flesh (Rom. 8:9-11). We make progress in this war only by His power operating in our lives.

Susan is an active member of her local church. She teaches Sunday School and attends a weekly Bible Study for young mothers. She and her husband are involved regularly with a small group that meets on Thursday nights. But Susan has always struggled with a sharp tongue and a critical spirit. She loses her temper and takes it out on her husband and children. Her tongue can be nasty and she knows it. It has caused problems in her marriage and she was convicted by a sermon the pastor preached some time ago on the tongue. She decided that she needed to change, so she arranged with a close friend to hold her accountable. She began to pray each morning that God would help her control her tongue. As she became aware of the problem she began to catch herself in the act. She would send up a quick arrow prayer for God to help her. Lately her husband has commented that she seems different, much gentler and less caustic. The side benefit is that their relationship is better. Oh, she still slips back into the old habit from time to time, but she is definitely getting better and enjoying the new Susan. At least she is making progress.

Progress, not perfection, is the mark of a normal Christian life. As we study God's Word, pray and seek God's help in our daily lives we grow more like Christ. This is the normal process of the Christian life. Growing holy is a daily process, not a once-for-all experience. Movement is the key to the normal Christian life. Paul wrote in 2 Corinthians 3:18, "We all, with unveiled face, beholding as in a mirror the glory of the Lord, are being transformed into the same image from glory to glory, just as from the Lord, the Spirit." Sanctification is a progressive transformation whereby we are being made like Christ that will only be completed in glory. God has given us many resources to use, but we are being transformed on an ongoing basis as we seek Him. The normal Christian life is progressive growth process.

Romans chapters 6-8 teach this progression. Paul teaches us in Romans 6 to think straight about our personal holiness. If we are not thinking straight about holiness, we will not make progress in our spiritual lives. Thinking straight is necessary to living right. The first step in the process is thinking straight about holiness, sin and grace. Paul teaches us in Romans 7 about the frustrations of willing ourselves to holiness. Willpower alone won't make holiness happen. It doesn't take us long to learn this truth. New Year's resolutions accomplish little in our spiritual lives. The selective nature of legalism leads to a selective righteousness as we pick and choose our characteristics from the smorgasbord of holiness. The end result of willing ourselves to holiness is always frustration and defeat. The solution is found in Romans 8. Here is the pinnacle of Paul's progression. Living by the Spirit is the only way to make progress in our spiritual lives. Living by the Spirit is a daily process of trusting God's power for victory. We will fail sometimes but we will make progress too and, in our failure, we fall back on our security in Christ's love and grace.

WHAT IS ADOPTION?

Paul culminates his section on the Christian life by explaining the importance of our adoption in Christ (Romans 8:15-17). Adoption was a legal act in Roman law, whereby a child or even a slave was chosen to be a legal son with all the legal rights of sonship. Paul is the only writer in the New Testament to use this metaphor to describe the Christian life. He refers to adoption five times (Romans 8:15, 23; 9:4; Ephesians 1:5; Galatians 4:5) in the epistles. Francis Lyall writes: "The metaphor points to the selection of believers as sons: their justification is the entry into sonship, and from the point of conversion on they are members of God's family, under His guidance and authority (in legal terms, under his "potestas"), irrespective of how they actually live."[2]

We have been adopted into God's family and we must learn the ways and values of our spiritual father as His adopted children. We are no longer slaves but sons (Galatians 4:5-7) and as sons we are being transformed into the image of our Father. Our failures do not revoke our sonship returning us to the spirit of slavery that leads to fear (Romans 8:15). We can run into the arms of our Father, where we find security in His love. The Spirit of God testifies with our spirits that we are His children even when we fail (Romans 8:16). We are being transformed by our adoption to become the sons God chose us to be in Christ.

WHAT IS HOLINESS?

Peter writes in 1 Peter 1:14-16: "As obedient children, do not be conformed to the former lusts which were yours in your ignorance, but like the Holy One who called you, be holy yourselves also in all your behavior; because it is written, 'You shall be holy, for

---

[2] Francis Lyall, <u>Slaves, Citizens, Sons: Legal Metaphors in the Epistles</u>, Academie Books, Zondervan Publishing House, 1984, p.68).

I am holy.'" He is quoting from Leviticus 11:44 (cf. Lev. 19:2, 20:7, 20:26, 21:8). There are three Hebrew terms used in the Old Testament for holiness. All three terms focus on separation. The emphasis in biblical holiness is first on separation from the profane to the pure. Israel was holy because she was set apart from the world to be God's possession. Holy things and holy people are set apart for God. However, this separation is not merely positional. It is ethical and moral in nature. If people are set apart for God then their behavior should correspond with God's will. There is a strong moral component to all holiness in the Old Testament. The same is true in the New Testament. Saints (holy ones) are set apart for God. The result of this separation leads to moral behavior. The word for "sanctification" is derived from the word for "holy" and is often connected directly with moral living. For example, sanctification is the will of God for all believers and is demonstrated in our abstention from sexual immorality among other sins (1 Thess. 4:3; cf. Rom. 6:19, 22).[3]

A good definition of sanctification is found in the Westminster Catechism. Sanctification is "the work of God's free grace, whereby we are renewed in the whole man after the image of God, and are enabled more and more to die unto sin and live unto righteousness." Salvation is always a work of God's grace, for we do not deserve salvation as sinners. We accept the doctrine of supernatural grace when it comes to conversion but often neglect the doctrine of supernatural grace when it comes to sanctification. We cannot be holy apart from God's grace any more than we can be regenerated apart from God's grace. Both are supernatural works of God in the human heart. Yet sanctification, unlike regeneration, is best described as an enabling process whereby God stimulates and energizes us to die to sin and live to righteousness. God not only

---

[3]For an excellent analysis of the biblical terms see, George Zemek, A Biblical Theology of the Doctrines of Sovereign Grace: Exegetical Considerations of Key Anthropological, Hamartiological and Soteriological Terms and Motifs, B.T.D.S.G. 1615 Dorado Beach Drive, Little Rock, AR 72212-2685, 2002, pp. 203-211).

gives us life spiritually but He also enables us to live that life once we are alive. Charles Hodge said it well when he wrote that "the cooperation of second causes is not excluded" from the supernatural work of God in sanctification. "Men work out their own salvation, while it is God who worketh in them to will and to do, according to his own good pleasure. ... As however, the effects produced transcend the efficiency of our fallen nature, and are due to the agency of the Spirit, sanctification does not cease to be supernatural, or a work of grace, because the soul is active and cooperating in the process."[4]

Sanctification is the business of a pastor. Spiritual leaders equip believers "until all attain ... to a mature man, to the measure of the stature which belongs to the fullness of Christ" (Ephesians 4:13). The job of a pastor is not to grow the church numerically or run the church administratively. There is nothing wrong with these tasks but these tasks should not be the focus of pastoral ministry. The job of a pastor is to help people toward holiness and helping people toward holiness means dealing with sin.

WHAT IS SIN?

Our human tendency is to define sin selectively but this will not do if we are going to understand God's call to holiness. Defining sin properly is critical to practicing holiness effectively. Charles Hodge writes "that sin consists essentially in the want of conformity

---

[4] Charles Hodge, Systematic Theology, Volume Three, Wm. B. Eerdmans Publishing Company, reprinted 1975, p.215. Monergism (God alone works) and synergism (God and man cooperate in the work) is not an either/or doctrine when it comes to progressive sanctification. Complete monergism is fatalism since the human is merely a passive pawn in the process. This is not consistent with the many commands and exhortations to put off sin and put on the qualities of holiness. Extreme synergism turns God into a personal aide for us to use at our beck and call. Biblical sanctification teaches us that God initiates and energizes us to act but we are called to obey and put into practice the will of God for our lives.

on the part of a rational creature, to the nature or law of God."[5] I will use this definition as the working definition for the study of Romans 6-8. It should be painfully obvious from this definition that we can never achieve perfection or total freedom from sin if sin is any lack of conformity to the very nature of God. We will always be a work in progress during our lifetimes. The irony is that the closer we walk with God, the more we see sin in our lives. The law reveals the obvious sin in our lives but the more we learn of God the more aware we become of how far we are from the nature of God. His character reveals our flaws and seeing our flaws drives us to God's grace.

WHAT IS GRACE?

Grace is God's favorable disposition toward us that results in favorable actions we receive in spite of the fact that we do not deserve the favor. Grace is related to a grand word in the Old Testament transliterated "Chesed," which means loyal love, lovingkindness and mercy. In the New Testament it is related to the mercy and compassion of God. All of salvation is dependent on God's grace. Grace is the free, unmerited favor that God shows to us in Jesus Christ and that we enjoy by faith (Eph. 2:8-10).[6] Paul has been developing his argument that salvation is based on the grace of God in Romans 4-5. Paul calls this grace a "free gift" (Romans 5:15) which results in justification. Those who receive this free gift enjoy the "gift of righteousness" (5:17). The Law of God increases our sinfulness (5:20) as we realize how far we fall short of His perfection but grace is sufficient to cover all sinfulness. Paul concludes with the famous statement, "Where sin increased, grace abounded all the more" (5:20).

---

[5] Charles Hodge, Systematic Theology, Volume Two, Wm. B. Eerdmans Publishing Company, reprinted 1975, p. 181.
[6] For an excellent summary of the Hebrew and Greek terms see, George Zemek, A Biblical Theology of the Doctrines of Sovereign Grace, pp. 112-118.

God's grace is sufficient for all our sins. Our conversion is solely by God's grace but Paul does not stop there. Beginning in Romans 6 Paul will say that our sanctification is also by God's grace. The operative power in the Christian is still an act of grace – favor from God that we do not deserve. Our Christian lives can only be lived by grace. John Piper writes in his book, *Future Grace*: "By future I do not merely mean the grace of heaven and the age to come. I mean the grace that begins now, this very second, and sustains your life to the end of this paragraph. By grace I do not merely mean the pardon of God in passing over your sins, but also the power and beauty of God to keep you from sinning."[7]

Ben talked a good talk. He could quote Scripture well and was very passionate about his faith. Most people were impressed with Ben but they did not know the Ben at home. Ben and his wife were both on their second marriage and her son lived with them. Ben despised her son and was very controlling and dictatorial with his wife. The son was a constant irritation to him since his wife often defended her son. Finally, Ben divorced his wife to live with another woman. Ben greeted me cautiously one day at the mall. He wanted me to know that he was getting married and that they were doing well. He had found a church that accepted him. I looked Ben in the eye and commented that his behavior was sinful. Ben responded quickly. "I know it is sin but God will forgive me."

Really?!

---

[7] John Piper, <u>Future Grace: The Purifying Power of the Promises of God,</u> Revised edition, Multnomah Books, 2012, p. 5.

2
GRACE ABUSE

Romans 6:1-4

1 What shall we say then? Are we to continue in sin so that grace may increase? 2 May it never be! How shall we who died to sin still live in it? 3 Or do you not know that all of us who have been baptized into Christ Jesus have been baptized into His death? 4 Therefore we have been buried with Him through baptism into death, so that as Christ was raised from the dead through the glory of the Father, so we too might walk in newness of life.

Gregory Rasputin was a Russian monk in the court of Czar Nicholas II during the closing days of his reign in the early 1900s. He was highly influential and powerful but was also known as a man who had an insatiable appetite for wine and women. He taught that man experiences the greatest salvation by sinning horribly so that he can be forgiven wondrously – again and again. Those who sin the most enjoy the most forgiveness, so the way to experience the greatest salvation is to sin the most. The more a person sins, the more grace he receives from God. Experience the sin so you can enjoy the grace.

Few would preach the doctrine so blatantly and yet pastors today know how common this teaching is in more subtle forms. There is a personal catharsis that takes place in the process of confession that actually exalts the sin and the sinner. Donald Grey Barnhouse, the famous pastor of Tenth Presbyterian Church in

Philadelphia for many years, tells about a wave of public confession meetings that swept America in the 1930s. Many would attend these revival meetings where people would gather in great hotels to bare their souls of all sorts of lurid sins, thereby doing great harm to many others who were implicated by these confessions. A journalist named Heywood Broun was invited to attend and he wrote a column about the experience. He said that he had finally found the type of religion he could go for in a big way, because "the next best thing to committing a sin is telling about it afterward. 'A pint always becomes a quart in the telling.'"[1]

Grace is abused whenever sin is promoted. There is alive and well in modern Christianity this notion that to experience grace you must sensationalize sin. The more you sin, the more you understand grace and the deeper your spiritual experience, according to some false thinking. It is the ancient heresy of antinomianism. According to antinomianism, we are saved by grace on the basis of faith, so the only thing that matters is your faith not your behavior. You are no longer subject to the Law of God as the rule for behavior. You do not have to live right to be saved by grace; all you have to do is claim His grace by faith and your sins are covered. You are living on a higher plane of spiritual life by faith.[2] However, Paul writes in Romans 6:2 that we no longer live in sin because we died to sin.

Paul lays out a principle that is foundational to the Christian life but to understand this principle we must first understand what he has taught in the first 5 chapters of Romans. He has been teaching on the subject of justification. We are all sinners and God saved us by His grace. None of us deserved His salvation. It is a free gift we receive by faith. All our sins are wiped clean. We are justified forever before God. He will never judge us for our sin because we stand

---

[1] Donald Grey Barnhouse, <u>Romans</u>, vol. 3. *God's Freedom, Romans 6:1-7:25: Expositions of Bible Doctrines Taking the Epistle to the Romans as a Point of Departure.* Wm. B. Eerdmans Publishing Company, 1959, p.67.
[2] Benjamin B. Warfield, <u>Studies in Perfectionism</u>, Presbyterian & Reformed Publishing Company, 1958, p. 301.

perfectly righteous before Him in Christ. This leads into the trap of antinomianism – a trap we still face today. If we are guaranteed our salvation by grace, then what we do no longer matters. We are free to live as we please because, if we sin, our sins are covered by His blood which we accept by faith. We are already guaranteed forgiveness so where is the incentive to live a holy life?

I took an 8 week course in intermediate Greek during a very hot summer in Indiana many years ago. I would go to class every day from 8-12. Then I worked on a paint crew in the hot sun until supper time. Then I would memorize forms, vocabulary and all sorts of detailed rules of grammar until midnight. I would get a few hours of sleep and start all over again. Each day began with a test over the material we had memorized the day before. To top it all off, I got sick with the flu that affected me for several of the hottest weeks of that summer. What if my professor had said to me at the start of the course, "Dave, I have already entered an "A" in my grade book for you. You are guaranteed an A no matter what you do in this course." How hard do you think I would have studied that summer? This is precisely the theological problem Paul raises in Romans 6. Why work for sanctification when justification has already been guaranteed?

STAGES OF SANCTIFICATION

Justification is the act of God whereby He declares us perfectly righteous. This is a legal act – a courtroom term. We are acquitted by the judge of all the earth. How can God declare the unjust just? According to Romans 4 and 5, God does so because He applies our sin to Christ and Christ's righteousness to us. This is all by grace. We do not earn it. We accept it by faith and in God's eyes we are now declared righteous. We sometimes say that it is "just as if I'd never sinned." Justification is the first stage of sanctification. Initial sanctification is a positional reality equated to justification. Paul describes the immoral behavior of those who do not inherit the kingdom of God and then writes, "Such were some of you; but you were washed, but you were sanctified, but you were justified in the

29

name of the Lord Jesus Christ and in the Spirit of our God" (1 Corinthians 6:11). Justification is initial sanctification, but initial sanctification leads to progressive sanctification.

Progressive sanctification is the process whereby God makes us perfectly righteous. Paul teaches us about sanctification in Romans 6-8. We know and God knows that we are not actually righteous even though He declared us righteous; sanctification is all about the process of becoming holy. Justification and sanctification are married. We cannot divorce one from the other. Paul ties the two together and argues this: Justification that does not lead to sanctification is not justification. Something real does happen that undergirds our justification. Paul says that we died to sin. The old person died. The Greek language uses a form here that tells us this is fact not possibility. The old man truly died. The death is a fact. If the old man died, then he cannot live in sin any longer. The person who has been justified – a Christian – does not continue in sin because his old man is dead. Cadavers cannot feel. They cannot act. They cannot function. The old man is dead. By definition, a Christian is a person whose old man has died to sin. Sin no longer controls him. *The first act of grace is an execution. Grace kills the old man.*

This means that the true believer will not continue to live in sin. The word means to persist or remain as you were in a sinful state. Christians are changed. They will not continue to sin. This does not mean that Christians won't sin, as we shall see in our study and we all surely know in our experience, but it does mean that real Christians do not live in sin on an ongoing basis. If that happens we would have to question whether they were truly justified in the first place. What do we do with those who profess faith in Christ yet continue to live in sin? We often hear the popular phrase, "once saved, always saved." I believe that is true, but there is an important condition to that statement - if truly saved. Justification leads to sanctification or it is not justification. If a person is truly saved, then he or she died to sin, and that should become evident in life. If a person confidently persists in a sinful lifestyle, then we must treat that person as if they were not truly saved to begin with for we are never saved to live in sin, Paul argues.

We died to sin when we identified with Christ. Paul wonders aloud if those who think grace abounds the more we sin are simply ignorant. We fail to understand the doctrine of grace when we think that behavior no longer matters and we can do as we please. Justification is based on a real execution. The old man – the person you were before Christ – is executed. He or she no longer lives. Paul was writing to the Romans, who knew much about death being entertained watching prisoners enter a "door of death" into the Roman Coliseum. All prisoners who entered this door would die on the floor of the Coliseum while the crowds cheered. These prisoners were executed. So is your old man! He is dead, Paul tells us.

When did this happen? It took place when you were baptized into Christ's death. He was executed, and you were executed with him, when you were baptized into His death. Baptism is the sign of your union with Christ. The early Christians were quite familiar with baptism for baptism at that time was done the moment a person believed in Jesus Christ. It celebrated the person's entrance into eternal life. But Paul is not talking about water baptism here. He is using baptism as a metaphor, a figure of speech, for what happens to a person spiritually on becoming a Christian. The word "baptize" literally means to dip, plunge or immerse a person. Paul points out that Christians have been plunged into Christ at conversion. Baptism symbolizes our union with Christ. We identify ourselves with Christ in baptism.

If we are united with Christ, then we are united with Christ in His death. Union with Christ means that we spiritually died in His death. Who you were before coming to Christ has been executed in the death of Christ. The old you no longer lives. This principle is the foundation for Paul's whole doctrine of sanctification. We died when we identified with Christ at conversion. This is the decisive turning point of our lives. We can never be the same again. Paul goes on to emphasize this point in the first part of verse 4.

Not only did we die with Christ but we were buried with Him. We were baptized into His death and into His burial. The moment when death is most certain is when we place that body in the grave. We must understand that when we come to Christ we die and we are placed in the grave. The old life is over. This is what baptism symbolizes for us today.

In Israel's Negev there is an ancient town called "Shivta" (Subeita) which may have been a way station for pilgrims on their pilgrimage to St. Catherine's Monastery in the Sinai. The ruins of three Byzantine churches dating to the 5th century are located in the village. The remains of an ancient baptismal are well preserved in the South Church. It is shaped in the form of a cross. There were steps carved into the east and west arms of the cross. The new believer would enter the baptistery, going down the steps on one side and be plunged into the water, symbolizing his burial. Then he would walk up the steps on the other side, symbolizing his resurrection to new life. All of this is done when we accept Christ's work on the cross and we identify with Him in His death. This is the foundation for our sanctification.

The "me" who now lives is not the "me" who died so I must live a new life, a sanctified life. The whole idea of intentionally continuing to live in sin is repulsive. The new person is no longer dominated by sin. The Christian will certainly commit sin but the Christian cannot continue in sin indefinitely without guilt because his new life will constantly clash with his old desires and the Holy Spirit will continually bring conviction. The person who continues in sin and abuses grace by claiming to be forgiven is not a normal Christian, for grace executed the person who lived in sin. Is it possible for a Christian to live in sin? Yes. As a pastor I have seen Christians who never seem to break out of the spin cycle of sinful behavior. They live defeated lives with no peace. They are tormented by guilt and despair (Romans 7:24). A Christian persisting in sin will eventually, if not immediately, be miserable. The misery is evidence of the reality of new life in Christ but it is hardly normative for a Christian.

The normal Christian life begins with the death of the non-Christian life. There is a famous story about Augustine that illustrates this principle. St. Augustine had lived an immoral life before he became a Christian. Before his conversion he had a mistress named Claudia. Shortly after he found Christ, Claudia saw him on the street in the city. "Augustine! Augustine!" she cried after her old lover. Augustine paid no heed. "Augustine! Augustine!" she cried out again. "It is Claudia!" "But it is no longer Augustine," he replied, as he continued to walk away without looking back.[3] Augustine had grasped the truth of this passage.

NEW LIFE

The result is that we identified with Christ so we can live like Christ. Here is the theme of chapters 6-8. Sanctification is living the reality of the resurrected life. How do we do that? We will explore that process in these next few chapters. Do you want to live a holy life? Paul will tell us how in these chapters. Do you want to stop being defeated by unholy habits and sinful desires? We will learn how to do that in these chapters. The starting point is our identification with Christ in His death, burial and resurrection. New life begins with our death, burial and resurrection in Christ.

The old person you once were is dead. You have become a new person in Christ. This does not mean that your personality changed. We are not talking about physical DNA here. If you were prone to depression before conversion then you will still be prone to depression after conversion. Your brain does not get rewired with conversion. If you were an extrovert then you will still be an extrovert. If you were analytical then you will still be analytical. God does not change your personality, your looks, or your genetic makeup. We must be very clear about this because there is a lot of confusion over these matters in Christian circles. God does not

---

[3] William M. Greathouse, Romans: Beacon Bible Expositions (Beacon Hill Press, 1975), p. 103.

make you a new person physically. We are talking about spiritual DNA here. The spiritual genes that you will need to live like Christ are all there in you at conversion. The new person has all the spiritual DNA that he or she needs to live the life God wants – to be holy.

Paul uses a careful grammatical nuance in verse 4 to set the stage for what he will develop. It is translated in the expression "we too might walk in newness of life." A new person comes to life but the new life is not guaranteed. In the Greek language there was a different form for speaking of something as fact or as possibility. When Paul spoke of Christ being raised from the dead he used the mode of fact. We call it the indicative mode of speaking. The implication is that we were raised with Christ and this is a spiritual fact. But when he spoke of walking in newness of life, Paul used the subjunctive mode of speaking. This mode of speaking looked at it as a possibility not a fact. We have the possibility of walking in newness of life because we have been raised with Christ.

The Christian life is lived between the reality – we have been raised – and the possibility – we might walk with Christ. We are caught between "Just as I am" and just as God wants me to be!! We come to Him as we are, but we are called to live as He wants us to live. It is by God's grace that the just as I am can be changed into just as you want me to be. Grace is the foundation for holiness. *At conversion, we are in possibility what we will become in actuality!* That is what sanctification is all about.

Michelangelo, the great sculptor and painter, was pushing a heavy rock up a small incline to his work area so that he could do some sculpting. A neighbor watched him for over an hour as he worked to get this rock in place. Finally he asked, "Michelangelo, why do you labor so hard over that ugly, heavy piece of rock?" Michelangelo said, "Because there is an angel inside that wants to come out."[4] That is what God wants you to hear as we start this study in Romans. There is a holy man or woman of God inside of you

---

[4] Dave Stone, "Keep the Dust off the Highchair," A sermon recorded by Preaching Today, Tape #43.

who God wants to bring out. All the ingredients are there already. You will be a beautiful expression of God's glory one day by God's grace.

The great New England Puritan preacher, Jonathan Edwards wrote these words:

> The tendency of grace in the heart to holy practice, is very direct, and the connection most natural, close and necessary. True grace is not an unactive thing; there is nothing in heaven or earth of a more active nature, for it is life itself, and the most active kind of life, even spiritual and divine life. It is no barren thing; there is nothing in the universe that in its nature has a greater tendency to fruit. Godliness in the heart has as direct a relation to practice, as a fountain has to a stream, or as the luminous nature of the sun has to beams sent forth, or as life has to breathing, or the beating of the pulse, or any other vital act; or as a habit or principle of action has to action; for it is the very nature and notion of grace, that it is a principle of holy action or practice.[5]

These chapters in Romans are a powerful testimony to the transforming work of God's grace. He wants to make us into His glorious image. He wants us to be perfect – and we will be one day, not just in position but in practice. God's grace will change us in His time, but not without steps we must take to grow in grace.

---

[5] Jonathan Edwards, *A Treatise Concerning Religious Affections: Part Three, Showing What are Distinguishing Signs of Truly Gracious and Holy Affections. XII. Gracious and Holy Affections have their Exercise and Fruit in Christian Practice.* Logos Research Systems, Inc.: Oak Harbor, WA, 1996.

3
FIRST STEPS

Romans 6:5-11

5 For if we have become united with Him in the likeness of His death, certainly we shall also be in the likeness of His resurrection, 6 knowing this, that our old self was crucified with Him, in order that our body of sin might be done away with, so that we would no longer be slaves to sin; 7 for he who has died is freed from sin. 8 Now if we have died with Christ, we believe that we shall also live with Him, 9 knowing that Christ, having been raised from the dead, is never to die again; death no longer is master over Him. 10 For the death that He died, He died to sin once for all; but the life that He lives, He lives to God. 11 Even so consider yourselves to be dead to sin, but alive to God in Christ Jesus.

Ali "is a young man with little money and no wife. He takes a ninety-minute bus ride from his village to Baghdad. As soon as he arrives, the 21-year-old Iraqi heads straight to Abu Abdullah's. There it costs him only $1.50 for 15 minutes alone with a woman. Ali sees the easy and inexpensive access to sexual favors as a big improvement over the days when Saddam Hussein was in power. The dictator strictly controlled vices such as prostitution, alcohol, and drugs. The fall of the regime gave rise to every kind of depravity. Iraqis also have their choice of adult cinemas, where 70 cents buys an all-day ticket to view pornography.

Referring to all the newly available immoral activities, Ali grins and says, 'Now we have freedom.'"[1]

What the world defines as freedom, God defines as slavery – slavery to sin. God offers us freedom not just from the guilt of sin but also from the power of sin. We do not have to live like Ali, enslaved by our appetites and addicted to our lusts. God opens the door to a new life not by laws of a dictator but through the grace that comes in Christ. God does not want us to live with our guilt any longer. God does not want our past to control our future. Nor does God want us to be defeated by our addiction to sin. He wants to free us from both the guilt and the power of sin. How does He do that?

The basis of our victory is the cross of Christ. Paul expands the doctrine he taught in verse 4. When a person comes to Christ and accepts His payment for sin on the cross, that person dies with Christ. The old person is dead. Paul uses a verb in verse 5 that means literally to grow together in the likeness of His death. The verb means that we are so united to Christ's death that our death is innate, congenital or perfectly natural. The person we once were before Christ is, by nature, executed with Christ when we trust Him as Savior. The first act of grace in our lives is an execution of the old man. This execution is viewed as past in this verse. It has already happened for the believer, but this past act has continuing results in our lives, as the Greek construction makes very clear.

Verse 5 is better translated "Since we have become united with Him in the likeness of His death." Since we are united with Christ in death, then we are also congenitally joined with Christ in His resurrection. Paul is not talking about the future bodily resurrection here, as some might think. He is talking about our moral, ethical and spiritual resurrection that takes place when we come to Christ. The old me dies and a new me rises. The future tense here tells us that this resurrection has started but is not yet complete, and we await the completion of the process whereby we become fully righteous in practice. That future is guaranteed in Christ.

---

[1] Christian Caryl, "Iraqi Vice," <u>Newsweek</u>, December 22, 2003.

Paul is once again marrying the doctrines of justification and sanctification. Everything in Romans 6, 7 and 8 will build on this foundation. Justification is the act of God whereby He declares us perfectly righteous. Sanctification is the process of God whereby He makes us actually righteous in opposition to the teachings of antinomianism. Antinomianism is an ancient heresy that taught that our behavior as Christians is not important because we are under grace not law. What we do is already forgiven in Christ. Every sin is already covered by the blood of Christ so all we have to do is claim that forgiveness and live as we please. This is terribly wrong–headed thinking. It is cheap grace. It is like taking only half the gospel. God didn't save us to continue in sin. *Justification that does not lead to sanctification is not real justification at all.*

SANCTIFICATION BY SPECIAL EXPERIENCE

There is an error opposite to antinomianism that has crept into Christianity regarding our sanctification. We will meet these two opposite errors again and again in our study of Romans 6-8 and we must walk the middle road between the two if we are to live as God wants us to live. The second error has also been around in various forms since the first century but came to popularity in America with the rise of two related movements called the Higher Life Movement and the Holiness Movement in the late 1800's and early 1900's.

The Higher Life Movement and her sister the Holiness Movement spawned several Christian denominations in the early part of 20th century. Although differing from each other in important aspects, they shared a similar theological foundation with respect to sanctification. Justification and sanctification were two distinct experiences resting on two different acts of faith.[2] Justification

---

[2] Benjamin B. Warfield, <u>Studies in Perfectionism,</u> Presbyterian & Reformed Publishing Company, 1958, p. 284, cf. p.297. George Marsden, <u>Fundamentalism and American Culture: The Shaping of Twentieth Century Evangelicalism, 1870-1925,</u> Oxford University Press, 1980 pp. 72-101.

happened when you accepted Christ by faith and was called conversion or new birth. Sanctification happened sometime later when you accepted Christ as Lord of your life and entered a deeper or higher experience of holiness through a second act of faith. It was called by many in the Holiness Movement a second conversion or a second blessing. In the Higher Life Movement it was called "absolute surrender." Watchman Nee, in his popular book, *The Normal Christian Life*, actually combined the two into one. Total consecration to the Lordship of Christ coincides with the baptism of the Holy Spirit so that God takes total control of our lives, and this is an act of faith distinct from our conversion.[3] When you have this special experience of faith you reach a higher level of holiness whereby you are delivered from the power of sin in your life, and you will no longer consciously sin. If you do sin then you must go through this process of re-consecration in order to resume your special level of holiness by faith. Repeated revival experiences became necessary to live the higher life in Christ. Revivalism became a major part of the Christian heritage we share together as many walked the "sawdust trail" at revival meetings to consecrate themselves to God. I call it sanctification by special experience and it is still practiced today in many places. Have this special experience and you are back living in victory again and don't need to worry about the past. You are on a higher level of holiness again.

Justification is the union with Christ in His death. Sanctification is the union with Christ in His life. These are not two separate acts of faith but two aspects of the same saving faith. In justification we died to sin, and in initial sanctification we were raised to new life in Christ, but both are tied to the moment we come to Christ. We died and rose so that we might walk in newness of life (v.4). We don't have to die and rise again and again and again by faith. We died and so we will live as risen people in Christ. We cannot separate the two doctrines. Justification and sanctification

---

[3] Watchman Nee, <u>The Normal Christian Life</u>, Angus Kinnear, 1961, used by permission of Kingsway Publications, Eastbourne, England, pp. 61-68.

cannot be divorced. It is more accurate to say that sanctification begins with justification. We are like Him in life because we are like Him in death. We start the new life when we die to the old life, not at some later point in time. With that as our ongoing introduction to the Christian life, let us move on to Paul's next point.

Paul begins verse 6 with the words "knowing this." Knowing what, Paul? Knowing what I am about to tell you in this verse. Correct theology becomes the basis for correct living. A person's theology influences how he lives, so we had better think straight first. What do we know that helps us live the Christian life? We know that our old man was crucified with Christ. Our spiritual history, both justification and sanctification, begin at the cross. The word means literally that our old man was crucified together with Christ on that cross. Obviously Paul is not talking about our physical lives here but rather our spiritual lives. When we accept Christ by faith, the old man is executed on the cross of Christ. One of the critical first steps in sanctification is to know that my old man was crucified with Christ.

WHO'S YOUR OLD MAN?

So who exactly is this old man? We must answer that question accurately or we will have all sorts of problems with our theology of the Christian life. A common view is that the old man is our sin nature, and that our sin nature has been crucified on the cross and we are given a new nature in Christ. If our sin nature has been crucified, then there is nothing stopping us from achieving a level of spiritual life where we do not commit conscious sin. We can achieve by faith a level of holiness that is complete or "perfect." *The problem is that when we get to Romans 7 we realize that we still struggle with sin, so how could it have been crucified in Romans 6?* Perfectionism leads to frustration because we hear people talk about this higher level of holiness, but we see in ourselves the struggles we face with temptation and sin. We know we live in Romans 7, but we are told that if we had enough faith, or surrendered ourselves completely, then we would reach a spiritual level where we did not have to struggle with sin any longer. This leads to the frustration of perfectionism or the hypocrisy of selective righteousness. The sin nature is not eradicated when we come to Christ, as Romans 7 makes clear.

The old man is not our sin nature. I like John Murray's definition best. "Our old man is the old self or ego, the unregenerate man in his entirety in contrast with the new man as the regenerate man in his entirety."[4] The old man is not your nature but the whole you before you became a Christian. The old man is the unsaved man. The you, with all you were before Christ, is the person executed on the cross. A new you came to life at that moment. So – and here is the important point – sanctification is not about the renewal or transformation of an old, unsaved person. Sanctification is about the growth and development of a brand new person in Christ. That is why sanctification cannot be a separate event that occurs later than justification because the new life begins at the moment of the new birth. All you will become in Christ is yours the moment you believe. God has put His spiritual DNA in you at birth and is developing that spiritual genetic code into the person He wants you to become in life. The first step to growing in Christ is knowing who we are in Christ.

Paul writes in verse 6: "in order that our body of sin might be done away with." God's purpose in executing the old man is stated here – that the body of sin might be done away. What is the body of sin? Some have interpreted this to be our sin nature itself. According to this view, the sin nature was destroyed at this point. The KJV translates this word 'destroy' and the resultant doctrine became important in some parts of the Holiness Movement that taught the error of sinless perfection. This is the tragic error of the holiness movement when taken to its conclusion. This event was viewed as a separate event in your Christian experience, whereby sin is destroyed in you by faith. You have only to claim His grace and

---

[4] John Murray, The Epistle to the Romans, Wm. B. Eerdmans Publishing Co., 1965, One Volume Edition, 1968, p. 219.

you can live above right and wrong. Your behavior does not really matter anymore, because what you do is not really sin any more. You have reached a state that is above sin. You have arrived at the state of sinless perfection. If you "fall from grace" you have only to claim His grace by faith and resume your higher life in Him.[5] It is a tragic form of triumphalism, in which the person believes that he is above the struggle of the Christian life that others experience. It is a terrible theology that has led to some tragic consequences in Christian living.

WHAT IS THE BODY OF SIN?

So what is the body of sin? The best way to translate this is to understand the grammatical construction as meaning the body that is controlled by sin. This is our physical body itself. This will lead Paul to his argument in verse 12, where the body is clearly the physical or mortal body, and that we should not let sin reign in our physical bodies. Our bodies are the vehicles that carry out sin and, in turn, sin comes to control our bodies. *Any habitual, ongoing sin is a form of addiction.* We just notice it more with certain sins than with others. Sin is habit forming. Sin controls the body to the point that the sinner literally has to do what the sin demands. He or she is addicted to that flavor of sin that has come to control his or her body. Habitual sin, or serial sin, is a form of temporary insanity. It is addictive. The person caught in these powerful forces of sin cannot even think straight about life. The mind and body crave the sin.

Paul says that the purpose for crucifying the old man is that the body as controlled by sin might be done away. The word does not mean destroyed in the sense of annihilated. The word means to give someone the pink slip, to make of no effect, to nullify the power. *The body as controlled by sin is left unemployed when the old man is crucified.* This is God's purpose in executing the old man. Sanctification extends to my physical body and what I do with it.

---

[5] Warfield, <u>Perfectionism</u>, p.301.

What follows is a result clause in the Greek text – "so that we should no longer be slaves to sin.' The result of this event is that we are no longer slaves to sin. Our employer, Sin, has been nullified. Sin does not cease to exist, but the power sin had over us has been defeated. Our bodies are no longer employed by sin. We are no longer slaves to sin. A slave has to do whatever the master commands, so when any non-Christian sins he is doing what comes naturally. The master – sin – commands that his body fulfill the directives of sin, so the non-Christian sins. God's goal is our freedom from sin. When a Christian sins, he is choosing to allow sin to enslave him all over again. The Christian does not sin because it is natural to sin. The Christian sins because he chooses to return to what was natural before he became a Christian.

Grace is intended to change a person. Jesus illustrated this concept when the Pharisees brought the woman they had caught in adultery to him. He refused to condemn her before them. She already stood in shame. He told her that he didn't condemn her but then he quickly went on to say to her, "go and sin no more" (Jn. 8:11). Grace leads to right living or it is not true grace. Our behavior does matter. Paul illustrates the same principle in 1 Corinthians where he lists a series of sinners like thieves, homosexuals, adulterers, drunkards and swindlers, and says that these people do not inherit the kingdom of God. Then He tells the Corinthians, "such were some of you, but you were washed, but you were sanctified, but you were justified in the name of the Lord Jesus Christ" (1 Cor. 6:9-11). Such were some of you!! What a powerful statement of the transformation that God sets in motion in justification and completes in sanctification. Sanctification is even viewed here in the past tense just like justification, because the transformation of grace is already in process. We are changed people released from slavery to sin and led to holiness in Christ.

We have been justified, so sin has no legal power over us. Paul returns to his basic argument. Our justification is the foundation for our sanctification. The word translated "freed" in the NASB is the Greek word "justified." We are declared righteous in

Christ. Our guilt is gone. Justification frees us from the prison of sin and that is the basis for our sanctification – our new life in Christ.

THE TULIANUM OF SIN

Paul was writing this letter to the baby church in Rome. Only a few years later Paul would be imprisoned at Rome and eventually beheaded for his faith. According to church tradition Paul was imprisoned at the Mamertine Prison in Rome during his second imprisonment prior to his execution. This makes sense since this prison was the only prison in Rome during that time period. It was not called the Mamertine Prison in the first century. It was simply called the "Carcer" or "Prison." The prison was divided into two sections. There was an upper and a lower prison. The lower prison was called the "Tulianum." The only entrance in ancient times to the lower prison was through a sort of manhole in the floor of the upper prison. Today there is a separate entrance with stairs, but in Paul's day the guards lowered the prisoners into the cells through this manhole. When we visited Rome as a family we entered with other tourists down the stairs into the Tulianum. It is a small cell and today it is filled with religious icons. The day we visited was very hot, and the cool, damp cell provided relief from the heat. The girls would have liked to stay longer! However, this would not have been Paul's experience. Life must have been quite Spartan and uncomfortable for any man let alone one who was getting along in years. Paul certainly understood what it meant to be in prison. As a prisoner awaiting trial Paul knew what it meant to stand accused of criminal activity. His offense was a capital offense according to Roman law for he preached allegiance to a king other than Caesar. Paul uses this imagery to describe what God does for us in justification. We are in prison awaiting God's trial. We are guilty of crimes against God. God justifies us. He declares us righteous. He acquits us on the basis of what Christ has done for us. Justification sets us free from the prison of sin and the guilt of our crimes. We no longer have to wait in the Tulianum of sin.

There is no justification without death to the old life with its values and its goals. Just as a criminal who died is no longer liable for his crimes, so we are no longer liable for our crimes because we died. How and when did we die? We died in Christ's death. The old person who is guilty of the crimes against God is dead because he died in Christ's death. The starting point for our freedom from sin is the death of our old man. On that basis God declares us righteous. The guilt is gone. We are free. Grace releases us from our slavery to sin. Knowing this reality is the first step to victory in Christ. God tells us that in Christ we are free. We do not have to live in the prison of sin ever again. So ... why don't I act free? Why don't I feel free?"

King Edward VIII abdicated the throne of the United Kingdom on December 11, 1936, barely 10 months after being named as King but before his coronation. He abdicated to marry Wallis Simpson, and they were titled the Duke and Duchess of Windsor. Kenneth Harris interviewed them just two years before the Duke's death on May 28, 1972. Recalling his boyhood as Prince of Wales, he said: "My father [King George V] was a strict disciplinarian. Sometimes when I had done something wrong, he would admonish me, saying, 'My dear boy, you must always remember who you are.'"[6] You are royalty and your behavior should reflect your position. In Romans 6:11, God gives us the same message. We, Christians, must always remember who we are.

Paul has been leading up to his first main point in how to live the Christian life. Verse 11 is that point! Our theology of the Christian life begins with the verb to "consider" or "reckon." The Greek verb was originally an accounting term. It meant to calculate the interest on an account or to audit an account. An accountant would reckon or set down to one's account the money that should be

---

[6] Kenneth Harris, "Edward HRH Duke of Windsor," British Broadcasting Corporation, 27 March 1970.

deposited in that account.[7]   Later, the word came to mean more generally to count upon, calculate or conclude something. We are to count on the fact that we are dead to sin but alive to God. The first step in the Christian life is to count on the fact that you are a new person in Christ. Sanctification starts with your head not your heart; with your mind not your feelings. *Let what you know rule what you feel,* Paul tells us. Faith unlocks the door to new life as a Christian. We start to live the Christian life when we start to believe what God has done for us in Christ. Verse 8 is the foundation.

We were prisoners of sin. We were spiritual criminals who had been sentenced to death by the judge of the universe. Christ died on the cross to pay our price for sin. We are now acquitted or justified because we died in Christ. The penalty has been paid. The judge has nothing on us anymore. We are free to leave the prison as Paul has just said in verse 7. We have been declared just. This is grace. This is the message of the cross to a world dying under the curse of sin. We offer the gospel, the good news of salvation in Jesus Christ. Christianity is not a set of rules and regulations whereby we earn our favor with God. Salvation does not come to good people. Salvation is for sinners. Only sinners need to be justified by God's grace. God offers that forgiveness in the death of His son on the cross. Once we accept that payment on our account the judge has nothing on us. We are free in Christ.

So why do so many still feel like criminals? Why do so many Christians struggle with the shame of past sins and see God as some mean old judge who will throw us back into prison the minute we fail? And why do so many Christians live like miserable judges just waiting for someone to step out of line so they can nail them with their spiritual gavels? The answer is legalism. Christianity has always been prone to legalism. The error of legalism creeps in whenever we begin to turn the Christian life into a life of works not faith,

---

[7] James Hope Moulton and George Milligan, The Vocabulary of the Greek Testament Illustrated from the Papyri and Other Non-Literary Sources, Wm. B. Eerdmans Publishing Company, 1930, p. 377.

performance not grace. Live right or get zapped. Christianity is for good little boys and girls. *Legalism replaces the prison of sin with the prison of law.* Paul is battling the false doctrine of legalism in the book of Romans with the good news of the gospel of God's grace.

Unfortunately we live in a day when singers, writers and preachers have reacted to legalism with half a gospel. Many present the gospel as strictly a message of love. "The good news of Christianity," many teach, "is that Jesus loves you just as you are. God accepts you as you are. Jesus died on the cross to show you how much God loves you and how valuable you are to Him." And we feel all warm and good inside. We feel affirmed. Our self-image is lifted up. Our self-esteem is validated. But this is not the gospel. The Bible is not the gospel of self-esteem. The gospel is not that Jesus loves you and accepts you as you are. Yes, Jesus does love you as you are but He loves you too much to leave you as you are. God wants to change you. He wants to give you a new life, a fresh start, a brand new beginning. The gospel is that, because God loves you, Jesus died on the cross to pay for your sins so that you can begin a new life by faith in Him who rose from the dead to guarantee your future.

Do you see what we have done? We have taken a life-transforming truth and turned it into a sin enabling message. We have become a culture of enablers. The homosexual can now say that God loves me just as I am, and, since I am a homosexual, I can continue to live in my homosexuality. We have taken the good news that God offers a new life of purity and turned it into a message that allows me to feel good about my impurity. We have taken a message about total life change and turned it into a message about building up my self-esteem. We have taken a spiritual truth and turned it into a psychological technique. And we have missed the good news!

THE GOOD NEWS!

The truth of the gospel is found here in verse 8. We died in Christ on the cross, and we entered a new life with Christ in His resurrection. Paul has said this before, but now he adds an important emphasis in verse 8. He says, "We believe." The starting point for this radical life change is faith. This truth must be believed to be effective. Faith unlocks the door to a new life in Christ. Now this is truly good news. You are no longer under the condemnation of the judge. You don't have to be locked in your prison of guilt and sin any more. God accepts you as you are but changes you completely to become what He wants you to become. He sets you free. The starting point of that change is faith in what He says He has done and will do in you. You are not unfixable. God can change you. God can make you new, whole and pure again by His grace. It all starts not with your feelings but with faith.

Paul reminds us of what Christ did for us. He died and rose again. But Paul is not just reminding us of what we already know about Christ. He is reminding us of these facts because we died and rose again in Christ. Verse 11 ends with a key phrase that helps us understand verses 9-10. It is the phrase, "in Christ Jesus." What He did, we did in Him. This is the way we must read verses 9-10. There are three truths we must know about ourselves in Christ. *In Christ: we no longer live under a death sentence (v.9).* "Christ, having been raised from the dead, no longer dies. Death no longer rules over Him." Paul's emphasis shifts from the crucifixion of Christ to the resurrection of Christ. The resurrection is the basis for our sanctification. As Christ died we died. As Christ rose, we rose! Christ no longer dies and we no longer die. Death no longer rules over Him. Death is not His master. He has defeated death by His resurrection. So death no longer rules over us either in Christ. Certainly this is a wonderful message of hope regarding our physical life and death. Because Christ rose from the dead we know that we shall rise again one day even though we might die physically on earth. But this is not Paul's point here. Paul is arguing spiritually here. Jesus no longer dies and we no longer die spiritually. We may die physically, but we will never die spiritually once we are in Christ. Spiritual death no longer rules over us. Christianity does not view death as our friend. Death is the enemy of life. Death is the tool of sin and the curse of this world. Physical death is the result of sin. Spiritual death is the penalty for sin. Paul will say, in verse 23 of this chapter, that the wages of sin is death. When Jesus died on the cross He defeated death. When we accept Him as our Savior we no longer live under that death sentence. We will never die spiritually. Death can never again lord it over Him or us!! This is good news.

Paul presents this as a decisive act. The dying and rising of Christ is not a process. He does not die and rise again and again and again. The dying and rising are events that are decisive and finished. So our dying and rising in Christ are viewed here as decisive events we experienced in Christ. We died and we rose. We do not die and rise again and again and again spiritually. The mystical cults of Paul's day all had celebrations of dying and rising again. The religious people would celebrate the dying and rising again and again and again by sacrificing a bull and drinking its blood for new life. The member of the cult would have to go through this process over and over again to continue in this new life. Paul is laboring here to point out that this is not Christianity. Yes there is progress and growth in the Christian life, but it is not a process of dying and rising again and again and again. That happened for us in Christ once. He defeated death, and we no longer live under that death sentence.

Unfortunately, many Christians adopt the idea that whenever you fall into sin you lose your salvation and must come to Christ all over again. In essence you must die and rise again in Christ. This is a misunderstanding of the gospel and causes many to live in fear that they have lost their salvation and fallen again under the death sentence of the judge. When I was a child and going to a mission boarding school in Pakistan I was consumed with overactive guilt feelings. A legalistic tendency will produce a constant sense of guilt in us because we feel like we never measure up to Christ. We constantly feel like failures. I often had nightmares about the fires of hell, and whenever an invitation was given by a preacher I would raise my hand to receive Christ again. I wanted desperately to feel certain that I was saved from the death penalty. This went on for several years until I came to realize that I had been freed from the grip of death on my life. This was a decisive act of God. Every time

I failed I did not fall back under that death sentence again. I did not have to die and rise again in Christ over and over again.

NO LONGER UNDER A DEATH SENTENCE

We must by faith take hold of the truth that in Christ we no longer live under God's death sentence. *In Christ: we died once to the power of sin over us (v. 10a).* "For the death that he died he died to sin once for all." How did Jesus die to sin? He died to sin in the same sense that we die to sin or, more accurately, we die to sin in the same sense that He died to sin. Verse 11 tells us that Christ died to sin. Verse 2 tells us that we died to sin. The whole point of verse 2 is that we died to sin so sin no longer controls us. The whole point of this passage for believers is not just that we died to the penalty of sin, but that we died to the power of sin. Sin no longer dominates our lives. Sin no longer rules over us. Can the same be said for Christ?

How can Christ die to the power of sin over His life? He never sinned. He was perfect. How can sin be said to have had power over Him? Sin had power over Him not in making him sin but because he submitted himself to sin's power for our sakes. He was made to be sin for us, Paul says in 2 Corinthians 5:21. Death was the ultimate weapon of sin. Jesus chose to enter this world dominated by sin and live under sin's power during his earthly life, yet without actually sinning himself. Jesus submitted himself to carry our sin in all its power and surrendered himself to the power of death over him. When he rose again, he defeated death and he broke sin's power forever. When Jesus died he defeated the power of sin and when he rose from the dead he rose to live in a state of life no longer controlled by the sin of this world.

UNDER NEW OWNERSHIP

Why is that so important? Because when we die in Christ we die not just to the penalty of sin but to the power of sin. We enter a new life that is no longer controlled by the power of sin in this world.

Paul's point is that, in Christ, we become dead to the power of sin and this death is a once for all event. That leads right into Paul's third lesson regarding life in Christ. *In Christ: we live continually as those who belong to God (v. 10b)*. Paul writes: "The life that he lives he lives to God." This is the basis for our sanctification. It is the second half of the gospel. The good news is not just that God loves you as you are. That is an incomplete gospel. The good news is that God loves you so much that he will not leave you as you are. You become a new person in Him, no longer dominated and controlled by the sin that enslaved you in the past. We belong to God. We, who were once thieves, and liars, and fornicators, and homosexuals, and alcoholics, and gossips, and prostitutes, and embezzlers, are no longer slaves to those sinful desires. We who once lived only for ourselves and our lusts are now people who belong to God. He owns us and the lives we live are for Him.

We miss the power of grace if we only see Christ reaching out to the sinners of this world in love. Jesus did reach out to prostitutes and swindlers and all manner of sinful people, just as he does today. But Jesus didn't just offer them a "feel good about yourselves" religion. He didn't just help them with their self esteem. He said, "I love you and I don't condemn you. Now go and sin no more." He says the same today. We no longer live for ourselves but for Him. Our self esteem is based not upon feeling good about ourselves as we are, but upon feeling good about ourselves as Christ has changed us by His grace. Our self-image starts with an understanding of who we are in Christ, not an acceptance of who we were in ourselves. This is a radical transformation, and it all starts in our heads. So why, if we have been given new lives, do we struggle so much with our old bondage? This, of course, is the big question of Romans 6, 7, and 8. But we can start to understand it when we realize that the bondage starts in our minds. How we think determines how we feel. What we believe determines how we act. Knowledge is the foundation for behavior.

In his book *Teaching the Elephant to Dance*, James Belasco describes how "trainers shackle young elephants with heavy chains to deeply embedded stakes. In that way the elephant learns to stay in its place. Older, powerful elephants never try to leave—even though they have the strength to pull the stake and walk away. Their conditioning has limited their movements. With only a small metal bracelet around their foot attached to nothing, they stand in place. The stakes are actually gone but the elephants remain there!"[8] We live defeated lives as Christians because we do not really count on the fact that the chains that bound us are gone. It is only our memories of those chains that now enslave us. We have been so conditioned by sin's power that we live as if we are still under that power. So the first step toward victory in the Christian life is to reckon ourselves dead to sin but alive to God. Sanctification starts in our minds, not our feelings. Let what you know rule what you feel. Know who you are in Christ!

On January 28th, 1945, 121 Army Rangers slipped behind enemy lines in the Philippines in an attempt to rescue 513 American and British POW's who had spent three years in a hellish prison camp. When the Rangers arrived to free them, the prisoners were too mentally messed up to understand what was taking place. Some even ran away from their liberators. One particular prisoner, Bert Bank, refused to budge, even when a Ranger walked right up to him and tugged his arm. "C'mon, we're here to save you," he said. "Run for the gate." Bank still would not move. The Ranger looked into his eyes and saw they were vacant, registering nothing. "What's wrong with you?" he asked. "Don't you want to be free?" A smile formed on Bank's lips as the meaning of the words became clear, and he reached up to the outstretched hand of the Ranger. The Rangers searched all the barracks for additional prisoners, then shouted, "The Americans are leaving. Is there anybody here?" Hearing no answer, they left, but there was one more POW—Edwin Rose. Edwin had been on latrine

---

[8] James Belasco, <u>Teaching the Elephant to Dance: Empowering Change in Your Organization</u>, Crown Publishers Inc. 1990, p. 2.

duty and somehow missed all the shooting and explosions. When he wandered back to his barracks, he failed to notice the room was empty and lay down on his straw mat and fell asleep. Edwin had missed the liberation. But there was a reason why. Edwin was deaf. The freed prisoners marched 25 miles and boarded their ship home. With each step, their stunned disbelief gave way to soaring optimism. Even Edwin Rose made it. He finally woke up and realized liberation had come.[9]

Have you been awakened to the reality of your new life in Christ or are you still living with the mindset that you must carry out those sinful desires that dominate your life? God is telling you that you are free. Will you believe Him?

---

[9] Hampton Sides, Ghost Soldiers, Doubleday, 2001.

4

CHEAP GRACE AND THE NEW WALK

Romans 6:12-14

12 Therefore do not let sin reign in your mortal body so that you obey its lusts, 13 and do not go on presenting the members of your body to sin as instruments of unrighteousness; but present yourselves to God as those alive from the dead, and your members as instruments of righteousness to God. 14 For sin shall not be master over you, for you are not under law but under grace.

The movie, *Glory*, dramatizes the true story of the first black regiment to fight for the North during the Civil War. The 54th Regiment from Massachusetts, led by Colonel Robert Shaw, receives an important letter from Washington D.C. while the men are in basic training. The half-trained volunteers are assembled in the midst of a heavy rain late at night. As they stand soaking wet in the mud, Shaw reads the letter. "In accordance with President Lincoln's wishes, you men are advised that the Confederate Congress has issued a proclamation. Any Negro taken at arms against the Confederacy will immediately be returned to the state of slavery. Any Negro taken in Federal uniform will be summarily put to death." He looks up at his men, many of whom are freed or runaway slaves and cherish their freedom from slavery. Assuming most will not want to continue serving, Shaw says, "Full discharge will be granted in the morning to all those who apply." The next morning, Shaw emerges from his quarters buttoning his uniform jacket as the trumpeter blows reveille and the flag is raised. Major Forbes announces, "Sir, formed and ready, sir." Expecting a depleted regiment, Shaw turns to see the entire company standing at attention. No one has left. He gazes into their faces and in amazement blurts out, "Glory, Hallelujah!"[1]

These former slaves had been freed from their slavery but now were willing to fight against their former owners. In the same way, Paul tells us in Romans 6 that we are freed from slavery to sin but sin will try to enslave us again. We are freed to fight against our former master. Paul lays out three principles that guide us in our fight against sin. He is developing a carefully woven argument in Romans 6. In verse 2 Paul tells us that we died to sin. This is a statement of fact in the Greek text. In verse 6 he tells us that our old man was crucified with Christ. This is a statement of fact. In verse 7 he tells us that the person who has died – statement of fact – is freed from sin – statement of fact. On the basis of these facts, Paul exhorts us in verse 11 to consider ourselves dead to sin but alive to God. This is a command. We are to determine in our minds that we are dead to sin but alive to God.

WHO RULES?

Now Paul moves to a series of three commands in verses 12-14. The first command tells us not to let sin rule our lives (v.12). The verb means to be a king, to rule or reign. The Greek construction used here commands us to stop letting sin rule over us as a king. Sin is not our king any longer. We are dead to sin so don't let sin continue to dominate and control you. Sin will try to control the Christian. We must fight back against this tyrant. We must revolt

---

[1] "Glory" (Tri-Star Pictures, 1989) Script by Kevin Jarre and directed by Edward Zwick.

against the "would be" king because we have a new king and we are freed from our slavery to the old king. Just like the former slaves, we must be committed to fighting against the former master who would enslave us again. We must understand that the Christian life is a war and we must fight that war.

It would be silly and even insulting to tell a sinner not to let sin reign over him. Telling non-Christians not to let sin control them is useless. They are slaves of the powerful king called sin. Imagine walking up to a slave in the years before the Civil War and telling him not to let the master control him any longer. We would be mocking him, for he cannot change his status. However, we can say to a slave who has been freed from slavery, "Stop acting like a slave and fight back against your masters." In the same way, this command can only be given to Christians who have been freed from their slavery to the king called sin.

Paul is very specific. He commands us not to let sin control us in our mortal, or fleshly, bodies. Mortal means that which is subject to death. The battleground of sin is the body. It is in our physical bodies that the battle rages. Sin wants control of our bodies. God has set us free from that control, and God wants us to use our bodies for him. God has dethroned sin in our souls, but sin will continue to fight for control of our bodies. We must avoid any of the Greek dualism so common in the first century, which taught that the soul was all that mattered to God and the body was not important. God cares about our bodies and our bodies are the battleground of sanctification. Sin's hellish forces meet God's holy plans in our bodies!

Stop letting sin control your bodies, Paul says, so that you will not listen to your bodies' lusts. The word "lusts" simply means desires, passions, longings or appetites. These bodily yearnings may not be wrong in themselves. These feelings and desires may be right in the right situations, but if we let these longings control us we will be letting sin rule over us. The longings of our bodies are the ways sin gets control over us. Our feelings are the doors into our souls. Let sin use those feelings, and you will let sin control you once again.

We feel lonely. We long for intimacy, so we try to fulfill that longing through a sexual relationship outside of marriage, or through homosexuality or pornography. We have followed our feelings right into sin. The longings may vary in focus, but not in force, from one person to another. These feelings we have in our bodies, these longings can lead us into sin.

Dr. Louis McBurney, a medical doctor who has served for many years as a counselor to those who have become addicted to sexual sin in one form or another, writes: "A common path to sexual sin is the notion that feelings are not only all-important but also totally uncontrollable; they just happen to you."[2] This is a lie straight from the pit of hell. Your feelings are real, but they are not the real you. Just because you feel an attraction or a longing does not mean that you should fulfill that longing any way you want. Loneliness and intimacy are true longings, but those longings can lead you into slavery. Those longings can kill you spiritually if you let them. An anonymous writer who described a long struggle with sexual lust wrote these powerful words. "Lust … is the craving for salt by a man dying of thirst."[3]

JUST SAY "NO"

Paul tells us that we must stop letting sin control us through our feelings and longings. But that is not enough to gain victory over sin. Secondly Paul commands us: Do not offer your body to sin (v. 13a). The word "members" here refers to the members of our physical bodies – our hands and feet, our mouths and ears. Paul views sin as a master. We are no longer under the authority of that master in Christ. We have been freed from sin's authority. So Paul commands us to stop presenting the members of our bodies to sin. The verb means to supply or deliver something; to present or offer

---

[2] Louis McBurney, Leadership, Vol. 6. No. 3.
[3] Anonymous, "The War Within," Leadership, Vol. 13, No. 4.

something to someone. It was used in a military context where the soldier would offer his skills to the General for use in the battle. The word translated "tools" can mean "weapons." Paul tells us to stop offering the organs of our bodies to be used by sin as tools or weapons of unrighteousness. Your hands, feet and mouth are not to be offered for sin to use as sin sees fit.

Many years ago I was in a Bible conference where the speaker illustrated this principle from his own experience in the military. He said that he had served his tour of military duty under a particular sergeant who had ruled his life for those years. When he was discharged he happened to be walking down the street of the military town when he saw the sergeant walking toward him on the sidewalk. He instinctively straightened his shoulders and prepared to salute the sergeant as he had been required to do for years. Then he realized that the sergeant had no control over him anymore. So he deliberately slumped his shoulders, stuffed his hands in his pocket and walked up to the sergeant without a salute. He was free and would not put himself under his authority again.

So Paul tells us not to present our bodies to sin. Sin is no longer our master. A good description of a spiritually mature person is one who is able to control his own desires, passions and feelings, and who refuses to offer his abilities to be used by sin. One of the tests of our Christian life comes when we feel the attraction to something we know is wrong. Do we say, "No, I'm not going to give in to sin? Sin is not my master. I am free from his authority." Paul is telling us that unless we start with the reality that we are dead to sin we will end up offering our hands and eyes to sin all over again. When we sin we salute sin as our master. We are not forced to sin. We offer ourselves to sin. "Here take me!!"

The Christian who struggles with sexual attractions must choose not to offer his or her body to fulfill those attractions. The attractions, the longings, are real but the Christian does not have to fulfill those longings. The Christian who has been addicted to drugs no longer has to offer his body to drugs. The physical craving for drugs or alcohol may still be there. God does not necessarily remove those cravings. God does say that we as Christians can say no to those cravings.

Why must I say "no" to my longings? I'm single and I want sexual intimacy. Why should I say "no" to sex when others who are married can fulfill their longings but I can't? Why should I wait for marriage?" Paul will answer the question more fully in verse 16 but the quick answer is that sin will take control of my body. When we offer our bodies to sin, we think we are in control and we can satisfy our longings while still being free. But it is a lie. The sin will come to control my body. Indulging in sex outside of marriage will come to control me. I will wake up a slave by my own choice. This is why it is so important that you fight sinful desires. Those desires will come to control you, and you will regret the power they have gained over you. How many alcoholics thought that they were just indulging in an innocent drink, until the drink came to control them? Now they are sneaking drinks in the car and hiding drinks in the house. How many drug addicts thought it was just one joint? What could that do? Only to wake up one day to the knowledge that they couldn't live without the drug. You see Paul's point. Sin will enslave your body and destroy you, if you let it.

In the *The Lord of the Rings: The Two Towers*, Gollum is also known as Smeagol, a slimy, worthless creature in Middle Earth. Smeagol was once a normal man, but he has been turned into a pitiful creature by his obsession for the ring that has been cast in the fires of Mordor. He calls the ring "My Precious," and his longings for the ring have destroyed and enslaved him. Frodo, the story's hero, meets Gollum and offers him kindness. Gollum's old nature surfaces one night. His old self and new self have an argument. Old Gollum questions the hobbits' kindness. He says, "Sneaky little hobbitses, wicked, treacherous." But the new Gollum interjects, "No! No! Not Master!" "Yes!" the old Gollum hisses. "They will cheat you, hurt you, lie!" "Master's my friend," new Gollum says plaintively. Gollum's old self says, "You don't have any friends. Nobody likes you!" Covering his ears in defiance, new Gollum says, "Not listening! Not listening!" "Go away," the new Gollum begs. "Go away!" As this exchange continues, the new Gollum shouts out, "We don't need you!" "What?" asks the old Gollum in shock. Stronger now, the new Gollum asserts himself. "Leave, and don't come back!" To his amazement, the old Gollum is gone. He is unshackled from the wickedness of his old ways. Relief floods his face as he dances and leaps. "Gone! Gone! We told him to go away, and away he goes! Smeagol is free!"[4]

This is the path to victory in the Christian life. Don't offer your bodies to sin, for sin will come to control you. You say, "I've tried so hard to break the bondage. I've really tried to say "no," but I just can't seem to do it." I know. Once sin has regained power over the Christian it can be very hard to break that power again. But let me give you hope. It is not impossible. The key is to understand that there is more to victory then avoiding sin. Paul commands: present yourselves instead to God. This is the third command (v.13b).

THE REPLACEMENT PRINCIPLE

It is not enough to say "no" to sin. A life focused on the negative – not doing something – never works. Why? Because the more we focus on not doing something, the more attractive it becomes. The more we set up rules to keep us from sin, the more we want to sin. That is why laws, rules and regulations can never set you free. The more you say, "I don't want that drink," the more you want the drink. Life revolved around the bar but if you don't replace that life with a new one you will struggle to say no to the old one and all the best intentions in the world won't change a thing.

We must understand the "replacement principle." We must replace the negative with the positive. We must replace the sin craving with a new passion, or we will never gain victory. So Paul tells us to offer ourselves – same verb – to God. We are to stop presenting ourselves to sin and we are to present ourselves to God.

---

[4] The Lord of the Rings: Two Towers (New Line Cinema, 2002) directed by Peter Jackson and Tim Sanders.

We are to offer ourselves to God as living ones from the dead. We died and now we are alive. As new living beings, we are to offer our members, our hands, eyes and feet, to God as tools of righteousness. This is the key to victory.

You say, "I have these longings, what do I do? I have these needs, how do I get past them?" Here is the key. Starve the longings that lead you away from God. Feed the longings that lead you to God. Fill your life with good and productive activities that lead you to satisfy yourself in God. The fuller your life becomes with God's plans the less time and energy you have to fulfill sin's plans. Wives, when your husbands don't fulfill your needs, find ways to fill your life with God's joys. Substitute one longing for a new longing. When your desires are focused on God and your life is filled with usefulness then it is much easier to say "no" to sin. *I have found by personal experience that I am most vulnerable to temptation when I am least involved with righteousness.* The cliché is true. Idleness is the devil's playground. King David's great sin with Bathsheba, which led to the murder of her husband Uriah, all started with David's idleness. "Then it happened in the spring, at the time when kings go out to battle, that David sent Joab and his servants with him and all Israel, and they destroyed the sons of Ammon and besieged Rabbah. But David stayed at Jerusalem" (2 Samuel 11:1). The next verse says that David was walking along his roof when he lusted after Bathsheba. If David had been busy leading his armies in battle the sin never would have taken place. The more we are involved with God's plans the less likely we are to fall into sin's grasp.

THE PROMISE OF GRACE

The first three commands in verses 12-13 are a process. Verse 14 is a promise. The Greek construction used here is a statement of fact in future time. Paul recognizes that the battle continues even as the victory is certain for the Christian. Paul knows that we often sell ourselves into slavery to sin but He also knows that God's grace is so powerful that He will ultimately release us completely from that bondage. Sin shall not be your master. Verses 12-13 are our practice. Paul has given us our responsibilities in the Christian life. Verse 14 is our prospect. This is our expectation. Sin shall not be our master. We may give sin authority over us at times when we sin but, for the Christian, sin shall not be our master. It is fact. It is certain. God promises this victory.

Why? Because we are not under law but under grace. This is a theme Paul will develop later. For now he merely states it. We are not under law in a dependent manner. If you try to depend on rules and regulations to make you holy you are doomed to failure, for law can never set you free from sin. Grace, as the energizing force in your life, is the only power that can set you free from sin. John DeBrine, on the radio program *Songtime*, used to say, "Grow in grace so you don't groan in disgrace." Good advice for the Christian life.

5
UNDER NEW OWNERSHIP

Romans 6:15-19

15 What then? Shall we sin because we are not under law but under grace? May it never be! 16 Do you not know that when you present yourselves to someone as slaves for obedience, you are slaves of the one whom you obey, either of sin resulting in death, or of obedience resulting in righteousness? 17 But thanks be to God that though you were slaves of sin, you became obedient from the heart to that form of teaching to which you were committed, 18 and having been freed from sin, you became slaves of righteousness. 19 I am speaking in human terms because of the weakness of your flesh. For just as you presented your members as slaves to impurity and to lawlessness, resulting in further lawlessness, so now present your members as slaves to righteousness, resulting in sanctification.

A professor at Trinity Evangelical Divinity School, D. A. Carson, practiced his German with a young man from French West Africa. Carson learned that the man's wife was in London, training to be a medical doctor. He was an engineer who needed fluency in German in order to pursue doctoral studies in engineering in Germany. Carson also soon realized that once or twice a week the man disappeared into the red-light district of town. Eventually Dr. Carson got to know him well enough that he asked him what the man would do if he discovered that his wife was doing something similar in London. "Oh," he said, "I'd kill her." "That's a bit of a double standard, isn't it?" Carson asked. "You don't understand. Where I come from in Africa, the husband has the right to sleep with many women, but if a wife is unfaithful to her husband she must be killed." "But you told me you were raised in a mission school. You know that the God of the Bible does not have double standards like that." The man gave Dr. Carson a bright smile and replied, "Ah, God is good. He's bound to forgive us; that's his job."[1]

Paul addresses two parts of the same issue in Romans 6. In verse 1, Paul asks, "Are we to continue in sin that grace might increase?" In verse 15, he asks, "Shall we sin because we are not under law but under grace?" Both questions stem from a false view of sin that leads to a false view of grace. The theme of Romans 6 is this: a casual view of sin is the enemy of grace. Grace is not like a Staples "Easy button" that automatically solves your problem when you push it. God's forgiveness is not automatic. God is not obligated to forgive us under grace, for then we make God our slave, forced to meet our needs while we pursue our wants. Paul teaches us that we are not free to break the law under grace (v.15).

Paul has just taught in verse 14 that the Christian is not under law but under grace, so sin shall not be our master. But what does it mean to be under law or under grace? The preposition means under in the sense of control or dependence. If a person is living under law, then he is dependent on the law for his righteousness. The person under the law is controlled by the law. He lives by the law. If a person is living under grace, then he is dependent on grace for his righteousness and he is controlled by grace. He lives by grace.

---

[1] D.A. Carson, "God's Love and God's Wrath," <u>Biblicotheca Sacra</u>, (October 1999), p.387.

LEGALISM VERSUS LICENSE

Historically, there have been two extremes when teaching on law and grace. Like a giant pendulum, we tend to swing between these two extremes in trying to understand how the Christian life is to be lived. The first extreme is legalism. Legalism teaches that you must live by the law in order to please God. Rules and regulations control your life. We often learn legalism first in the home and then in the church. Everything is about performance – doing it right. Love is parceled out in response to performance. Live up to expectations. We transfer this mentality to God. Do it or lose it. Earn God's love by your righteous works. In legalism, our life revolves around works – being good enough for God and everyone else. It becomes a form of emotional and spiritual bondage. Paul has been addressing legalism throughout chapters 4 and 5 of Romans. We can never be good enough for God. We must accept His grace and stop trying to earn His love. We must receive His forgiveness as a gift and live by faith in His love for us. God loves us. He wants us to be free from legalism to enjoy His love by grace. However, all of this teaching has led to an equally dangerous extreme.

The opposite extreme is license. The Christian is not under law, so the rules do not matter anymore. You are free in Christ. Grace means that God has already forgiven you for all your sins, past, present and future. You will never have to pay for those sins, so stop worrying about it. Claim His forgiveness and enjoy His love. God's grace is so great that a few sins don't matter. He can handle your sins. Everybody sins. It is no big deal. Get over it and get on with your life. We sin. God is bound to forgive. What a convenient arrangement grace is!! Forgiveness is the "easy button" of the Christian life. Push it when you get in trouble and don't worry about any laws or consequences.

In the 1970s when I started out in youth ministry, the evangelical church was recovering from legalism. Some of you can relate to the way life was lived under control of laws and expectations that governed what a good Christian was supposed to be. The pendulum has now swung the other way in American Christianity. Sociologists documented the swing in the evangelical church beginning in the 1970s.[2] Worldliness was re-defined, and the lists of acceptable and unacceptable activities dismissed. Much of this swing was good because the old legalism was unbiblical. However, the swing continued until now it sometimes seems that nothing is wrong. Writers, singers and popular preachers have all been emphasizing grace with such power that we have begun to see the pendulum swing to the other extreme. Preachers speak crudely and call it being relevant. Christians publicize sin and call it being "real." Churches advertise the "no judgment zone" and call it love.

The truth is that neither extreme is biblical at all. The pendulum needs to stay in the middle. Balance is the key when it comes to the Christian life. The old hymn had it right – we must "trust and obey." We are not free to break the law under grace. The law tells us what God wants. It reveals God's character and His values. It is true and useful. We dare not depend on the law to make us righteous, but we still need to obey the law by faith in God. "Shall we sin because we are not under law but under grace? May it never be!" Such a view of sin leads to a false view of grace. Just because we live under grace does not mean we are free to violate God's law.

We had a law in our home when our girls were still eating in a high chair: "Thou shalt not deliberately pour your juice on the floor." We never had to invoke the law often but, when we did, a strong correction was necessary, along with an explanation of the law. It makes a sticky mess on the floor that mommy or daddy has to clean up and we don't like that. As the children grow up the law is never mentioned again. Why? Is it suddenly OK to pour your juice on the floor? NO WAY! May it never be!! If an adult child comes home from college and looks us in the eye while pouring out a glass of juice

---

[2] Richard Quebedeaux, The Young Evangelicals: The Story of the Emergence of a New Generation of Evangelicals, Harper and Row, 1974. The Worldly Evangelicals, Harper and Row, 1978. James Davison Hunter, Evangelicalism: The Coming Generation, The University of Chicago Press, 1987.

on the floor, we would be horrified. "But," he might say, "I am not under law any more. I am under grace and you are supposed to forgive me." This is a misunderstanding of grace. Grace means favor and it goes both ways. The law doesn't change. It is still wrong to pour your juice on the floor, but now you obey the law out of grace – a desire to treat another with favor because you have received favor from that one. This is why Paul tells us in Galatians 5:13-15 that the essence of grace is summed up in the royal law of love. Love is the motivating force of grace. We are free but not free to break the law. We are now free to love one another, and virtually every violation of the law is a failure to love!! If you truly loved someone you would not gossip about him, and if you truly loved God you will not break the law. When we sin we fail to love and so we fail to live holy lives.

FREE FOR WHAT?

We are free under grace. We are freed from slavery to sin but for what?!! We are free to become slaves by choice. We like to talk about free will, but the truth of the matter is that no man actually has free will in the sense of an uncaused or un-influenced choice. We all make our choices based upon the influences in and around us. There is no such thing as free will in the pure sense of the term. Furthermore, as Paul says here, there is no such thing as being free in the sense of having no master – of being your own master. No man is truly the master of his own soul. Paul lays out a general principle of human life here. Whatever influence you give yourself to obey becomes your master. If you present your hands and your mind to make money, then money becomes your master. If you present your mouth and your eyes to pursue pleasure, then pleasure becomes your master. Everyone is ruled by something or someone by choice.

Paul is returning to his theme of the two masters which he will use throughout Romans 6. The Christian has a choice to make between obeying sin and obeying God. If I present my hands to serve sin, then sin becomes my master. Sin controls me. If I present my mouth to be used for God, then righteousness becomes my master. The contrast is vitally important for understanding the Christian life. We are not free to be completely free and do whatever we please. This is not freedom but another form of bondage. We are free to choose our slavery. We can present our hands and feet to serve sin, or to serve righteousness. The choice of slavery is our choice, and the results are diametrically opposed to each other. Slavery to sin leads to death. Jesus said the same thing. "Everyone who commits sin is the slave of sin" (John 8:34). He also said, "No servant can serve two masters; for either he will hate the one, and love the other, or else he will hold to one and despise the other. You cannot serve God and money" (Luke 16:13).

The people who lived in Pompeii in the first century thought they understood Mt. Vesuvius. They also clung to their possessions until it was too late. They died because they refused to leave what they had. They were slaves to their homes and belongings, and that led to death. The ones who fled the fire of Mt. Vesuvius, leaving all they owned behind, were the ones who lived to tell about it, as did Pliny the Younger, who wrote an account of the event as an eyewitness who fled the area.

Slavery to sin leads to death. Paul will now emphasize this theme culminating in the last verse: "For the wages of sin is death" (Romans 6:23). You say, "I'm a Christian. God has saved me. I'm not going to hell. What does this verse have to do with me?" You are correct. You are not going to hell - but this verse doesn't say anything about hell. We commonly use this verse in a conversion situation, but the verse is really set in the context of Paul's discussion of sanctification. Here, death is death in all its ramifications. An employer does not wait to pay wages in a lump sum at the end. Wages are the ongoing compensation one receives for sin. Sin pays her wages throughout our lives, and sin is a very conscientious employer. When you choose to sin you put yourself under the death grip of sin. You will not go to hell, but you will reap the wages of death in your life. Everything about sin is deathly. Sin always pays deathly wages. It may be the death of trust or the death of a relationship. The wages of sin may be the death of a ministry or of a friendship. These are the ongoing wages that sin pays.

Paul is dealing with Christians who think that since they are under grace then they can sin once in awhile and it really doesn't matter all that much. They think, "I'm saved. A little sin is no big deal." Not true. Sin leads to death in one form or another. It might be the death of a new opportunity, or death to the joy of our fellowship with God. Think of death as slavery. Every time a Christian sins he surrenders himself to the slavery of sin, and sin can get such a grip on your life that you cannot break free. The Bible talks about Christians committing a sin unto death (1 John 5:16) meaning that God takes them home because they cannot break free from the power of sin that is destroying them and everyone around them. If we think we can play with sin and get away with it, we are wrong. Pursue drugs and drugs will become your master. Pursue money and money will master you. Pursue thinness and physical beauty and anorexia will control you. Sin is deathly and pays deathly wages. But there is a flip side to this principle. Slavery to sin leads to death, but slavery to obedience leads to righteousness (v.16).

The opposite master of sin is obedience to God. When we are mastered by obedience we will live right. Actually this is true in life as a whole. The best basketball players have disciplined themselves through obedience to the fundamentals of the game so that it becomes second nature to them. They no longer have to think about what to do next. The muscles develop memories based upon long hours of obedience in practice. So how do we become a slave to obedience? First, we must stop sinning. This is the point Paul made in verses 12-13. I sometimes hear people say, "I have prayed and prayed and prayed for victory over this particular sin, Pastor. I have asked God to remove this sin from my life." Where does it tell you to do that in the Bible? As far as I know there is no place in the Bible where we are told to ask God to remove some sin from our lives. We are often told to stop sinning. Simply stop sinning and start obeying.

Righteousness is habit forming too. Doing good becomes addictive just as much as doing evil. The more you obey God the easier it becomes to obey God. Just as lying, gossip and back-biting can become habitual through practice, so telling the truth, thinking pure thoughts and helping others through kindness can become habitual. Cultivate the habits God wants until they become the habits of your life. We must reprogram our desires, our thoughts and our habits until they become the natural response of our hearts. This is the battle we call sanctification. Read the kinds of books and magazines that will help you think righteously. Spend time with friends who will help you do the right things and encourage you to make the right choices. Stay away from the situations that will lead to possible sin, and put yourself in situations that will help you live right. Instead of lying, practice telling the truth. Instead of gossiping about someone, say something nice or don't say anything at all. If someone tries to get you to say something about someone else, just tell them you don't want to sin against that person and you won't talk about them outside of their presence. Reprogram yourself for obedience to God and you will learn to live righteously.

WHO WILL BE OUR MASTER?

We cannot avoid slavery. There is no such thing as total freedom. The question is who will be our master? Less than two decades after Paul's execution in Rome, Mt. Vesuvius erupted. August 24, 79 A.D. saw the city of Pompeii buried in ash. Many people died because they could not leave their possessions behind, even though ships had been available for rescue. The eruption had not come without warning. Sixteen years earlier, in 63 A.D., a great earthquake shook the region - a warning to the people below the cone. Many heeded the warning and left the city during those years. Many did not leave even when the mountain spewed death the day before the great eruption. It was easy to ignore the bad tempered mountain when life was so pleasant and sunny on the plain. Archaeologists have painstakingly excavated the city and found a decadent, affluent and sensual world. The archaeologists who first excavated the site tell us that early Christians who discovered it apparently tried to cover up the graphic images of sensuality because they were so bad. The people of Pompeii had all the pleasures of sin and struggled to leave them behind, even with the mountain spewing death. The haunting figures preserved by the ash and lava tell us how people clung to their world. Sometimes we resemble the people of Pompeii. Though Christ sets us free from sin and death, how often we choose to die in slavery to our treasures rather than live in newness of life. We go back to the sins that enslaved us. We can't let go even if it means death. Who will be our master?

Grace frees us to serve Christ. Paul has been developing this theme throughout Romans 6. Freedom does not mean freedom to do as we please. Grace does not mean we can grab whatever we want in life. In Romans 6:17-19, Paul teaches us that the gospel of grace transfers us to the control of Christ. We live under new ownership. We belong to Christ so we are not free to do whatever we want. We are free to serve Him. To follow Christ we must obey His teaching.

Paul begins with a doxology to God for the change that takes place in us when we become Christians – a change from what we were to what we are! We were slaves of sin. Sin owned us. But the Christian is a person who has obeyed God. Conversion to Christ is an act of obedience. When we come to Christ and accept His grace, we are committing ourselves to obey His teaching. Faith is more than mental assent to the truth of the gospel. We cannot divorce faith from obedience, or we end up with half a gospel. Many today want to preach a faith without obedience, forgiveness without repentance, and grace without responsibility. The fact of the gospel is that true grace transfers us to the ownership of Christ. We belong to Jesus. He has bought us with His blood. We are not free to do whatever we want. We are now free to serve Him.

Paul is very precise in his language here. Literally Paul writes that "you obeyed from the heart the type of teaching to which you were handed over." It is not that we obeyed the form of teaching that was given to us. The teaching is not being given to us to obey. We are being given to the teaching to obey. The Greek text says that we obeyed the type or form of teaching to which we were delivered. We were handed over to a form of teaching. The Greek verb means to be delivered or transferred, like you hand over a city or a person into another person's control. We were under the control of sin and all that it taught us to do, but now we are handed over to the control of a certain teaching that we must obey. We are transferred to a new master.

Obedience always requires a standard of truth or a set of doctrines that must be obeyed. We cannot obey without something to gauge our obedience. If we think of grace as lawlessness, we misunderstand grace. If we think of grace as freedom from all responsibility, we misunderstand grace. Grace has its own law. The law of grace is the law of love, Paul said in Galatians 5:13-15. We were handed over to the pattern of teaching on grace. The gospel of grace teaches us how we are to live under this new ownership. There is an objective standard that governs how the Christian life is to be lived. We are responsible to obey that standard to which we have been transferred by grace. We must understand that obedience is more than compliance.

OBEDIENCE OR COMPLIANCE

Paul writes, "You obeyed from the heart." There are many today who are trying to live the Christian life by complying with certain rules and regulations. This is the heart of legalism. Legalism wants us to believe that if you outwardly obey all the right rules and do the right things then you can be right with God. Legalism celebrates outward righteousness, and churches that are legalistic will focus on the outward signs of compliance with whatever rules are set up to govern righteousness in that church. So if you are compliant then you are viewed as a good Christian, and if you are not compliant then you are judged as a failure. But Paul is not talking about mere outward compliance. He is talking about obedience from the heart.

Obedience is more than compliance. Every parent knows that truth. Children can comply with the command but we can see in their body language and in their eyes that the child is still rebellious in the heart. This is not God's kind of obedience. Obedience is not doing what God wants outwardly while raging against God inwardly. Obedience is not complying because you have to, but doing it because you really want to. Obedience is not performing the right actions while avoiding the consequences for our behavior.

Living in Maine and heating with wood is a labor intensive task. As the saying goes, when you heat with wood you warm yourselves three times – when you split it, when you stack it and when you burn it. We usually bought our wood already split but it still had to be stacked for the winter. Stacking the wood was a family activity. Our daughters were expected to help stack the firewood for the winter. Needless to say this was not their favorite chore but it had to be done. The rule was if the girls whined, complained or argued they had to stack more wood by themselves. The rest of the family would be done and the whiner was responsible to stack a certain amount more from the wood pile. They learned not to whine, complain or argue but that did not mean that they were obedient as Paul talks about obedience. They learned to comply with their hands but their hearts were not in it. This is obedience while in rebellion and we have perfected the art in church. It is repentance without restitution. It is saying, "I'm sorry" knowing I am not sorry. It is treating my wife with respect at church while putting her down at home. It is outwardly living up to expectations while inwardly seething with resentment. It is hypocrisy. God does not want our compliance. God wants our obedience *from the heart.*

Obedience is more than compliance, and freedom is more than permissiveness. Slavery was common in the Roman Empire during Paul's life. Slaves were being bought and sold all the time. It was a common experience to transfer ownership of a slave, and so Paul uses what is a commonly understood experience to teach a spiritual truth. Salvation is not emancipation that leads to self determination. Salvation is emancipation from slavery to sin by transferring the ownership of our lives to a new master. We are still slaves, but now we are slaves to righteousness. The irony of Christianity is that we are free to be slaves to a new master. Under sin, we were not free to live right because sin controlled us in the end. Under grace, we now have the power to live right because we are freed from the power of sin that once enslaved us. God didn't free us to do whatever we want. He is not a permissive parent who encourages us to do whatever feels good at the time. God knows this is not good for us. Christ died to make us His own possessions. He paid the price to buy us back so we can live right in Him.

Saying "NO" to sex before marriage demonstrates that you have been freed from the power of sin and are living by the power of grace. You have a new master and He wants you to live righteously. Why? Because he doesn't want you to have any fun in life, or because He is a mean and harsh slave owner? No. Because God knows that sex before marriage will harm you and can haunt your joy in marriage later. Many studies done over the past few decades all show us that people who live together before marriage have a lower rate of successful marriages then people who say "No" until marriage. God knows that saying "NO" is better for you. Slavery to what is right is the greatest form of freedom in life.

To follow Christ we must obey His teaching, and to follow Christ we must offer our bodies for His use. Paul begins with an apology of sorts. He tells us that he is speaking in human terms because of the weakness of our flesh. Paul knows that his analogy to slavery has problems. The first problem with the slave analogy is mental. We, like the ancient Romans, have mental images of slavery that are not helpful to our understanding of Christianity. The slave owner analogy conjures up in our minds the wrong pictures. God is not like the evil slave owners we might imagine. Paul wants us to imagine a new form of slavery – slavery to righteousness. The second problem is more important, though. The problem is that we have a tendency to self-deception. We don't understand the power of sin or the call of God on our lives. We are dull spiritually and prone to excuse our sin as not very important or serious. After all, we are under grace not law, aren't we?! Paul uses a harsh picture of slavery to help us understand the importance of obedience and holiness in the Christian life. He knows that we are weak and prone to sin, so he wants us to see clearly the power of grace to transform our lives. He wants us to see that we are under new ownership. Listen to what Paul wrote to the Corinthians: "Do you not know that your body is a temple of the Holy Spirit who is in you, whom you have from God, and that you are not your own? You have been bought with a price; therefore glorify God in your body." (1 Cor. 6:19-20)

God owns us. And God owns not just our souls and minds. God owns our bodies. Don't fall into the ancient heresy of Docetism that argued for a distinction between body and soul. What you do in your bodies is not really all that significant because your soul is all that matters to God. Wrong!! God bought our bodies with the blood of His son on the cross. Therefore with our freedom comes responsibility – responsibility to our new owner. And that responsibility relates directly to how we use our bodies. The body is the battleground for sanctification. This is where the fight rages. What we do with our bodies has direct ramifications for our spiritual lives.

SIN POWER VERSUS GRACE POWER

Paul contrasts what we were under the power of sin with what we are under the power of grace. He draws a parallel between how we used our bodies for sin and how we use our bodies for righteousness. At the same time the parallel shows a contrast. The contrast is in the result while the parallel is in the method. As Christians, we have a choice. We can present our bodies to righteousness just like we once presented our bodies to sin. This is method. But the results of the two presentations could not be more opposite. Let's take a closer look. Paul tells us that impurity leads to lawlessness.

All sin is impure. Sin is filthy and dirty. The word translated "uncleanness" here was used of the foulness of a wound or sore when gangrene sets in and destroys the flesh. Sin stinks like an open cesspool to God. Paul pictures the person before he came to Christ as presenting the parts of his body to be used by the cesspool of sin. When you present your bodily parts to be used by sin you are surrendering to a vicious power that will control and dominate you. The non-Christian is unclean before God. Like a leper in Jesus' day, the non-Christian is rendered unclean by his sin. This impurity comes from lawlessness. The sinner has broken the law of God and so all sin is also lawlessness. Then Paul adds the result of this process. Impurity and lawlessness lead to more lawlessness. The power of sin grows as you give yourself to that power to control you. Sin is addictive. Sin seems so pleasant at first but slowly sin entangles the sinner until sin controls his desires. Lawlessness grows in the sinner until it consumes him, but obedience leads to holiness.

As Christians we serve a new master. Just as we gave our bodily parts to serve impurity and lawlessness before we became Christians, so we must give ourselves to serve righteousness now. How did we give ourselves to sin in the past? Well, we looked at sin and saw it was inviting. We wanted it. We took pleasure in that sin. Sin is pleasurable. Sin is enjoyable for the moment, so we give ourselves to enjoy it. But sin bites back hard. The aftertaste of sin is very bitter. Why would we want to present ourselves to that vicious power to control us all over again once we have been liberated? Instead we should give ourselves to serve righteousness with the same commitment. When we can see the right thing to do in a situation, we should give our hands to do what is right. When we face the choice to sin, we should use our feet to walk away from what is wrong, knowing the power of sin to enslave us all over again. We offer ourselves to God to do what we know is right to be done. We surrender our mouths to talk as God wants us to talk. We submit our eyes to look at what is God honoring. We discipline our ears to listen to music that is wholesome not impure. We focus our minds to think about what is pure. Self-discipline, not self-esteem, is the measure of grace. It is not so much how we feel about ourselves but how we discipline ourselves to use our bodies that determine our righteousness. What we do with our bodies is vital to our spiritual lives. How we manage our bodies is the test of spiritual growth.

God calls us to be responsible in the use of our bodies as a spiritual commitment. The result is sanctification, Paul says. Sanctification is not some theoretical concept that has little practical value. Sanctification boils down to how we live – how we use our bodies – what we eat and what we do. The word translated "sanctification" here literally means "holiness." What we do with our bodies and how we present our bodies to God in obedience to the teachings of the Bible is the method by which we grow in holiness. Obedience is the key to sanctification. The gospel of grace transfers us to the control of Christ. We will live for Him. That is what sanctification is all about.

I had the privilege of traveling with a friend through Morocco visiting Christians living in the country and learning about the underground church a number of years ago. I remember enjoying tea in the home of a Moroccan man who was a leader in his local church. He was a gracious host who served us tea and cookies in his modest home. He introduced me to his son, who was also a leader in the little underground church and was getting married soon. It would be a Christian wedding, which was very rare and exciting in this Islamic world. This wonderful, godly man shared his story with me. He had been an engineer by education and status with an excellent career that paid him well. He was well established in the middle-class lifestyle of Casablanca where he lived. Then he came to Christ and was faced with a hard choice. He had chosen to die to his old life and live for Christ but he was faced with a difficult situation for his family. His employer found out about his new faith because he was bold in his witness. He was given a choice. He could recant his faith in Christ and keep his job, or he would be fired for His Christianity. In Morocco, Christianity was legal but converting from Islam to Christianity was illegal. He refused to recant His faith in Christ, and was fired. He was blacklisted and could not find work in his field. Here was a well-educated engineer whom nobody would hire because he was a Christian. So he chose to start a business doing something nobody else would do. He would take his wagon around the city and pick up garbage. He learned to gather scrap metal which he could re-sell, so he eventually built up a business selling scrap metal that he collected. At first he pulled the wagon by hand but now, in his 60's, he had a little vehicle he could use to pull his trailer. He was filled with joy and never regretted the choice he had made many years earlier despite the hardships for him and his family. He lived under the control of Christ and was determined that the wedding of his son would honor His Lord. Sanctification is about making the choice to leave the old behind and live for Jesus. Our lifestyles, our desires, our goals, our careers are His. Jesus is our new master.

6
WHAT IS FREEDOM?

ROMANS 6:20-23

20 For when you were slaves of sin, you were free in regard to righteousness. 21 Therefore what benefit were you then deriving from the things of which you are now ashamed? For the outcome of those things is death. 22 But now having been freed from sin and enslaved to God, you derive your benefit, resulting in sanctification, and the outcome, eternal life. 23 For the wages of sin is death, but the free gift of God is eternal life in Christ Jesus our Lord.

Victor Frankl was a medical doctor in Vienna who was arrested by the Nazis less than a year after his marriage, in 1942, and was imprisoned at both Auschwitz and Dachau. His wife died at the Bergen-Belsen prison camp 3 years later but he never knew until after the war. Frankl was eventually liberated and went on to become a famous writer and professor before he died in 1997 at the age of 92. His most famous work was a book entitled *"Man's Search For Meaning."* Frankl once commented about the issue of freedom particularly as it related to America and the freedom we enjoy here. He said, "Freedom is not the last word. Freedom is only part of the story and half the truth. Freedom is but the negative aspect of the whole phenomenon whose positive act is responsibleness. In fact, freedom is in danger of degenerating into mere arbitrariness unless it is lived in terms of responsibleness. That is why I recommend that the Statue of Liberty on the East Coast be supplemented by a Statue of Responsibility on the West Coast."[1]   The "Statue of Responsibility Foundation" has plans to build a 300 foot tall stainless steel statue of locking arms designed by sculptor Gary Lee Price. The statue will be built in San Diego, San Francisco, Los Angeles or Seattle.[2] Freedom and responsibility must walk hand in hand, or we end up in selfishness and anarchy.

The philosopher John Locke wrote these words in the 1600's, "I have always thought that the actions of men are the best interpreters of their thoughts." It is what we do that really shows what we think. We talk much about freedom to watch what we want and do whatever feels good but what is freedom? Freedom is the chance to make choices and our choices reveal our goals and determine our destinies. Paul discusses two kinds of freedom as he concludes Romans 6.

Paul is answering the question he set up in verse 15. Paul is talking about Christians who think that because we are under grace and not under law that sin is not really a big deal any more. If you sin then grace covers your sin. God will forgive you so don't worry about it. Great news! We are free in Christ. Those Christians who are constantly preaching about holy living and righteousness don't understand grace, according to this view. They just want to put you back under bondage to the law. Grace means that if you sin you just have to claim His forgiveness by faith and you are free to get on with your life as if you never sinned. Paul addresses this kind of thinking by saying, "May it never be!" Paul is still continuing that theme in verse 20. Freedom without Christ means freedom to do what we want. Many think that freedom is the freedom not to feel compelled to live by someone else's standards, and certainly not to have to live by God's standards as set forth in the Bible. This is freedom to many who scream, "Don't impose your views of righteousness on me. I

---

[1] Victor Frankl, <u>Man's Search for Meaning</u>, Touchstone Books, 1984, pp. 209-210.
[2] Caleb Warnock, "Statue of Responsibility," <u>The Daily Herald</u>, May 8, 2005. See *statueofresponsiblity.com* for more information.

don't have to live by your old-fashioned views of morality contained in the Bible. I live by my own rules."

Imagine that you answered an advertisement for a transcontinental auto race and entered to win the first prize of $50,000. You had dreamed of winning such a race since you first saw the movie "Cannonball Run." You knew that Alex Roy and David Maher had set the record in their Mercedes M5 in 2006, a record broken by Ed Bolian and Dave Black in 2013 in their Mercedes CL55 AMG. The new cross-country road record was now 28 hours, 50 minutes and 30 seconds. You hoped to win the race and maybe come close to the record. The racers would leave Portofino Hotel and Marina in Redondo Beach, California in staggered starts three hours apart. They would follow a prescribed highway route with checkpoints along the way. You head out and soon overtake the lead cars. After 34 hours and 20 minutes you pull into Fort Williams Park in Cape Elizabeth, Maine – the finish line for the race. You know you are far ahead of your nearest competitors. What you don't know are the rules for the race. The fastest time is not the winner. The time closest to the official time set according to speed limits on the prescribed highways is the winner. It is not how fast you raced but how close you came to the right time. The winner was required to follow all the traffic laws along the way. You placed last because you did not follow the rules for the race. You prepared well and spent lots of money but you came in last. Why? You didn't know the rules. You lost out on the prize because you didn't follow the rules.

If you think that freedom is the right to run the race any way you want, then you are in for a surprise. God's rules for the race of life are opposite what the world expects. So Paul raises a business question. Basically Paul sets up a profit and loss analysis to examine if this kind of freedom is worth it. When you were free to do as you pleased and you did not feel compelled to follow God's rules for life what profit did you have from that freedom? What was the benefit? It was self-gratification. You could gratify yourself. The fruit or advantage you had in life was that you could feel free to pursue whatever you thought would make you feel better. So let's analyze this profit.

PROFIT OR LOSS

What did this freedom produce for you? Now that you can look back on your life before Christ and your freedom without Christ you feel shame. Sin feels good at the time, but later brings a sense of shame that is not pleasant at all. The world tries to tell us that this shame is only because of puritanical Christians who preach on sin but in reality the shame is built into the human psyche because a sense of shame is part of what it means to be a human created in the moral image of God. We can suppress that shame. We can deny it. We can avoid it, but in the end the shame will get to us when we least expect it. Shame often drives people to realize that there is more to life than self-gratification. Shame and guilt drive people to Christ. After coming to Christ we look back on our lives before Christ with shame. Was it worth it, Paul asks.

The result of sin is death. The downward slide of this profit and loss analysis ends in death. Ultimately the sinner will die and face God's judgment. This is the result of freedom to do what we want in life. Is it worth it? Paul is talking to Christians here. These Christians were looking at sin with longing eyes. He asks, "Do you really want to be free to go back to the stuff that brought you shame and led to death?" When a Christian sins, he is choosing to return to the profit and loss business that leads to death. Sin kills. If we try to hang on to our desires for self gratification we are surrendering to sin and sin leads to death. Freedom in Christ is the opposite of freedom without Christ.

When we come to Christ, we are set free from slavery to sin. Every Christian has been emancipated, liberated, and released from sin. We don't have to sin. We don't have to feel obligated to fulfill our needs to be obsessed with the self-gratification that led to shame. Whenever we decided to make ourselves feel better by getting drunk or fulfilling our sexual desires, we actually ended up feeling ashamed of what we did afterward. Some seek fulfillment through making money or pursuing fame, but Hollywood doesn't bring happiness either. All this stuff only brings more shame in those private times when no one else is looking. When we felt shame we then suppressed and avoided that shame. How did we do that? We did it by anesthetizing our sense of shame with more self gratification. We think that since we're not happy we need to do whatever it takes to make ourselves happy, and that leads into more sin, which leads to more shame, and the downward spiral goes on.

Paul says we have been set free from this slavery. We don't have to run that race anymore. We are free to win by doing less for self and more for God. We run the race by God's rules, and the result is a much better profit for us. The irony of Christianity is that when we are set free from sin we are enslaved to God, but slavery to God is the greatest form of freedom for us. Freedom in Christ means freedom to do what God wants. Paul sets up the same profit and loss analysis to show us what this means.

We have right now – present tense – a profit as Christians. We have an ongoing benefit built into our lives in Christ. We are free to make good choices. These good choices lead to more good choices, just as the bad choices led to more bad choices under sin. As we make good choices with our freedom in Christ, we are really making choices that serve God and follow God's rules for the race. These good choices open up new opportunities to live as God wants us to live. This produces real fulfillment for us. We find our greatest significance and fulfillment when our choices lead us to want what God wants. John Piper wrote in his book *Desiring God*, "I know of no other way to triumph over sin long-term than to gain a distaste for it because of a superior satisfaction in God."[3]

What do these good choices produce in our lives? They produce sanctification. The word means holiness. Whereas before Christ we pursued self-gratification now we can make good choices.

---

[3] John Piper, Desiring God: Meditations of a Christian Hedonist, 25th Anniversary Edition, Multnomah Books, 2011, p.12.

We can want what God wants. Whereas before Christ we felt shame in our sin, now, in Christ, we can see the holiness of our actions and grow in holiness by our choices. What is the end or the goal of this new freedom in Christ? When we do what God wants we are living holy lives, and when we live holy lives then we know that the end result is eternal life. Whereas before Christ we were on a path to death now, in Christ, we are on a path to living forever. Which profit margin is better? Obviously it is much better to be freed from sin and a slave to Christ. The payoff both now and in eternity is rich.

This is why God commands us in verse 19 to present our bodily parts to God as slaves of righteousness. It is worth it. The profit and loss analysis shows us that giving ourselves to God, and doing what God wants, leads to great reward now and forever. Why would we want to go back to what we had before Christ? Essentially when the Christian chooses to sin the Christian is choosing to throw away what he has in Christ, and reenter the bondage that led to shame and ultimately to death. Paul does not mean that the Christian goes to hell, only that the Christian is choosing to become a slave to sin, shame and death all over again. We throw away our freedom in our pursuit of sin.

CONTRASTS

This brings us to Romans 6:23. Paul draws two sharp contrasts in this verse. He draws a contrast between the wages of sin and the gift of God, and a second contrast between death and life. Death is earned by sin. We deserve to die because of our sin. No man can ever claim that God is unfair in sentencing him to death, because death is exactly what sin earns – no more and no less. Death is inevitable. Death here includes all aspects of death. There is physical death, which came into this world because of sin. There is eternal death, which is separation from God forever, and there is the principle of death that overshadows sinful experiences on earth. Sin brings death. Death is earned but life is a gift from God. God does not pay us what we deserve, but in Christ He gives us the gift of eternal life. We cannot pay him for this gift. We do not deserve it. We can only receive it from God on the basis that Christ has died in our place, and so paid the price we owed.

We use Romans 6:23 in a way that focuses on conversion – the beginning of the Christian life – but Paul sets this verse in the context of sanctification – how we live the Christian life. This verse summarizes his answer to why Christians should not continue in sin under grace. We should not continue in sin as Christians, because sin pays death but God has given us life. We have eternal life right now. The verb is present tense. We don't have to wait for eternal life until we die. We enjoy eternal life beginning the moment we come to Christ. God's gift of life frees us from the grip of death. Why, if we have been freed from death, do we continue to do the things that lead to death? This is Paul's argument.

Sin is viewed here as a slave master who pays out wages on an ongoing basis. These are not the wages we receive for our sins from God. These are the wages that sin pays to us. Sin is the slave master who pays out the wages we earn when we sin and those wages start in this life. Sin does not need to wait until eternity to pay its wages. The word "wages" is a very specific word. The word was used in a military context not for a once-for-all salary payment or premium due a soldier at the end of his service but for the daily ration for food allowance paid periodically to the soldiers. The word was also used with respect to slaves. Many slave owners paid their best slaves pocket money as a reward for good service. This pocket money was paid out on an ongoing basis, and many slaves in the Roman Empire actually saved up enough money over time to buy their freedom. Paul is talking here about sin as a slave owner paying out pocket money to those who sin. *The pocket money that sin pays is death.* Ultimately, apart from Christ, sin leads to eternal death but here we learn that death casts its shadow over our lives on an ongoing basis. When Christians sin, they are not in danger of hell but they will feel the shadow of death in their lives because of the pocket money that sin pays. Pursue sin as a Christian and you will reap some deathly reality from that sin in your life. Sin kills. Sin is a harsh paymaster so we must not play around with sin as a Christian.

THE WALLS WE BUILD

In the movie "The Shawshank Redemption," Andy Dufresne is a banker convicted in 1946 of the murder of his wife, Linda, and her lover, despite his claim of innocence. Andy is sentenced to a life term at the Shawshank State Prison in Maine. He meets another lifer named Ellis "Red" Redding, and the two become friends as they work together to survive the horrors of prison life. There is a scene where the prisoners are talking together in the prison yard about another prisoner named Brooks. Brooks, the prison librarian, almost kills another prisoner with a knife so that the prison will revoke his upcoming parole and keep him in prison. He has been at Shawshank for 50 years. The inmates discuss why Brooks would want to avoid leaving the prison after 50 years. Red explains, "These prison walls are funny. First you hate 'em, then you get use to 'em. Enough time passes, gets so you depend on them." Later Brooks is given his parole, but he cannot handle life on the outside and hangs himself.[4]

Sometimes we are like that as Christians. We can't get away from our past even when we have a bright future. We choose to sin and the patterns of sin become so ingrained that they become our own prison walls. We build those walls ourselves, brick by brick, through our choices in life. We "hate 'em" but we come to depend on them! Those walls are comfortable. We know what to expect inside those walls, and we forget that the walls are the walls sin uses to control us. We will not go to hell, but sin will cast the shadow of death over our lives. Sin may pay the wages of death in the form of physical addiction. It may be death to a relationship we once treasured. Sin may bring death to our service in the church. Sin may kill our opportunities for witness. Sin kills. The wages that the

---

[4] The Shawshank Redemption, Columbia Pictures, 1994, directed by Frank Darabont based on a story by Stephen King.

employer sin pays are always deathly wages, even in this life. Sin kills by enslaving us in the prison walls we create by our sinful choices as Christians.

Sin is addictive, trapping us in the physiological and psychological forces of our own bodies. This is exactly why Paul warned us in Romans 6:12-14 not to let sin rule our physical bodies by presenting the members of our physical bodies to sin. When we use our bodies to sin, our own bodies addict us to the sin. Sin controls us through our bodily desires. Natasha Dow Schull, from the Massachusetts Institute of Technology, spent several years studying how slot machines are used to addict humans. In her book, entitled *Addiction by Design*, she explains "the machines' pulsating rhythms and rapid repetitions: Press the button and get the jolt, occasionally a very large jolt, over and over ... Very talented people design these machines. They know their neuroscience. They know that addiction to substances (or) experiences both involve chemical and metabolic changes in the addict."[5] Sin kills by trapping us like suckers and exploiting our own desires against us. We have to ask ourselves as Christians, what are we feeding? Are we feeding sin that leads to death? Are we feeding our lives in Christ with good choices? What are we feeding by our choices?

Romans 6 is the first stage in our process of sanctification. We must be thinking straight about who we are in Christ. Our old man – the person we were before Christ – has been executed. A new man has come to life in Christ. We must count on this reality. We must reckon that this is true for us. We are no longer enslaved by the old master but we must choose to yield ourselves to the new master. The battleground is our bodies. Our physiological and psychological personalities are the battleground for sin. We have a choice. We can surrender our bodies to sin or we can yield our bodies to

---

[5] Natasha Dow Schull, Addiction by Design: Machine Gambling in Las Vegas, Princeton University Press, 2012. Cited by M.D. Harmon, "No Harmless Game, Casino Gambling an Exploitive 'Sucker Trap,'" Portland Press Herald, January 31, 2014.

righteousness. Each time we yield our bodies to sin we are allowing sin to become our paymaster again. Sin pays the wages of death. As we yield our bodies to righteousness we enjoy the gift of life by God's grace. This is a daily process of life. So we must think straight. Stay on course for life. Sin will try and tempt us to come back into his employment and we must flee that temptation by making good choices.

John Bunyan's <u>Pilgrim's Progress</u> is a classic study in sanctification. There is a conversation between Apollyon and Christian that masterfully illustrates this choice.

> Apollyon: Whence came you, and whither are you bound?
>
> Christian: I am come from the city of Destruction, which is the place of all evil, and I am going to the city of Zion.
>
> Apollyon: By this I perceive thou art one of my subjects; for all that country is mine, and I am the prince and god of it. How is it, then, that thou hast run away from thy king? Were it not that I hope thou mayest do me more service, I would strike thee now at one blow to the ground.
>
> Christian: I was indeed, born in your dominions, but your service was hard, and your wages such as a man could not live on; for the wages of sin is death, therefore, when I was come to years, I did, as other considerate persons do, look out if perhaps I might mend myself.
>
> Apollyon: There is no prince that will thus lightly lose his subjects, neither will I as yet lose thee; but since thou complainest of thy service and wages, be content to go back, and what our country will afford I do here promise to give thee.

Christian: But I have let myself to another, even to the King of princes; and how can I with fairness go back with thee?

Apollyon: Thou hast done in this according to the proverb, "changed a bad for a worse," but it is ordinary for those that have professed themselves servants, after a while to give him the slip, and return again to me. Do thou so too, and all shall be well.

Christian: I have given him my faith, and sworn my allegiance to him, how then can I go back from this, and not be hanged as a traitor?

Apollyon: Thou didst the same by me, and yet I am willing to pass by all, if now thou wilt yet turn again and go back.

Christian: What I promised thee was in my non-age: and besides, I count that the Prince, under whose banner I now stand, is able to absolve me, yea, and to pardon also what I did as to my compliance with thee. And besides, O thou destroying Apollyon, to speak truth, I like his service, his wages, his servants, his government, his company, and country, better than thine; therefore leave off to persuade me farther: I am his servant, and I will follow him.[6]

---

[6] John Bunyan, The Pilgrim's Progress From This World to That Which is to Come; Delivered Under the Similitude of a Dream. Oak Harbor, WA: Logos Research Systems, Inc., Part 1, The Fourth Stage.

SECTION TWO:

Willing Ourselves to Holiness?

7
HOLINESS BY CHECKLIST

Romans 7:1-6

1 Or do you not know, brethren (for I am speaking to those who know the law), that the law has jurisdiction over a person as long as he lives? 2 For the married woman is bound by law to her husband while he is living; but if her husband dies, she is released from the law concerning the husband. 3 So then, if while her husband is living she is joined to another man, she shall be called an adulteress; but if her husband dies, she is free from the law, so that she is not an adulteress though she is joined to another man. 4 Therefore, my brethren, you also were made to die to the Law through the body of Christ, so that you might be joined to another, to Him who was raised from the dead, in order that we might bear fruit for God. 5 For while we were in the flesh, the sinful passions, which were aroused by the Law, were at work in the members of our body to bear fruit for death. 6 But now we have been released from the Law, having died to that by which we were bound, so that we serve in newness of the Spirit and not in oldness of the letter.

I am sitting in the dentist's office for my regular cleaning and my hygienist takes my blood pressure. It is very high. She is concerned and tells me to go to my doctor. I meet with my doctor for my annual physical. My blood pressure is high so he tells me to buy a pressure cuff and start checking my blood pressure regularly. I am to keep track of it and in two weeks I have another appointment. I track my blood pressure and it is normal. I visit the doctor and it is high. Why? He calls it the "white coat syndrome" although no one actually wears a white coat! I determine to control my blood pressure on my next visit. I will simply relax and lower my blood pressure. It doesn't work. Why? The more I will myself to relax the more stress I feel from trying to relax! My blood pressure goes up the more I try to keep it down.

This is precisely the problem with willing ourselves not to sin. I sin. This is my reality. I want to live a holy life. This is my goal. So … I resolve to control my sin with discipline. I will myself to be holy. I make a list of some sins that people commit and resolve to control those sins. I will not do them. My checklist is selective, of course. I focus mostly on external sins that are easily measurable. My list tends toward activities that I can control. I avoid smoking and drinking, but I really didn't have a problem with those activities anyway. It makes me feel good by comparison, but I'm not sure that this is what holiness is really about. So I add to my checklist positive tasks I can measure like attending church regularly, reading my Bible and praying every day. This is better. I feel better about my holiness. I look pretty good at church. If someone asks me how I am doing spiritually I can note the checks on my checklist. This works pretty well for measurable markers, but I notice that I am developing a sense of pride about my spirituality. Furthermore I still struggle with love, gentleness, kindness, longsuffering, and joy. I still struggle with impure thoughts, a quick temper and a judgmental spirit. In fact, my judgmental spirit is worse since I started my checklist. The more I try to control these areas of my life the more I notice how often I fail. I feel worse for trying so hard. Willing myself to holiness is not working. "Checklist spirituality" breeds sin in me!

A checklist measuring our spirituality is what the Bible calls legalism, and it is a way we try to control our sin. Paul addresses legalism in Romans 7. Grace does not mean that we are free to sin.

We are free from sin but not free to sin. We must not use our freedom to excuse our sin. Paul addressed this matter in Romans 6. Paul is addressing the flip side of that problem in Romans 7. Thank God we are free from sin, but now we want to control our tendency to sin so we use the law to control our sin. We create a checklist. We fall into the trap of legalism. Legalism is born from the desire to be holy. The desire to be holy is a good desire, so legalism is motivated by good desires. The Pharisees of Jesus' day did not start out to be hypocritical. The party of the Pharisees historically began out of a desire to purify themselves and the nation. Legalism today is born out that same zeal for purity. We try to earn our holiness by our works and we live by codes and rules that dominate our lives with a performance mentality.

When I was in Israel we stayed in a nice hotel in Jerusalem. We enjoyed the accommodations very much and the hotel certainly catered to our needs. It was a busy hotel and sometimes the wait for the elevator was lengthy. There was one elevator that never seemed to have a line and we found out why. It was the "Shabbat" elevator. There were no buttons in the elevator because it stopped at every floor. You could not choose your floor. The reason for the "Shabbat" elevator was to assist those honoring the Sabbath (Shabbat). It was considered "work" to have to push the elevator buttons to select your room, and this way they did not have to work to take the elevator. The cafeteria was modern and well equipped and the food was excellent. It was served buffet style. However, on the Sabbath all the choices were cold choices and there was no hot coffee or tea. The hotel was observing the Sabbath "laws" and did not want to violate those "laws" by heating food or drink. Yet all the other aspects of hotel life including heat and lights were still operational. Telephones still worked and the staff had to clean up in the cafeteria after we ate our cold meals. This is the way of legalism. Legalism leads to inconsistency in life.

Paul teaches us in Romans 7 that we died to the law to live for God. He is picking up in his explanation from Romans 6:14. We are not under law but under grace. He starts chapter 7 with a basic principle of life. Everyone knows that a law can only control you as long as you live. Once you die the law ceases to rule over you. This is true no matter what law system you live under. It does not matter whether it is the Mosaic Law or the Roman law, the same principle applies. Once you die the law no longer rules over you. Paul uses a well known fact to illustrate this principle in verses 2-3. In a marriage the husband's death frees a wife to marry again. The woman is bound by the law to her husband. She is under the law that tells her she is subject to him until he dies. If her husband dies, then she is released from the law of the husband so that she can marry again. If she were to enter into any relationship with another man before her husband dies, then she would be called an adulteress. She will be labeled or branded as an adulteress for that new relationship because she is under the law of her husband.

DON'T MARRY THE DEAD MAN

Paul returns to his image of the law as judge. When you are under the law the law controls you – the law rules over you - the law condemns you when you break it. You will be branded as an adulteress. Some today are offended at Paul's illustration because, they say, the gender should not make a difference. The man could be used as an example just as well as the woman, so why does Paul pick on the woman and present her as under the rule of her husband? This is a rather modern view about what is an historical illustration. The reality is that in Paul's day, the woman literally was under the law of the husband. In Jewish law she did not have the same right of divorce, for example, as did her husband. She was controlled by the law in a way that he was not. This serves Paul's purpose in the illustration here. He is not saying that this is right or good. He is simply using a common reality to illustrate a spiritual principle and the wife illustrates being under bondage to the law much better than the husband in that cultural setting.

The wife truly was under bondage to the law in Paul's day. She was controlled and condemned by the law and so were we before

Christ. We are no longer under the law as a way of life but we are under grace. Grace has set us free from the law. Some have taught that the husband is an illustration of the law and the woman is an illustration of the Christian. When the law dies then we are free from the law like the woman is free from her husband. However, this is not correct. The husband here cannot be the law because Paul makes very clear in the next verse (and later in the chapter) that the law did not die. We died to the law but the law remains very much alive and true. We are not to put ourselves back under that law like the legalist says. *The legalist who makes law keeping his way of life is actually marrying the dead man all over again.*

A tragedy in 1959 is the basis of a strange law in France. When hundreds died after a dam burst, President Charles de Gaulle passed a law that allowed a young woman to marry her fiancé who was one of those killed. Such marriages have continued over the years so Christelle Demichel decided to marry her fiancé who had been killed in a traffic accident. She appeared before a city official in Nice, France, wore black, carried a bouquet of yellow roses, and stood alone. Her absent bridegroom had been dead for 17 months. Demichel insists she is not in denial. "My husband is dead. I accept that. Even if I wish he had lived much longer and we had had children, I'm not fighting reality or the fact of his death…. The wedding day was "lots of fun," Demichel said. "I was determined that it shouldn't be The Funeral Part Two."[1] The legalist marries a dead man.

Paul stretches the marriage illustration by adding a twist to it. He writes, "You were put to death to the law." The law did not die. We died to the law but the law remains very much alive. How did we die to the law? We died to the law "through the body of Christ." When Christ died on the cross we died on the cross with him. Paul has already taught this idea in chapter 6. He tells us that our old man or woman was crucified with Christ (6:6) and that we died to sin

---

[1] Philip Delves Broughton, "Bride Wears Black: Marries Man Who Died 2 Years Ago," Chicago Sun-Times, (2-23-04).

(6:2). Our old man or woman died with Christ (6:5) so that we could come alive as a new person in Christ (6:5). Now Paul adds that the death of Christ meant that we died with Him to the law that controlled us. What is the purpose of this death to the law? The purpose is so that we could be "joined to another, to the one who was raised from the dead." Our death to the law in Christ allows us to marry again. We can be married to Christ in our new lives. We are no longer under the law but under grace. We are free to live in Christ.

Now you can see why we must not make the husband into the law and why Paul could not have the wife die. If the wife died then she could not marry again. If the law died then God's law would cease to be true. Neither of these options is what Paul is teaching. The illustration is an illustration of a principle. The death of the woman's husband freed her from the law to marry again. The death of Christ freed us from the law to belong to another, namely Christ. In both cases, the person had to have a direct relationship with the one who died. So it is only in Christ that we are free from the law to live again. Why go back to the law as a method for trying to earn righteousness with God? That is like marrying the dead husband all over again.

What is the end result of this process? Paul tells us that the result is for us to "bear fruit for God." Christ's death frees us to produce fruit for God. The fruit Paul is talking about here has to do with our spiritual character and our moral behavior. Paul goes through the same process in Galatians, and he concludes with the same result. "But the fruit of the Spirit is love, joy, peace, patience, kindness, goodness, faithfulness, gentleness, self-control; Against such things there is no law. Now those who belong to Christ Jesus have crucified the flesh with its passions and desires" (Galatians 5:22-24). Paul is talking about a life transformation here, not compliance to selected artificial standards that people can manufacture for others to view. This is the classic problem with legalism. The legalist thinks that we must set up measurable standards to determine a person's spirituality. We demonstrate that we are good Christians by living up to these artificial standards. Since it is hard to measure love, joy, peace and kindness, the legalist looks for specific performance markers that will prove spirituality. The performance markers are attendance at church meetings, clothing, avoiding certain activities that have been branded as wrong like movies or dances. We can measure these markers, so the motto of the legalist has been ridiculed by the saying, "I don't smoke and I don't chew and I don't go with girls who do!!"

EXTERNAL MARKERS OR SPIRITUAL REALITIES

Pastor John Ortberg writes: "Conforming to boundary markers too often substitutes for authentic transformation. The church I grew up in had its boundary markers. A prideful or resentful pastor could have kept his job, but if ever the pastor was caught smoking a cigarette, he would've been fired. Not because anyone in the church actually thought smoking a worse sin than pride or resentment, but because smoking defined who was in our subculture and who wasn't—it was a boundary marker. As I was growing up, having a "quiet time" became a boundary marker, a measure of spiritual growth. If someone had asked me about my spiritual life, I would immediately think, Have I been having regular and lengthy quiet time? My initial thought was not, Am I growing more loving toward God and toward people?" [2] You see what we have done? *We have taken external markers and made them more important than spiritual realities.* This is the way of the legalist. Attending a specially designated prayer meeting is more important than real prayer. We don't intend for that to happen but it does and this is the danger of legalism as Paul goes on to explain in verses 5-6.

The argument of the legalist is that we will only produce holiness by enforcing laws and maintaining measurable standards. It sounds good, but in reality, as Paul, who lived by the law more than anyone, points out, the law actually energizes sin in us. In the flesh

---

[2] John Ortberg, "True (and False) Transformation," <u>Leadership</u>, Summer 2002, p. 102.

the law excites our passions even as the law tries to suppress our passions. Controlling our bodily passions by the law is like squeezing a balloon full of water. The more you squeeze in one place the more sin pops up somewhere else. It is incredibly frustrating to try to be holy by living out the letter of the law. The more resolutions we make the more we find new and creative ways to sin. The flesh becomes more insidious then we can imagine as we seek to eliminate the flesh through the law.

SHILOH

On a sandy hill overlooking the Androscoggin River in southern Maine stands a still impressive structure known as Shiloh Chapel. Shiloh Chapel was founded in 1896 by Frank W. Sandford and was originally called "The Holy Ghost and Us Bible School." The ministry grew rapidly into a Christian community of 500 residents who sold their personal property and came to live on site. Shiloh became a prayer center for worldwide missions. The building and surrounding property are all that remain of what once was the center of a global evangelistic organization simply called "The Kingdom." The prayer tower still reaches heavenward and the relatively small chapel with its balconies is still a place of worship today. I have preached in the chapel which is home to a small but vibrant evangelical church led by a fine evangelical pastor. Shiloh Chapel left "The Kingdom" and reincorporated as an independent evangelical church. A drum set stands next to the place where Frank Sandford once preached against worldliness – a sight that would surely make him turn over in his grave.[3]

Frank Sandford led with absolute authority and the community zealously pursued holiness in every detail of life. Life at Shiloh involved periodic purgings or cleansings. Whenever there was a crisis brought on by illness or financial need, the community would go through a period of intense purging looking for any signs of

---

[3] www.shilohchapelmaine.org

sinfulness in the hearts of the Christians. Nothing short of absolute cleansing for everyone through confession and prayer was needed before God would provide for the community. In 1900, the community participated in what came to be called the "Fair, Clear, and Terrible" purge based upon Frank Sandford's message from the Song of Solomon 6:10. "Who is she that looketh forth as the morning, fair as the moon, clear as the sun and terrible as an army with banners?" Frank Sandford taught that this verse described the Christian whose human nature had been completely transformed into Christ's holy nature. Tickets were printed that would allow the bearer to attend the service of celebration, having passed the "cleaning out" of sin in their lives. Each person would go through continuous day and night examinations that included intense public criticism aimed at rooting out the fleshly attitudes inside the person until the person responded with the right attitude and he or she earned a ticket to the celebration.[4]

The residents soon learned that the flesh is not so easily rooted out, and, in fact, the unrelenting legalism only led to the discovery of new sins – "holy sins" that the average Christian didn't face. The residents could control the outer sins, but the inner sins were more subtle to discern and yet more important to eliminate. To be spiritual meant to be transformed inwardly so that the flesh had no hold on you. This was considered measurable so everyone sought to look spiritual before their peers. Shirley Nelson describes the problem.

> Willfulness meant nothing so simple as breaking the house rules, but rather resistance to God's leading. Laziness meant cheating at bearing a burden in prayer, letting the mind wander. Fear was any pulling back that might inhibit Spirit-filled action, and doubt was giving in to the sneaky thief called reason.

---

[4] Shirley Nelson, <u>Fair, Clear, Clear and Terrible: The Story of Shiloh, A Strange Fragment of American History</u>, British American Publishing, 1989, pp. 148-150.

Covetousness in ordinary circumstances might be easily defined – desiring someone else's overcoat or wife. But to be filled with envy because God had answered someone else's prayers and not your own, or had given someone else the privilege of leading a particular soul to Christ, even conferring that honor on someone less earnest than yourself, this was far harder to scout out and identify, simply because it was integrated with the highest spiritual standards of the school – and complicated even more by the fact that it was often difficult to distinguish between Mr. Sandford's approval and God's.[5]

THE FLESH

What is the flesh? Paul is introducing the business of the flesh versus the Spirit in this verse, so we must define the flesh if we are to understand how it is controlled by the Spirit. The flesh is human nature willingly given to sin. It is the "self," the "ego," the "I" whose disposition tends toward sinfulness. A former professor of mine, S. Lewis Johnson defines it well. The flesh "refers to man or man's human nature, considered from the standpoint of his weakness and creaturely state in contrast to God, and also as the seat of sin ... the flesh has absolutely no good in it. This is because it is ruled by the sin principle, not because there is inherent evil in the flesh."[6]

Every time we surrender to the power of sin we are letting our flesh take over in life. Before we were Christians, the flesh controlled us. The "Old Man" was dominated by the flesh. Our decisions were directed by self and sin. This does not mean that the

---

[5] Nelson, The Story of Shiloh, pp. 112-113.

[6] S. Lewis Johnson, "A Survey of Biblical Psychology in the Epistles to the Romans, " Unpublished Doctor of Theology Dissertation (Dallas Theological Seminary, 1949), p.75.

non-Christian cannot do anything good, but rather that the non-Christian lives ultimately for self-fulfillment. He may rise above his desire for self-gratification many times, but ultimately he is focused on self and the flesh. Periodically the passions pop out in new ways and the sin leads always to death in the end. Death is the fruit of sin. When we become Christians the "Old Man" is executed. We are no longer under the rule of sin but we still have the flesh. We do not cease to be human and to possess a human nature, which is the "seat of sin" in our lives. Our human nature is prone to sin and we will battle the flesh throughout our lives.

So how do we produce righteousness? The argument of the legalist is that we have to control the flesh, so we must make and enforce many laws to keep us righteous. The goal is wonderful but the reality of this kind of thinking is that it never works. We can make all the best laws we want in our society but those laws will never produce a righteous person. The only way to produce righteousness is to change the heart of the sinner. Death is the fruit of sin. Bondage is the fruit of law keeping. Righteousness comes only through grace. Paul tells us that we are released from the law "so that we may serve in newness of the Spirit and not in oldness of the letter." We are freed from the law to serve by the Spirit. Here is the key to victory. Some have argued that the word "spirit" here should mean our human spirit. This is grammatically possible, but it is better to see this as the Spirit of God because Paul is leading up to chapter 8 where it is the Spirit of God that gives us the power to live victoriously. Furthermore, Paul uses this contrast between Spirit and letter over in 2 Corinthians 3:6 to teach us the same lesson. "Not that we are adequate in ourselves to consider anything as coming from ourselves, but our adequacy is from God who also made us adequate as servants of a new covenant, not of the letter but of the Spirit; for the letter kills but the Spirit gives life."

THE LETTER OF THE LAW

When we try to live by the letter of the law we die inside. There is no end to the rules and regulations that can govern our lives. We end up in bondage to the expectations of others and we always fall short so we always feel guilty. There are many guilty Christians running around who feel like they can never measure up to all the holy people who sit in church. Churches that major on the letter of the law damage the very lives they seek to protect. God isn't interested in killing our dreams and our desires through libraries of rules and regulations. If you have been there, you know how devastating it can be to live up to the expectations of others. It is a "no win" life. You always feel like you let someone down. You always feel defeated and depressed because you aren't as good as someone else at playing the performance game of the Christian life. Every time something bad happens in life or you face a new crisis, you look inward, convinced that God is punishing you for some failure. The legacy of legalism is constant guilt and fear.

Paul tells us that God set us free from the law so that we can live in the newness of the Spirit of God. The word means "freshness." God wants us to live our lives in the freshness of the Spirit. Seeking the freshness of the Spirit in our lives by avoiding legalism is vital to our Christian lives. Yet many a Christian running away from the legalism experienced in life falls into the trap of reverse legalism. We can look down our long spiritual noses at the legalists as we pride ourselves on the freedom we have in Christ. We can begin to measure spirituality by the freedoms we flaunt and in the process we become "Pharisees" of a new order. Measuring holiness is always tricky business.

Philip Yancey was teaching a class on the life of Christ and the discussion focused on how the legalism of the church presents barriers to non-Christians. The class quickly erupted into many members recounting their experiences growing up in legalistic churches and Christian colleges and laughing about the hypocrisy they had witnessed. Philip Yancey told of his own experience with

Moody Bible Institute in the 1970s. He was amused by the school which banned all beards, mustaches and hair below the ears for all male students while a large painting of D.L. Moody hung on the wall depicting him breaking all three rules! The class enjoyed a good laugh about the hypocrisy of such legalism. All laughed except one young man. He spoke up in anger. "I feel like walking out of this place. You criticize others for being Pharisees. I'll tell you who the real Pharisees are. They're you (he pointed at Philip Yancey) and the rest of you people in this class. You think you're so high and mighty and mature. I became a Christian because of Moody Church. You find a group to look down on, to feel more spiritual than, and you talk about them behind their backs. That is what a Pharisee does. You're all Pharisees." They were caught in reverse legalism. The arrogance that measured spirituality by one set of ideals had been replaced by an arrogance measuring spirituality by another set of ideals. It was a healthy corrective, and the class, including Philip Yancey, quickly responded in love toward this young man. The class ended by looking at their common ground at the foot of the cross, sinners all in need of God's grace.[7]

Holiness by check list never works no matter who chooses the check list.

---

[7] Philip Yancey, <u>The Jesus I Never Knew</u>, Zondervan Publishing House, 1995, p.148.

8
SIN'S GAME PLAN

ROMANS 7:7-11

7 What shall we say then? Is the Law sin? May it never be! On the contrary, I would not have come to know sin except through the Law; for I would not have known about coveting if the Law had not said, "You shall not covet." 8 But sin, taking opportunity through the commandment, produced in me coveting of every kind; for apart from the Law sin is dead. 9 I was once alive apart from the Law; but when the commandment came, sin became alive and I died; 10 and this commandment, which was to result in life, proved to result in death for me; 11 for sin, taking an opportunity through the commandment, deceived me and through it killed me.

There have been many odd laws enacted in America to control human behavior over the years. "In Maine, it is illegal to have Christmas decorations up after January 14. ... In Wisconsin, it is illegal to serve butter substitutes in state prisons. ... In Idaho, it is illegal for a man to give his sweetheart a box of candy weighing more than 50 lbs. ... In North Carolina, Bingo games can't last more than five hours."[1] What do such laws accomplish? Do they make citizens more righteous?   No.   They

---

[1] Katia McGlynn, "17 Ridiculous Laws Still on the Books in the U.S." Huffington Post, 05/02/2010 updated 05/02/2011.

might actually incite us to break the law. Laws can never make us righteous; instead, laws show us our unrighteousness. Paul argues in Romans 7 that we are not under law but under grace. He points out that the law actually incites sin in us producing death (vs. 5). Does this mean that the law is sinful? So laws are bad? We should do away with laws and be free?! No. The Law's job is to expose sin. The purpose of the law is to show us our sin. Paul uses himself as an example of all mankind. We all struggle with the same things that Paul expresses in this chapter, so his example is a universal example. Paul would not even have known what sin was except that the law defined sin for him; his knowledge of sin came through the law. The law reveals sin to the sinner. God's law wouldn't be the law unless it condemned sin. This is what God's law does.

Here is the crux of the debate over gay rights today. Those who practice homosexuality don't want their actions condemned by the law. They want the law to affirm that homosexual behavior is acceptable, and insist that our society should give gays the right to live as they please. The gay rights movement hates the condemnation of society and craves acceptance. They argue that no law is going to make homosexuals stop pursuing their homosexuality, so why not do away with all such laws? Why not? Do we really think that a law against homosexuality will stop homosexuals from sinning? No. Homosexuality has been around since the fall of Adam into sin. When Paul wrote the book of Romans, homosexuality was very common throughout the Roman Empire. A law would not stop it then and it won't stop it now. We cannot make anyone do what is right by having a law against what is wrong. So why did God ordain laws in the first place? God's law tells us what is wrong. It does not make us right. The law condemns sin. This is why we stand against legalization of homosexual behavior. We stand for the law that condemns homosexual behavior because God stands for the law against homosexuality. If we do away with that law then sin becomes acceptable. We stand for the law for the same reason the gay person stands against it – the law condemns homosexual behavior as morally wrong. The law does its job when it condemns sin.

THE SECRET SIN

We face the same condemnation of the law in other matters, Paul writes. He chooses as his example the law against lust. The 9th and 10th commandments both prohibit coveting what belongs to others. Paul says, "I came to know that coveting was wrong because the law told me it was wrong. The law condemned coveting, so when I coveted, I saw my sin. The law revealed my sin to me." The word translated "covet" here is simply the word that means desire or passionate longing. It is an emotional word indicating an appetite or a yearning for something - anything. Such longings are not necessarily wrong. Lust or coveting is wrong because it is yearning for something that is not ours to have. Lust wants anything that is not ours to possess. This covers a wide variety of topics and Paul does not identify any particular objects of the lust here precisely because he wants to leave it wide open. We lust whenever we want something that is not ours to have.

Why does Paul use lust as his example? Because first of all it is a common sin to all of us, and, second, it is a hidden sin. The legalist likes to point out external or visible sins because these are easily identifiable, yet the legalist himself can hide his sin of lust from others. The moralist rails against homosexuality but glosses over lust. We don't often condemn lust because we cannot see it in others. We can lust after something or someone and nobody else might even know about our sin. So Paul uses this example because he wants to reinforce that the law addresses real sin, not just our selective self-righteous attempts to condemn others while looking good ourselves. We all sin, and the law condemns all of us and lust is a prime example of how the law works. Lust is a sin of the mind and we only know it is sin because the law condemns lust as sin. Otherwise we can easily rationalize lust away as simply our fantasy or longing. The law won't let us do that. The law points out that it is sin and the ancient Rabbis pointed out that the law against coveting is at the root of almost all sin. We generally lust after something in our minds long before we act on it with our bodies. So lust is a serious sin of the mind.

"There is a story of two Buddhist monks walking in a drenching thunderstorm. They came to a stream, and it was swollen out of its banks. A beautiful young Japanese woman in a kimono stood there wanting to get to the other side but was afraid of the currents. In characteristic Buddhist compassion, one of the monks said, "Can I help you?" The woman said, "I need to cross this stream." The monk picked her up, put her on his shoulder, carried her through the water, and put her down on the other side. He and his companion went on to the monastery. That night his companion said to him, "I have a bone to pick with you. As Buddhist monks, we have taken vows not to look on a woman, much less touch her body. Back there by the river you did both." The first monk said, "My brother, I put that woman down on the other side of the river. You're still carrying her in your mind."[2] Isn't that the very essence of lust? Lust is not the initial thought or even the initial sight. Lust is dwelling on that thought, rolling that image around in our minds, enjoying the stimulation of a desire that is not ours to have.

Pornography is the lust business. It is lust incorporated and marketed to willing participants. The internet has expanded the lust business exponentially in recent years. The statistics for 2011 are staggering.

> 12% of the websites on the internet are pornographic
> $3,075.64 is spent on pornography every second
> 28,258 internet users are viewing porn every second
> 40 million Americans are regular visitors to porn sites
> 33% of porn viewers are women
> 70% of men aged 18-24 visit porn sites in a typical month
> Internet porn rakes in $2.84 billion per year in the U.S. and $4.9 billion worldwide

---

[2] John Claypool, "The Future and Forgetting," <u>Preaching Today</u>, Tape No. 109.

25% of all search engine requests are pornography related (68 million per day)
35% of all internet downloads are pornographic
The most popular day of the week for viewing porn is Sunday.[3]

Pornography is lust and God's law tells us that lust is sin. It is just as much sin for the Christian as it is for the non-Christian. Just because we are under grace not law does not mean the law ceases to condemn pornography as sin for the Christian. Quite frankly, *this is the secret sin that is consuming America and is a far greater threat to our society than homosexuality, yet we don't see much of a battle over this issue because it is hidden and people wrongly think it is not harming anyone.* Lust is destroying marriages today at an alarming rate and the law reveals to all of us that lust is sin. But that is not all that the law does. The law stimulates sin in the sinner.

THE LAW STIMULATES SIN

If we think that laws will make people more righteous, we are sadly mistaken. Paul uses himself as an example again. He knew the law better than anyone, yet Paul points to the fact that the law actually excited his lust even more. Oddly enough this is part of the job of the law. The law brings sin out into the open. The law prods sin into action so all can see its fruit in our lives. Most of us don't think that we would ever do certain sins. We look at someone who has sinned in some egregious way and we think, "I would never do that." Those of us not caught up in pornography think that we would never do that. And we are dead wrong, as Paul points out. We wake up one day and the law has exposed our sin, sin we thought impossible. The law prodded sin into action and suddenly we realize that we are no different from any other human being and we are

---

[3] Ed Stetzer, "Pornification: Just the Facts, The Exchange, Christianity Today, August 10, 2011.

capable of all kinds of sin. So the law does its job by stimulating sin in our lives and, as a result, showing us to be sinners.

How does this work? Paul gives us a brilliant summary of how sin gets a grip on our lives in this one verse (vs.8). "But sin, taking opportunity ...," Paul writes. Paul uses a military word here. The word can generally mean a "starting point" or an "occasion" but was used in a military context for a "base of operations." We are at war with sin. Throughout this whole section sin is personified as either a slave owner or a military commander attacking us. Sin establishes a base of operations in our lives. Sin establishes a beachhead in our souls. All sin begins with a point of attack where sin gets a grip, a hold, on some part of our emotions or our minds. Sin puts its paratroopers down on the soil of our soul and from that point attacks us where we are most vulnerable. Often sin attacks where we think we are strongest. The very place in your life that you think you have got it all together is the very place where sin will attack when you least expect it. It is so subtle and yet so powerful. From this base of operations in your soul, sin will fan out to create a revolt inside of you that you never thought about before. Sin begins with rebellion.

"But sin, taking opportunity through the commandment ..."! It is not in the areas where we don't know right from wrong but in the very area where we do know right from wrong that sin will bring about a revolt. Because we know something is wrong does not mean that we will not rebel and do what we know is wrong. Parents this is an important lesson for all of us. Some in the family counseling profession seem to give the impression that if you are a good parent then your children will make the right decisions as they grow up. Guess what? It isn't necessarily true. The very things you teach your children are wrong are the very areas that sin will attack them later on, and we cannot guarantee that our instruction or love will protect them from sinful choices. Each person makes his own choices in life, and each person is responsible for those choices, and often children grow up with the right teaching only to rebel against that very teaching in adulthood. Why?

Sin uses the law to stimulate sin. It is through the very commandments themselves that sin is incited into action. We rebel against the law. Sin is rebellion against God's instruction. Sin is not a mistake. We know it is sin but we do it anyway. Sin is a choice to rebel against God's law. Many have called this the "forbidden fruit syndrome." That which is forbidden is the very thing we want most. This is why lust is so exciting. The "forbiddenness" of it actually makes sin more appealing. Our thinking runs something like this: the law limits our freedom. God doesn't want us to enjoy something we want. We feel trapped. Why should others have all the fun? Why am I stuck in this situation? Why do I face these limitations or why don't others meet my needs? We look around and it seems like others are enjoying something we long for in our own lives, so the law looks bad. The law condemns us and we don't want the law to condemn us. We don't want to feel bad. After all, we deserve to fulfill our desires too! So we sin. We rebel. We revolt. Sin establishes a little beachhead in our lives that breaks out into open revolt precisely against the limits the law places on our lives.

We can see the anatomy of sin in Adam and Eve, the very first people to sin. Many think Paul was actually thinking about Adam and Eve here. Adam and Eve lived happily in the garden until one commandment was instituted. "Thou shall not eat of the tree." Ah, lust now started. But that fruit looks good. Why should I eat from all the other trees but not that one? And then the Serpent started from this base of operations. The law was the base of operations for the temptation. God is just trying to limit you. God is stopping you from fulfilling your needs in life. He is keeping you from becoming like him. God didn't really say you would die, did he? Doubts were sown. Rebellion sprouted. Sin came into power and resulted in death. Sin begins with rebellion by working up lust. James writes about lust. "What is the source of quarrels and conflicts among you? Is not the source your pleasures that wage war in your members? You lust and do not have; so you commit murder. And you are envious and cannot obtain; so you fight and quarrel." (James 4:1-2)

Paul tells us in verse 8 that sin works up lust in us. In fact, Paul says, sin works up every kind of lust in us. Lust is not only sexual. We may lust for money or a nice home. We may lust for a higher position in the company or to be a star football player. We may lust for recognition as a singer or musician. We may lust for the lifestyle of someone else we know rather than our own. We think, "Life is passing me by. I want more than what I have. Look at what John has over there. If I didn't have all these family responsibilities I could be like Susan over there, free to go where she wants to go and do what she wants to do." We get the gimmes!! "Gimme. Gimme. Gimme." I want. I want. I want.

The problem with lust is that it is never satisfied. Lust always wants more. Lust is addictive. Finally, in 2004, after denying the truth for 14 years, Pete Rose admitted that he bet on baseball during his days as the manager of the Cincinnati Reds. In his autobiography, *My Prison Without Bars*, Rose tells his story. Betting became an addiction that led to losing hundreds of thousands of dollars. "I didn't realize it at the time, but I was pushing toward disaster," he wrote. "A part of me was still looking for ways to recapture the high I got from winning batting titles and World Series. If I couldn't get the high from playing baseball, then I needed a substitute to keep from feeling depressed. I was driven, in gambling as well as in baseball. Enough was never enough. I had huge appetites, and I was always hungry." He was a guaranteed Hall of Fame baseball player who let lust destroy his life and his chance at the Hall of Fame.[4]

Sin works up lust in us through the law and "Apart from the law, sin is dead," Paul says. I don't think Paul means that sin is nonexistent apart from the law. He means that sin is inactive, inert. Sin is not doing anything until it is aroused by the law to fight back. Sin is there in our lives, but when the law pokes at this sleeping bear, sin erupts. Sin attacks. There is something about knowing it is wrong that increases the excitement of doing it – and the hatred of

---

[4] Ronald Blum, "Rose Admits Betting on Baseball in Book," Associated Press, 01/05/2004.

those who condemn it. The law pricks our pride. We don't like someone telling us we can't do that, so we begin to lust for the very thing that we are told we can't do.

To summarize: Sin begins ... with rebellion ... by working up lust ... being prodded by law. So this is the problem with trying to use the law to make us righteous. The legalist thinks that if we just enforce more laws then we will become righteous and create righteous people but the opposite is what happens. The law gives sin a base of operations in our lives to stimulate lust and open rebellion against the law. The ironic reality is that because of laws there is more sin, and the more the sin the more the laws. This is why legalism never works.

Columnist Steve Kloehn began his article on the vitality of the religious community in Chicago with this line: "Rev. John Alexander Dowie left little to chance a century ago, when the charismatic preacher founded the city of Zion as a carefully ordered religious utopia: He immediately outlawed sin."[5] That vision worked out well for the Chicago area! Laws never change hearts. We cannot eliminate sin by outlawing it but the law is not sin just because it fails to make us righteous. The law's purpose is to reveal sin, and even stimulate sin, so that we realize we are sinners and turn to the only one who can save us from our own sinfulness – Jesus Christ. He alone can set us free from the slavery of sin, and He alone can give us the power to fight sin in our lives.

SELECTIVE VISION

I have heard the often repeated story about D.L. Moody who preached a sermon against the evils of tobacco in the presence of C.H. Spurgeon, the great Baptist preacher. Spurgeon, a well-known cigar smoker, walked to the pulpit when Moody was done and said, "Mr. Moody, I'll put down my cigars when you put down your fork." While the story may be apocryphal, it is consistent with what we

---

[5] Steve Kloehn, "Spirits Soaring in Chicago," <u>Chicago Tribune</u>, 09/22/2000.

know about both men. Moody was very overweight and Spurgeon publicly defended his cigar smoking. A major controversy developed in the fall of 1874 when an American preacher named Dr. Pentecost was invited by Spurgeon to preach in the Metropolitan Tabernacle. Dr. Pentecost preached against smoking and how God had freed him from the habit. Charles Spurgeon stepped up to the pulpit afterward and said that he did not consider smoking to be a sin and he hoped to enjoy a good cigar before going to bed that night. The "scandal" was reported in detail in "The Daily Telegraph" and a church magazine called the "Christian World." The controversy was widely discussed in the papers, and Spurgeon was quoted as saying: "I know that what a man believes to be sin becomes sin for him, and he must give it up. ... Why, a man may think it a sin to have his boots blacked. Well, then, let him give it up, and have them whitewashed. I wish to say that I'm not ashamed of anything that I do, and I don't feel that smoking makes me ashamed, and therefore I mean to smoke to the glory of God."[6] One critic of Spurgeon's smoking, W. M. Hutchings, wrote a public tract attacking Spurgeon. He argued that if Spurgeon could argue that there was no commandment in Scripture against smoking then others could use the same logic to defend behaviors like enjoying the races, gambling, cards and attending the theater.

The truth is that we are very selective about how we measure spirituality whenever we fall into legalism. Charles Spurgeon himself strongly criticized Christians who attended the theater for being worldly while he enjoyed a cigar before going to bed at night.[7] D. L. Moody enjoyed eating and his rotund figure proved his gluttony but he didn't preach against over eating like he preached against smoking. I am not suggesting that either gluttony or smoking is a healthy habit. I am merely pointing out that *legalism is always selective*. Legalism leads to selective vision and self-righteousness as we measure spirituality according to the standards that suit our lifestyles.

---

[6] "Spurgeon's Love of Fine Cigars," in <u>The Spurgeon Archive</u>, www.spurgeon.org.
[7] C. H. Spurgeon, "The Case Proved," <u>Sword and Trowel</u>, October 1887.

We are sinners but we hide behind our self-righteous spirituality until we face the law of God. The law exposes all of us for what we really are – sinners. Your flavor of sin might be different than my flavor of sin, but we are both sinners. I can hide behind some form of legalism for a while. I may fool you and many others by my zeal for the law, but inside, where only God sees; I know I'm a sinner just like anyone else. This is Paul's testimony in this verse. He begins with where he was in his legalistic self-righteousness. He writes, "I was once alive apart from the law." Now Paul does not mean that no law existed, for he knows that the Mosaic Law was given back in Exodus long before he lived on this earth. Paul also knows that he was brought up living the Law of Moses. Listen to his testimony in Philippians 3:5-6. "(I was) circumcised the eighth day, of the nation of Israel, of the tribe of Benjamin, a Hebrew of Hebrews, as to the law, a Pharisee; as to zeal, a persecutor of the church; as to the righteousness which is in the Law, found blameless." Here was the heart of the legalist. Paul believed that he kept the Law without failure and that he in fact had mastered the Law of God. He was blameless in his mind. How can this be? He was blameless because he saw the Law as a legalist sees the Law – selectively applied to his life. This is what led him to search and destroy all Christians. Imprisoning and murdering Christians was morally acceptable in his legalism. He was zealous for the law and there is nothing as insufferable as self-righteous zeal. He would eliminate all who did not measure up to his legalistic application of the Law and he would do it all for God and in the name of God. Legalism is always blind to her own sins and there is nothing as insufferable as legalistic zeal in the name of God.

So when Paul said that he was alive apart from the Law he meant the Law as it indicted or condemned him in any way. Sin was quiet in his life not because it wasn't there but because he didn't see it. Paul was complacent in his legalism. He was-self righteous. He felt secure. Legalism makes us feel secure in our self-righteousness. This is why we as churches find legalism so easy to fall into. We can feel good about ourselves, and sin is quiet in our complacent, contented spiritual lives. We have it all together and we can look down our holier than thou noses at everyone else.

So what happened, Paul? "When the commandment came, sin became alive." This is a specific commandment because of the definite article here - the command against lust that he just spoke about in verse 8. Paul could zealously attack everyone else about their sin but completely miss this particular sin in his life. It was dormant until he applied the law against lust to his own life. Then lust came alive in him – all kinds of lust: lust for power, lust for sex, lust for fame, lust for control, he doesn't tell us what he lusted for, only that lust came alive when the law pointed out what he was feeling was wrong. The command that brought Paul down was the command against lust. The law exposed his sin and when he saw his sin then he could no longer feel self righteous. Sin punctures our self-righteous security.

DUST IN THE PARLOR

In John Bunyan's classic tale – Pilgrim's Progress – he tells about the time when the interpreter took Christian by the hand and led him into a very large parlor where everything was covered in dust, thick layers of dust. The interpreter calls for a man to come and sweep the dust away, but as he sweeps the dust fills the room so that Christian is choking in the dust that is flying all about him. Then the interpreter calls for a woman to bring water and sprinkle it on the dust, and after that the room is swept clean without a problem. The interpreter then explains the meaning to Christian. The parlor is the heart of man and the dust is his sin. The sin has corrupted him but lies still in his heart until the law comes along. The sweeper is the law that condemns us, but, instead of cleansing the heart, actually revives and increases sin in our souls. Sin comes to life in a choking swirl because of the law. The water is the sweet gospel of Christ which when sprinkled on our hearts allows God's grace to clean us up.

Is this not true in our lives? Watch a child when corrected for a wrong and see the defensiveness that rises quickly as the sin is pointed out. Watch yourself as you come face to face with your sin and realize that your sin is rising up in you even as you realize it is sin. You have been struggling to stuff the sin away in a closet somewhere, but the law points out your sin so you try to control your sin by the law and it just gets worse. Paul says, "Sin became alive and I died." The law doesn't solve the problem. It only makes you feel worse as you realize what you have done. You start choking on your own sin. You die inside. You come to hate yourself for doing what you never thought you would do. This is the tragedy of legalism: what I hoped would bring life brought death instead.

Paul literally writes: "And I found for me the commandment unto life this unto death" (vs. 10). The original intent of God's law was life not death. Paul is reflecting the ancient Rabbinic teaching on the law. In Leviticus 18:5, God tells His people: "You shall keep My statutes and My judgments, by which a man may live if he does them; I am the Lord." Jewish teachers said that studying the law enabled one to defeat sin because the law brings life not death. Paul believed this with all his heart and he had devoted himself to the study of the law in an attempt to live right before God. The tragedy of Paul's experience is that he found the law to actually bring death. He thought he would find life but instead he found death. Why? Because while it is true that the law can bring life, it can only bring life when lived perfectly - and none of us live perfectly. The result is condemnation, guilt and death, not life because inevitably we fail. This is the tragedy of all legalism. What we hope will bring us life actually ends up condemning us to death because we are not perfect.

In the early 400s there were two men who encapsulated this matter for us. The first man was a monk named Pelagius who came to Rome from Great Britain. He saw the Roman Empire and the church disintegrating into immorality and corruption. Pelagius wanted to reform society and the church. He was a moralist. Pelagius taught that man is basically good in his nature and has the capacity to choose to do "good." He taught that "ought equals can," so if God said we ought to do something then we can do it. We must constantly emphasize good works. The law must be rigorously taught and enforced. This is our only hope for society because Rome and the western church are becoming increasingly corrupt. Pelagius taught that we do not need grace because we can do right ourselves. Preaching grace opens the door to sinful living because it allows people an out for their sins. We can keep the law perfectly, for why else would God tell us to be holy as He is holy. So Christ died as our example of perfect love, not our substitute for sin. Be good and God will love you. This is legalism. It is the essence of religion.

Another man came on the scene during this time. He was not a righteous man. In fact, he was well known for his licentious, womanizing, immoral lifestyle before he became a Christian. His name was Augustine and Augustine took up the battle with Pelagius, more precisely, the disciple of Pelagius named Julian of Eclanum. Augustine taught that man is sinful from birth and cannot choose to be righteous. While man can choose to do good things at times, he can never be perfect by keeping the law. We need grace. Grace is unearned favor from God. Christ died in our place to pay our guilt for sin so we can be righteous in Him. Righteousness is a gift from God to us. We accept it by faith. The debate raged throughout the church for several years but eventually five different church councils and seven or eight Protestant creeds and confessions condemned Pelagius as a heretic.[8] You cannot be good enough for God. Salvation is by grace through faith alone. The law cannot make you righteous.

LEGALISM'S LURE

Yet the lure of legalism persists. Martin Luther struggled with legalism and found the same experience as Paul. What he hoped would bring life only brought death. Luther wrote: "If ever a monk could obtain heaven by his monkish works, I should certainly have been entitled to it." He tried so hard to live out the law as a monk in the Roman Catholic Church, but instead he only became more

---

[8] R. Scott Clark, *Pelagianism*, unpublished notes from Westminster Seminary California, 2001.

miserable with his failures. He would spend 6 hours a day in confession and spoke about hating God because the burden of his sin was so heavy upon him. The tragedy of legalism is that what we hope will bring life only brings misery and death instead.

It's amazing what some people will do to be spiritual. Pelagius advocated asceticism, and Christianity has a long history of ascetic practices in the pursuit of holiness. Anthony of Egypt (c. 251-356) came from a wealthy family but renounced his wealth and took up life as a hermit. He moved deep into the desert near the Red Sea and overcame sin by fasting and prayer. When he returned to civilization he was revered as a holy man. Pachomius was a communal monastic who established 8 monasteries and 2 convents in Egypt, with 7,000 residents who prayed 12 times a day and dedicated themselves to poverty and chastity. By the sixth century as many as 50,000 monks were living in monasteries in Egypt. Asceticism flourished as Christians sought holiness by rejecting the world. One form of asceticism was practiced by the "stylites" or "pillars." Hermits would live on the top of pillars. Simeon Stylites (c. 390-460) was one of the most famous. He built a pillar 60 feet high with a platform on top that was only 3 feet in diameter. He lived on that pillar for 30 years and fought the demons through prayer and meditation. Many pilgrims came to see him to seek his advice and prayer as a holy man. Even emperors and representatives of the church councils sought his perspective. His disciple, Daniel the Stylite, lived on the same pillar after Simeon was gone. It was said that his legs were totally atrophied by the time of his death 3 decades later.[9] Can we really achieve holiness through asceticism? Can we earn holiness by our works? We may not be as extreme as the ascetics but we can slip into the same trap of legalism. The tragedy is that what we hope will bring us life – what we hope will help us alleviate our guilt if we just pay for our sin – only brings more guilt and death in our lives.

---

[9] Robert G. Clouse, Richard V. Pierard and Edwin M. Yamauchi, <u>Two Kingdoms: The Church and Culture through the Ages,</u> Moody Press, 1993, pp. 110-112.

Paul explains the result of legalism – sin deceived me to destroy me. Paul uses the same word that he used in verse 8 when he says in verse 11, "Sin taking opportunity through the commandment." Sin set up a base of operations in his soul through the commandment producing lust (vs. 8). Here he speaks of sin deceiving him to kill him (vs. 11). The word means to "seduce" someone into doing something that is wrong, or to "cheat" someone into believing something that is false. Sin used the commandment to deceive Paul into false thinking. What was the deception? The deception was the doctrine of legalism. The fault is not with the law, but how sin makes us think about the law. Sin leads us to believe that if we just could follow the law we would find life, but that is pure deception, Paul says. What we find out is that the more we build our lives around the law, the more we sin and the guiltier we feel about what we have done. We think that if we just go to church and do all the right things that we will feel better about our lives and we will atone for our sins. We try so hard to be good little Christians, but only find bondage, not freedom, and guilt, not forgiveness.

The result of legalism is that sin deceives us to destroy us. Paul writes, "Sin deceived me and through it killed me." The "it" is the commandment. Sin uses the law to kill us. Sin uses the law to defeat us. Why are there so many defeated Christians around? Because we are trying to follow the law to victory over sin, and instead the law makes us feel worse until we don't want anything to do with it any more. All sin is an attempt to fill our deepest desires with substitutes – to fill the ache we feel inside with temporary relief. So many walk away from church and try to fill life with substitutes in an attempt to anesthetize the guilt in their souls and to fill the ache they feel with something – anything. This is why so many who know the law turn away from the law so they won't have to feel guilty anymore. Yet Paul will say in the next few verses that this killing process is good and necessary. We must face our guilt and the law's condemnation, because then we are ready to receive grace as God offers it. As long as we remain legalists and point the finger at everyone else then we are not ready to receive the grace we need for ourselves. It is only when we have been killed by our guilt and condemned by the law that we see our sin as God sees our sin and we are ready to accept the grace He offers in the blood of Christ.

The world was shocked in May of 1996 when 3 climbers died on Mt. Everest. One of the most disturbing aspects of that event was the story of two Japanese climbers who bypassed the 3 injured; starving and freezing climbers camped below the summit. The Japanese climbers did not want to jeopardize their own ascent by stopping to help the men. They passed them on the way up and camped next to them on the way down and never offered to help. As a result all 3 men died. One of the Japanese men said afterward, "Above 26,000 feet is not a place where people can afford morality." James Edwards, a Christian writer and teacher, spoke of this event and often criticized the self-centered nature of these climbers until he saw sin in a new light. He was leading a college study tour to the Middle East, and they were hiking up 7,500 foot Mt. Sinai early one morning when they came upon two Bedouins carrying a man down the mountain. James Edwards suspected that the man was suffering from pulmonary edema caused by the high altitude and needed to get down to the bottom quickly or he would die. For a brief moment he considered stopping and helping the Bedouins, but they seemed to be doing all right and he really wanted to get to the top and see the sunrise with his students. So he gave them a flashlight and went on to the top. He wrote in his book *The Divine Intruder:* "The sunrise from the summit was glorious, but it was overshadowed by what transpired on the way down. Not far below the place where we had passed the Bedouins, a figure draped with a blanket was lying on the ground. Two shoes protruded from under the blanket. The man carried by the Bedouins was dead. Whether he died while being carried down, or was put down and died, I do not know. I do know, however, that every step down the mountain smote my conscience. What I had found so loathsome in the two Japanese climbers on

Everest had been essentially repeated in my own action on Mount Sinai."[10]

The mask of self righteous legalism must be ripped away before we can see our sin as God sees our sin, because sin uses the law to kill us. Legalism promises life but produces death. The death is necessary for the life to begin. As long as we try to live by the law we will die by the law, but when we die by the law we are ready to accept the grace that comes through the blood of Christ. We must stop trying to be good enough for God – to clean ourselves up. We must come to Him as we are and let Him clean us up.

The law will never make us righteous, so what use is the law for holiness?

---

[10] James R. Edwards, <u>The Divine Intruder</u>, NavPress, 2000, pp. 103-104.

9
THE ROLE OF THE LAW

Romans 7:12-13

12 So then, the Law is holy, and the commandment is holy and righteous and good. 13 Therefore did that which is good become a cause of death for me? May it never be! Rather it was sin, in order that it might be shown to be sin by effecting my death through that which is good, so that through the commandment sin would become utterly sinful.

The notorious Nazi Adolph Eichmann escaped from Germany after the war and was captured many years later in Argentina. In the movie, *The Man Who Captured Eichmann*, based on the memoirs of Israeli agent Peter Malkin, who had tracked and captured him, he was shackled and guarded by another agent named Maxi while they waited to smuggle him out of the country. Eichmann pleaded his case with the agent by arguing that he had sworn an oath to Hitler and that he was only released from that oath when Hitler died. "He was like my father. Whatever I did I always asked myself, 'If the Fuhrer hears of my actions, will he approve?'" Maxi replied, "And the answer was always yes. When the Fuhrer said, 'Kill the Jews,' you killed the Jews." Eichmann clarifies, "No, I did not kill any Jews. I was in charge of transport. Nothing more. My sole responsibility was shipment, transportation, and organizing the trains." Shocked, Maxi stood up, and said, "But you knew where those trains were going. You knew you were sending millions of people to camps." "Yes, I know that but—" "You knew that these camps had gas chambers and crematories. You knew that every Jew you shipped would be gassed or shot or starved or worked to death. You knew that." Eichmann responds, "That was not my province. Once the shipments were complete, my responsibility ceased. My duties ended at the gates of the camps. Besides, hundreds of thousands survived. That's a fact, Maxi. I had nothing to do with the concentration camps." Maxi reiterated, "You knew that" as he left the room. Eichmann said, "You misunderstand me, Maxi."[1]

The greatest horror of the Nazi mass murders was its normalcy. "I'm just doing my job," the government bureaucrats argued. "I'm carrying out my duty." The holocaust was implemented behind the desks of mundane office buildings and carried out with business-like attention to detail. When we toured Dachau with our girls and two other families I was struck by the cold, clinical efficiency of the prison camp. The normalcy of prison camp order was mind numbing. It led Hannah Arendt to coin the controversial phrase "the banality of evil" to describe what Eichmann and others were doing.[2] We are incredibly gifted at self-deception and self-vindication. The greater our sin, the greater is the temptation to rationalize the sin. To explain sin is to excuse sin in some way. "If you just understood my circumstances," we protest, "then I wouldn't seem so bad." This is precisely why we need the law. The law is necessary to expose sin. Evil can be excused until it is exposed by the law. The role of the law is to expose sin.

Paul is still answering the question he raised back in verse 7. Is the law sinful? Paul answers that question by giving his personal testimony. Verses 7-12 are best understood as Paul's explanation of

---

[1] *"The Man Who Captured Eichmann,"* Turner Pictures, 1996.
[2] Hannah Arendt cited by Jonah Goldberg, "Where is the moral outrage surrounding the Sochi Olympics?" Portland Press Herald, 02/15,2014.

what he was like before he became a Christian. Paul was a moralist – a legalist. He lived by the law and he considered himself a righteous man. He believed he was blameless according to the law, and he made it his life goal to root out sinners who were violating the law so that society would be good and moral. The problem was that the law began to condemn him for his lust. Lust was something no one else could see. Paul tried to vindicate himself as a righteous man by pushing even harder to obey the law, but the harder he tried the worse he felt. Inside he knew that he lusted and the law condemned his lust. No one else might know but Paul did. Sin, Paul writes, seized a beachhead in his soul through the law against lust and deceived him into thinking that he was OK when lust was killing him. Paul stood condemned by the law he tried to live. All his good works were useless when he finally faced his sin. He could always excuse his failures until the law backed him into a corner with no way out. He was caught.

HOW IS GOD'S LAW GOOD FOR US?

God's law is good for us! Paul tells us that the law is good and holy, and each commandment, especially the specific command not to lust, is good for us. Why? Who wants laws that make us feel guilty? Surely it is not good for us to have our failures exposed? We should get rid of any laws that condemn us, shouldn't we? Our cultural mindset is that laws are manmade impositions curtailing our right to be free to fulfill our desires in life. This is wrong, according to our modern world. Since there are no moral absolutes, humans should be free to do whatever makes them feel good as long as it doesn't hurt someone else. Self-fulfillment is good. Guilt is bad. No one should ever make us feel guilty about our choices by imposing a law on us that condemns our actions. How can the law be good for us if it makes us feel guilty? The Bible teaches that God establishes moral absolutes through His law and this law condemns us when we violate it. God intends His law to show us our sin so that we can change our behavior and in this way God's law is good for us.

What are we to do with God's law? There are three options available. First, we could conclude that the law is bad for us not good for us. Let's get rid of the law that makes us feel guilty so we don't have to feel bad any more. The first option is to redefine what is right and wrong so that we can feel accepted by others. This is the approach of the gay rights movement. Let's just redefine society's moral code so that our behavior will be accepted by society. The goal is to normalize homosexual behavior.

I participated in a civic event a number of years ago in Portland, Maine designed to bring various leaders together to discuss the social issues in our area. Representatives of the Center for Preventing Hate (now dissolved), the NAACP, the ACLU, a local gay rights leader and a representative of the Islamic community, along with local business leaders gathered for the symposium. I was the token evangelical church leader in the group. Light refreshments were served in a large well appointed conference room amidst a pleasant atmosphere. We were to discuss the social issues facing our area. The two hot button topics were gay rights and the need for Islamic students to practice their faith in the public schools. I attempted graciously to express the Christian perspective but was promptly told that any statement against homosexuality was a hateful statement despite the fact that I had been invited to join this symposium to discuss the matter! Condemning homosexual behavior was hate speech. I responded that disagreeing with someone's moral values is not hate. I can love a person and still disagree with what that person does. Just because I disagree with you does not mean I cannot love you. I told them that I don't hate anyone in the room, but I still must disagree with what people do based upon what the Bible says. Furthermore, I said, how can we discuss the issue if I am not allowed to express my views on the issue?

At the conclusion of the meeting, each person was asked to express what they had learned from the symposium. I was seated next to a thoughtful, articulate young man who was the leader of a local gay rights group. When it was his turn to speak, he said, "I learned today something that I had never thought about before. I learned that someone can disagree with you but still love you. That is the one new idea that I will take away from this meeting." After the meeting we talked informally, and one of the participants thanked me for participating because she said that they have a hard time finding evangelical Christian leaders willing to participate. I thought but did not say, "I can see why!" The leader of the NAACP chided me and said that if we want our churches to grow we need to be more inclusive and stop condemning people for what they do. If we would get rid of these outdated moral limitations then our churches would grow and our influence in society would grow.

The first option in regard to God's law is the idea that we must eliminate the law because it condemns our behavior. God's law is hateful so it is bad for us. There are two problems with this line of thinking. (1) No matter what we redefine here on earth it, doesn't change God's law one bit, and we all must face God some day. Feeling good now may be temporary relief, but God's law is absolute. This is the Christian bedrock. Our world does not understand that God's law is not our law to change. (2) There is no hope of change – what God calls redemption – until we actually agree with the law of God about our behavior. Only then can we hope to change. So this option is just a band-aid on a mortal wound deep in the soul. If there are no moral absolutes, then we have no hope of change. The fact that the law condemns our wrong behaviors opens the door to changing those behaviors. God's law is good for us because it opens the door to redemption by the grace of God. *If there is no sin there is no grace! Grace needs sin to be gracious.*

Secondly, we could conclude, as the moralist concludes, that we must enforce the law to make ourselves and others righteous. The legalist is zealous for the law, as Paul was zealous for the law. The moralist argues that law does not merely condemn what is wrong but shows us what is right. If we exert our wills to the task, we can will ourselves to moral perfection. The problem is that that this doesn't work. We cannot make ourselves righteous by keeping the law, for inevitably we fail. Paul found this out, and countless moralists have discovered the same throughout history. We end up miserable in our failed self-righteousness.

Benjamin Franklin was a classic moralist who wrote in his unfinished autobiography: "I conceived the bold and arduous project of arriving at moral perfection. I wished to live without committing any fault at any time; I would conquer all that either natural inclinations, custom, or company might lead me into. As I knew, or thought I knew, what was right or wrong, I did not see why I might not always do the one and avoid the other. But I soon found I had undertaken a task of more difficulty than I had imagined. While my care was employed in guarding against one fault, I was often surprised by another; habit took the advantage of inattention; inclination was sometimes too strong for reason. I concluded, at length, that the mere speculative conviction that it was our interest to be completely virtuous was not sufficient to prevent our slipping; and that the contrary habits must be broken, and good ones acquired and established, before we can have any dependence on a steady, uniform rectitude of conduct."[3] So Benjamin Franklin set himself to the task. He studied all the writings he could find and summarized moral perfection in 13 virtues.

> 1. TEMPERANCE. Eat not to dullness; drink not to elevation.
> 2. SILENCE. Speak not but what may benefit others or yourself; avoid trifling conversation.
> 3. ORDER. Let all your things have their places; let each part of your business have its time.
> 4. RESOLUTION. Resolve to perform what you ought; perform without fail what you resolve.
> 5. FRUGALITY. Make no expense but to do good to others or yourself; i.e., waste nothing.

---

[3] Benjamin Franklin, The Autobiography of Benjamin Franklin, www.earlyamerica.com/live/franklin/chapt8.

6. INDUSTRY. Lose no time; be always employ'd in something useful; cut off all unnecessary actions.
7. SINCERITY. Use no hurtful deceit; think innocently and justly, and, if you speak, speak accordingly.
8. JUSTICE. Wrong none by doing injuries, or omitting the benefits that are your duty.
9. MODERATION. Avoid extreams; forbear resenting injuries so much as you think they deserve.
10. CLEANLINESS. Tolerate no uncleanliness in body, cloaths, or habitation.
11. TRANQUILLITY. Be not disturbed at trifles, or at accidents common or unavoidable.
12. CHASTITY. Rarely use venery but for health or offspring, never to dulness, weakness, or the injury of your own or another's peace or reputation.
13. HUMILITY. Imitate Jesus and Socrates.

Franklin created a little book with one page for each virtue. The pages were ruled with red ink and set up in seven columns, one for each day of the week. He practiced this process of self-examination until he was 79, when he wrote his autobiography. His success was uneven but progressive. He believed that this process made him a better man and helped him live a better life. However, the more he tried to practice the virtues the more his pride grew. He concludes chapter 8 with these words: "In reality, there is, perhaps, no one of our natural passions so hard to subdue as pride. Disguise it, struggle with it, beat it down, stifle it, mortify it as much as one pleases, it is still alive, and will every now and then peep out and show itself; you will see it, perhaps, often in this history; for, even if I could conceive that I had compleatly (sic) overcome it, I should probably be proud of my humility."[4]

---

[4] Ibid.

No matter how successful the moralist becomes, he always fails in the end. Willing ourselves to holiness never works. We can be successful in some areas of life while failing in others. This does not mean that the moralist does not improve himself through the process. A moralist like Franklin leads an exemplary life and accomplishes much while never achieving moral perfection. Moralism is the way of most religious people. They seek to control vice and practice virtue through the exercise of their wills, but no one ever succeeds in the end.

The third option is God's way. We can see that the law is good because it exposes our guilt and so opens us up to receive God's grace. A moralist has no room for grace. His refuses to accept grace. This is what Paul explains in verse 13. Our sin is exposed through God's law. The sinner wants to blame the law for his pain. "I'm dying inside so let's get rid of the law. I feel guilty so there must be something wrong with the law that condemns me. I don't want to feel bad anymore, so let's get rid of the law." This is simply human nature trying to vindicate itself. But God's law is much more like a CT scan. It shows us what is really wrong so it can be corrected. The sin inside of us is killing us but we can't see it without the law.

GOD'S CT SCAN

A young couple had been coming to our church for a short time when they made an appointment to see me about performing their wedding. I went through the normal interview process getting to know them better. It was soon apparent that they were living together so I addressed the matter with them. They were honest in answering my questions. They had been living together now for a couple of years. I asked them if they understood that this was sin. They were uncomfortable and evasive so I opened my Bible and had them read 1 Thessalonians 4:3-5. "For this is the will of God, your sanctification; that is that you abstain from sexual immorality; that each of you know how to possess his own vessel in sanctification and honor, not in lustful passion, like the Gentiles who do not know

God." They responded that they understood that the Bible called their sexual union sin. So I went on to explain my standard practice in these matters. The sexual relationship is sin so they needed to agree with God's assessment of their union as sin. Once they agreed with God about their sin then God is a God of grace and we could proceed in one of three ways. 1) They could get married immediately in a quiet ceremony without the church wedding and then have a public reception at another time. 2) They could separate and live apart until the wedding, pledging to abstain from sexual immorality. 3) They could continue to live together but agree to abstain from sexual intercourse until the wedding night. I explained that I would consider that a sacred pledge before God. Although others would not know, God would. The purpose was so that they could learn to "possess their own bodies in honor." I have offered this option to many and have seen some remarkable transformations in the relationship. Often the bride will confide in me as the wedding approaches that she feels pure and honored for the first time in a long time.

This couple became quite angry. The woman in particular was deeply offended at my offer. They told me that this was totally unacceptable and left my office quickly. I never saw them in church again, but the next week I received a phone call from the mother of the bride, a woman I had never met before. She and her husband attended a church in another part of the state, and had been quite concerned for their daughter for several years. They had been delighted to hear that she was attending our church and talking to me about a church wedding. They had high hopes that this would draw their daughter back to Christ. Now I had ruined it all. The mother was very angry with me. How could I destroy her daughter's life by refusing to perform a church wedding? I was driving them away from church. Here was a mother who believed that the best way to get her daughter back to Christ was to ignore her sin. God's grace, to her, meant the grace to pretend no sin took place. The truth is that there is no grace without the law and the law had done its job. The woman was confronted with sin and offered a way to receive God's grace for that sin. If there was no sin then there was no need for grace. The mother wanted me to look at it as temporary mistake that I could help them correct. This is the wrong diagnosis. A wrong diagnosis only leads to a wrong remedy and that is why the law is so important. We need the law to diagnose what is wrong with us. The law is designed to show us our sinfulness so that we can go to the only one who can fix what is wrong in our souls – Jesus Christ.

Sin uses the good to reveal our evil. The real problem is not the law but our sin. Paul writes: "In order that (sin) might be shown to be sin by effecting my death through that which is good." The power of sin inside of each of us is so insidious that sin can take what is good and use it for evil. All sin essentially takes something God intended for good and turns it into something bad. To use Paul's illustration of lust, the law says that we should not lust after our neighbor's boat, car, house, snowmobile, position, wife or anything else that is not ours. Is there anything wrong with those things themselves? No, of course not. Sin takes what is perfectly good and holy and pure, and turns it into that which is dirty and evil. Now follow Paul's progression of thought here. We don't think there is anything wrong with these good things until sin uses the good to actually show us our own evil. We think we're doing pretty well. We don't go around murdering people, so we feel smug in our selective self-righteousness until sin uses something good in our lives and turns it into dirtiness, and then we see our sin as God sees our sin. The word translated "shown to be" means to expose to the light, to strip bare or disclose what is hidden.

SIN UNDER COVER

Sin thrives in secret. Sin grows in darkness. Sin takes something good, and under cover of our own secret world we let sin take over. Slowly sin grows in the secret areas of our lives until it kills us. Sin always kills in the end. What is it Paul said? "The wages that sin pays are death wages!" Sin kills us with what was once good. How does sin kill us? Sin kills us by strangling us with our own sinful choices. We come to realize that we chose to follow sin's lead and we died because of our sinful choices. Our relationships die. Our ministries die. Our families die as long as sin is our employer and pays her wages to us.

So, the moralist argues, we must enforce the law. The problem is that the law has been ignored. But Paul points out that the law actually stirs sin to erupt. The purpose of this process from God's perspective is "that through the commandment sin might become utterly sinful." The law doesn't actually end sin in our lives nor does it make us righteous. Actually, the law does exactly what God designed the law to do. The law provokes more sin. The law aggravates sin in us. The law provokes our pride. "Nobody is going to tell me what to do or not to do. You have no right to impose your moral values on me. I'm going to live my way and do my thing." So sin that was relatively benign in us before suddenly becomes malignant in our souls. The law does this in us so that what we really are becomes evident to all especially us. God wants to expose sin. What better way to expose sin then to aggravate sin inside of us until it erupts like a volcano and spews its evil where all can see.

This is true of society as a whole. Paul tells us in Romans 1 that God sometimes gives a society over to pursue its evil until the society implodes by its own sinfulness and all can see the depravity of that culture. The same process happens in each of us. As long as we can rationalize our behavior, as long as we can make ourselves feel good, then we don't have to face our own sin. But God lets sin grow in the darkness of our secret souls until – WHAM! – the sin erupts against the law. Our pride drives us to go after what we know we shouldn't do and suddenly the whole world sees us for what we really are – sinners in desperate need of a Savior. Our sin is exposed through God's law. What could not be seen before is now evident. We feel dirty. We know we need a good cleaning.

Pet owners know that they can purchase a simple ultraviolet flashlight, otherwise known as a black light, to use for locating pet urine in the carpet. Wait for night. Turn off all the lights in a room and then turn on the black light. The black light causes the urine crystals to glow. Even old urine crystals usually show up under the black light. Every drop and dribble can be seen, not only on the carpet but often on walls and furniture. The offending urine was there all the time but it was invisible until the right light exposed it. The black light does not fix the problem. The pet owner needs to use special carpet cleaning supplies to correct the problem. The purpose of the black light is to reveal what is otherwise unseen so that the owner knows where to clean. In the same way, God shines the light of his commandments not just to make us feel guilty and leave us that way. He has a cleaning service to offer – the cleansing grace of Jesus Christ – but the cleansing grace of Christ cannot clean the sin until the law reveals the sin. The purpose of the law is to reveal sin. *The law is God's black light for our souls.*

Paul is giving us his testimony beginning in verse 7. Verses 7-13 tell us Paul's story before he became a Christian. These are all past tense verbs. Starting in verse 14 Paul tells us his story as a Christian. These are all present tense verbs. Paul was a moralist before he became a Christian. He lived and taught the law. He zealously tried to enforce God's law on others. He thought he was righteous – a good man – until the law pointed out his own inner lust. Then he saw that the law could not make him righteous. Instead sin used the law to prove how guilty he was. He became miserable in his sin. He knew how super exceedingly sinful he was because he came face to face with the fact that he could do awful things just like anyone else. The whole point of the law is to show us our sin. Sin gets worse and worse until eventually the law proves how utterly sinful we really are.

GUILT LEADS TO GRACE

God doesn't take joy in making us feel guilty. The whole point of guilt is to lead us to grace. God's law exposes our sin until we welcome His grace. Paul does not tell us about grace here because he has spent many chapters telling us about grace earlier in Romans. Paul's point here is to emphasize that we can never find forgiveness until we face our sinfulness. As long as we continue to make excuses or offer explanations we will never experience grace. As long as we try to stay in control we will never enjoy forgiveness. As long as we hang on to our pride we will never know His mercy. Pride is the enemy of grace. Grace cannot be accepted until need is acknowledged. As long as we are trying to earn it by our good works there is no grace. *We must face the enormity of our sin before we can appreciate the greatness of His grace.*

I worked for two years as the grading assistant for the Chairman of the Greek and New Testament Department at Grace Theological Seminary while I was completing my Th.M. degree. As his grading assistant I proctored his exams and graded the tests and papers. So I was the grader for his students but I was also a student myself. This dual role made for some awkward relationships with other students at times. They were my fellow students but I gave them their grades in class. One year I was proctoring an exam for a Greek grammar class when I became suspicious that one student was cheating on the exam. I watched closely from the front desk and the student kept checking something in his hand before writing the answer on the test. The room had two doors with windows so I slipped out the front door and walked to the back door. I could now see what the student was holding below the desk. He was most definitely cheating with a sheet where he had recorded the answers. I went back into the room and when the student came forward to turn in his exam I confronted him and asked to see what he was using. He showed me the cheat sheet, so I asked him to come with me. We left the room and went to the Dean's office just down the hall. There I reported what I had seen and gave the Dean the cheat sheet. The student was angry and defensive, but it was now out of my hands. He was subsequently dismissed from school. I never saw him again, but I hope that he repented and returned to complete his degree without cheating.

I had a good friend who was a student taking one of the Greek classes that I was responsible to grade. He was an excellent student but struggled with his grades. I remember one particular exam that he flunked. I graded the exam and turned in his grades to the professor. He had flunked the exam, but his other grades in the course were good enough to earn a barely passing grade. I remember talking with him at his home that weekend. He was embarrassed by his failure on the exam. He knew that I knew and it bothered him, so he talked with me about it. I knew that he struggled with his grades because of the incredible schedule he was trying to carry. He was married and had several young children. He was working 40 hours a week and taking a full load of graduate classes. He was determined not to be in school any longer then he had to be so as not to put his family through that stress. He told me that it bothered him to do poorly on the test, but he had had little sleep because one of the children had been sick and he had no time to study. He believed that his higher priority was his wife and children, and grades were not as important to him in those circumstances. I agreed. I told him that I respected him even more for what he was doing and that God would honor his faithfulness.

I was the law to both those men. I was the grader who determined whether they passed or failed the course. One man responded to the law by cheating. He was circumventing the law. He was avoiding the law and ignoring what the law said about his responsibilities. When I, as the law, exposed his failure he became angry and defensive. He tried to avoid the punishment but in the end the law punished him for his wrongdoing. If he did not repent and agree with the law then he would never experience the grace of God. He could not be forgiven and used for God's work until he agreed with the law. The other man responded to the law correctly. He did not like the hardness of the law but he obeyed it even if it cost him dearly. He might not look as successful as the one who cheated to get good grades but he was determined to live right. When I, as the law, exposed his failures he agreed with the law's assessment of his work. He accepted the results with grace and trusted God to use him even if the grades were poor. And use him is exactly what God has done over the years. He has been a highly successful pastor and teacher serving God faithfully for many years now. God has honored him with grace. The purpose of the law was fulfilled in both cases. The law reveals failure. It does not fix problems. The response to the law is critical. When we agree with what the law exposes then we can enjoy the grace God gives – and not before.

As a pastor I often have to confront sin in the lives of people I shepherd. No pastor enjoys being the enforcer of the law – the policeman for the church – yet using the law to expose sin is necessary for grace to be offered. How we respond to the law when it exposes our sin is a key marker of spiritual growth. I see it in myself and I see it in others when the law exposes sin. There are three responses to the law's exposure of sin. 1) Rejection – some respond to the law by rejecting it. When we rebel against the law and refuse to accept the law's assessment of our behavior then we will never experience grace. Many people refuse to agree with the law's evaluation. "I don't feel that what I did was wrong." "That is your interpretation of the Bible, not mine." "I don't have to do what you say." "I'll just find another church." 2) Deflection – some respond to the law by deflecting it. People deflect the law by agreeing with what the law says but then pointing the finger at others. "I was wrong but you should have handled it differently." "The church didn't treat me right." "What I did was wrong but you were angry when you confronted me, so you were wrong in being angry about it." All of these are common deflections and the result is no different than rejection. Deflection is just a clever attempt to reject the law's exposure but look good while doing it. 3) Confession – this is the only way to grow spiritually out of failure. Confession is agreement with God. Confession is acknowledging that the law's assessment of what I did is true and accurate. When we respond to the law's exposure with confession we receive God's grace in abundance. The law has accomplished its purpose by driving us to grace.

How do you respond to the law?

10
SIN'S GRIP AND INFLUENCE

Romans 7:14-16

14 For we know that the Law is spiritual, but I am of flesh, sold 'into bondage to sin. 15 For what I am doing, I do not understand; for I am not practicing what I would like to do, but I am doing the very thing I hate. 16 But if I do the very thing I do not want to do, I agree with the Law, confessing that the Law is good.

arl Sandburg wrote: *"There is an eagle in me that wants to soar and there is a hippopotamus in me that wants to wallow in the mud."* Every Christian experiences this conflict. There are times when we soar and times when we wallow. We experience this conflict but we struggle to understand, especially as we compare our experience with the lofty ideals expressed in the Bible. The pivotal passage in the New Testament for understanding this conflict is Romans 7:14-25. How we interpret Romans 7:14-25 speaks volumes about our theology of the Christian life. In general there are four ways that Christians have understood this passage over the years and the way we understand what Paul is telling us in this passage will define our view of the Christian life. A brief survey will help us grasp the importance of this passage.

THE HOLINESS MOVEMENT

The "Holiness Movement" developed in the late 1800's and had a profound influence on American Christianity. The roots of "Holiness" teaching can be traced back to John Wesley in the 18th century. Wesley's work on "Christian Perfection" was foundational to the later holiness views on sanctification. Methodist holiness taught that God's grace freed us from even the disease of sinful motives and the power of sin in our lives. A Christian could achieve a state of "entire sanctification," often through a dramatic spiritual experience, which allowed the Christian to have a "perfect love" and be free of known, voluntary sin. A person could fall from this state of perfection, and so need to experience God's grace often through a dramatic spiritual experience which allowed the Christian once again to have a "perfect love" and be free of known, voluntary sin.

Charles Finney refined and popularized this teaching in Reformed circles through revival meetings in the middle 1800s. Finney and Asa Mahan developed what came to be known as the Oberlin Theology – a view of the Christian life based on the concept that nothing is sinful or righteous unless it is performed as a free act of the will. A person is never commanded to do something beyond his capacity to do it, therefore he must have the ability to choose to do right and could attain a state of entire sanctification in his life through a special work of the Holy Spirit. Phoebe Palmer popularized Methodist holiness renewal through her "Tuesday Meetings" and the "National Camp Meeting Association for the Promotion of Holiness," formed in 1867. She spoke of a "second blessing" which was achieved through an act of total consecration to God. Once that took place a person was saved now from all sin. The revivalism spawned by Methodist holiness teachings later split with the arrival of Charles Parham and his insistence on the "Baptism of the Holy Spirit" in 1901. He argued that speaking in tongues was the sign of the Pentecostal experience. The Azusa Street Revival in Los Angeles in 1906 led by Parham and W.J. Seymour popularized the eradication of the sin nature through a second blessing of the Holy

Spirit followed by a third blessing - the baptism of the Holy Spirit - which was demonstrated by speaking in tongues.[1]

The Holiness Movement in its various forms generally argued that Romans 7:14-25 could not be describing the experience of a Christian. This passage was Paul's description of his pre-Christian experience. Once he came to Christ and experienced the power of the Holy Spirit in his life, his sin nature was eradicated and he was free from the power of known sin. The view depended on a definition of sin limited to known or voluntary sin and the free will of the person to use the power of the Holy Spirit to eradicate it in his life. Obviously Romans 7:14-25 was talking about known sin, so Paul must not be talking about his experience as a Christian. If this passage describes your experience then you have fallen from grace and need to receive Christ ... again.

THE HIGHER LIFE MOVEMENT

The Higher Life Movement can be traced to the teachings of William Boardman, who wrote *"The Higher Christian Life"* and Hannah Whitall Smith, who wrote *"The Christian's Secret of a Happy Life."* They were involved in a series of meetings in the English town of Keswick in 1875 which became an annual event, so the movement is sometimes called the "Keswick Movement." They had a profound impact on D.L. Moody who, although he did not follow Keswick theology precisely, taught very similar views of sanctification. The Keswick teachers rejected the holiness teaching of perfectionism and entire sanctification. They argued that the sin nature was not eradicated, leading to perfection as the holiness movement taught, but that it was also not merely suppressed, leading to constant conflict in the Christian life, as taught in reformed theology. The

---

[1] George Marsden, <u>Fundamentalism and American Culture: The Shaping of Twentieth-Century Evangelicalism 1870-1925</u>, Oxford University Press, 1980, pp. 72-93. Robert Clouse, Richard Pierard and Edwin Yamauchi, <u>Two Kingdoms: The Church and Culture through the Ages</u>, Moody Press, 1993, pp. 526-528.

Higher Life Movement emphasized the "fullness of the Spirit" as critical to "victorious living" and "abiding in Christ." There were two stages of the Christian life. The first stage was the "carnal" Christian stage and the second stage was the "spiritual" Christian stage. A person moved from the first stage to the second stage through an act of consecration. The consecration was an act of "absolute surrender" where one yielded his life totally to the Holy Spirit resulting in a fullness of the Spirit. The Spirit-filled life was a life of victory over sin. They called their view "counteraction," meaning that sin was counteracted through the fullness of the Spirit and the Christian lived on a higher plane of the Christian life.

A Christian had two natures which battled one another. The sin nature was in conflict with the spiritual nature. The "Higher Life" was achieved through an act of total consecration, so that the sin nature no longer ruled. This event was a repeated and repeatable event in the Christian life, so revivalism emphasized regular acts of consecration whereby the Christian would die to self and be filled with the Spirit all over again ... and again ... and again. D.L. Moody would often exhort audiences to "Get full of the Holy Spirit." Preachers would exhort Christians to examine themselves to see if there was any sin in their lives, and to be cleansed once again by the Holy Spirit. Popular hymn writers like Fanny Crosby, Frances Havergal and Philip Bliss wrote songs based on the concepts of total consecration. Hymns like "Oh, to be Nothing," "Dying with Jesus," and "Take my Life and Let it Be Consecrated Lord, to Thee," became popular songs in Christian circles. A Christian must empty self of self to be filled with the Spirit. Once the Higher Life was achieved through consecration, it became almost passive in nature. "Let go and Let God" thinking permeated the teachings. "Resting in Jesus" was equivalent to living the Higher Life.[2]

The Higher Life Movement generally teaches that Romans 7:14-25 pictures a stage of the Christian life that we can grow out of through revival or consecration. This passage speaks of a carnal or

---

[2] Ibid.

backslidden Christian who needs revival, or of a baby Christian who needs to consecrate himself totally to the Lord, so as to live on a higher plane of the Christian life. This passage is not normal for the Christian. A person who lives the Romans 7 experience is a carnal Christian who needs to re-dedicate himself to the fullness of the Spirit and rest in the higher life of a Spirit-filled Christian by faith.

NEW MAN THEOLOGY

In recent years a step-child of the Holiness Movement has developed. I call this the "New Man Theology." It is a reaction against the two nature view of many in the Higher Life Movement, without accepting the perfectionism of the Holiness movement. A Christian is a new creation in Christ who has crucified the old nature. The Christian does not have two natures, but one – a spiritual nature. This spiritual nature is essentially holy and good, and the Christian can live victorious over sin on a consistent basis because he no longer has an old nature. The normal Christian life is a victorious Christian life, and the reason we see so much failure in the lives of Christians today is that they have bought into the lie that we have two natures in conflict with one another. If we would just realize who we are in Christ, we would rule with Him over sin by the power that God provides. We do not have to struggle with sin in our lives any more. New Man Theology argues that Romans 7:14-25 is Paul telling his story of a pre-conversion struggle with sin. Many have popularized this view today. David Needham wrote a readable and cogent defense of this position in his book entitled, *Birthright: Do You Know Who You Are?*[3] The crux of the argument in support of Romans 7:14-25 being Paul's pre-conversion experience is that Paul admits total defeat in his battle with sin, and Paul would never admit total defeat because it runs counter to the rest of the New Testament.

---

[3] David Needham, Birthright: Do You Know Who You Are?, Multnomah Books, 2005. I agree with many of the arguments Needham makes but I think he has missed the point in Romans 7:14-25.

147

Paul is indeed admitting total defeat in his Christian life *as he lives it apart from the Holy Spirit.* The New Man alone cannot win the victory over sin in this life. In the flow of Romans 6-8 this is precisely Paul's point. We experience total defeat whenever we try to live our spiritual lives apart from the supernatural work of the Holy Spirit. Sanctification is a supernatural process of growth in the Christian life, but Romans 7 remains a normal part of the struggle of every Christian.

As a pastor I evaluate my interpretation of Scripture by two tests. I view Scripture through two lenses. *1) Is the interpretation exegetically defensible? 2) Does the interpretation reflect the real world of real people?* After all the arguments are said and done, the crux of the matter is that it must answer these questions. I believe Paul is talking about his Christian experience of attempting to live his life as a new man in Christ apart from the power of the Holy Spirit in Romans 7:14-25. This interpretation is exegetically defensible because the verbs in this passage are present tense verbs. Romans 7:1-13 uses past tense verbs, but Paul switches in verse 14 to talk about his present ongoing experience as a Christian. I do not think the change is merely to a gnomic or generic expression. I take the present tenses as continuous and descriptive of the ongoing struggles that Paul experiences in his Christian life. For me this is a critical exegetical argument in the interpretation of this passage. The interpretation also reflects the real world that I deal with everyday as a pastor. Pastors deal with sin constantly in the lives of their people. Christian leaders struggle with pride, selfishness and lust all the time. I am no longer surprised by what I see and hear from fellow Christians and I see the same things in me. Even the spiritual giants of history never gained permanent victory over their struggles with sin. There are times in every life when we, like Paul, face total defeat because we are trying to win the battle with our flesh by our own abilities as a new man. I know this experience well. Determined to be invincible, I soon discover that I am quite vincible! New man triumphalism never works.

AUGUSTINIAN THEOLOGY[4]

These viewpoints were all reactions against the doctrine of sanctification as taught in much of evangelicalism. The leaders of the reformation like Martin Luther and John Calvin followed Augustine in arguing that this passage teaches the regular, ongoing battle of the Christian life. Paul is giving his testimony about his life after he became a Christian in these verses, and we experience the same struggles today. This is normal and to be expected. Christians are positionally perfect in Christ but experientially struggle with sin. The Christian life is a war against the flesh. Sanctification is progressive meaning that we can grow – we can make progress in our personal holiness, but we will never achieve perfection in this life. The way we progress in the Christian life is not through special experiences where we throw ourselves on the altar; treat ourselves as nothing and get full of the Holy Spirit. Carnal Christianity is not a stage in the Christian life we grow out of by consecration. Carnality (fleshly living) is a reality we all face every day of our lives. We win the victory over the flesh moment by moment and day by day as we turn to the Holy Spirit and use His power to fight sin. We face a battle with the flesh every day of our lives (Romans 7). Christians must constantly use the power of the Holy Spirit for daily victory (Romans 8). These are not two stages of the Christian life, but two descriptions of our battle with sin.

I believe that this is the correct understanding of what Paul is saying here. Paul is giving his testimony as an illustration of what we all experience. In verses 7-13 he tells about his experience before he became a Christian because the verbs are all in the past tense. In verses 14-25 he speaks in the present tense of his ongoing experience as a Christian. These verses are not a stage we grow out of but the reality of our lives as Christians. Non-Christians don't struggle with

---

[4] J. I. Packer, <u>Keep in Step with the Spirit</u>, Fleming H. Revell Company, 1984, pp. 122-129.

these things. Some of these descriptions can only be said of Christians. Who am I anyway?! I am a saint who wrestles with sin.

A SAINT WHO WRESTLES WITH SIN

When Paul began his letter to the Romans he called them "saints" (1:7). We are all saints if we are believers in Christ. We are holy ones. We are saints by virtue of Christ's righteousness not ours. We are saints positionally but we are not perfect experientially. Real saints wrestle with sin throughout their Christian lives.

I am freed from sin's grip but I am not free from sin's influence (vs. 14). We know that the law is spiritual. We cannot ignore the law of God. Paul then makes two statements that confuse us until we understand them properly. He says that we are of the flesh. What does this mean? Some think it means that we are not Christians so Paul must be speaking about non-Christians but this is not what the word "flesh" refers to. In fact, this particular word literally means "of the flesh" or "like flesh." Paul uses this word in 1 Corinthians 3:3 to refer to the Christians at Corinth as fleshly because they were jealous and bickering. They were Christians but fleshly Christians. At the end of this section Paul writes clearly writes from the perspective of a Christian. "Thanks be to God through Jesus Christ our Lord! So then on the one hand I myself with my mind am serving (right now) the law of God but on the other, with my flesh (I am serving) the law of sin."

Paul is clearly a Christian here. He serves the law of God with his mind but he serves the law of sin with his flesh. This is the reality of his everyday life. So what is the flesh? *Flesh means human nature as the willing instrument of sin.* I am a new person in Christ but I still possess a human nature. My human nature is predisposed toward sin because of original sin. The flesh is my human nature subject to and directed by sin. It is not a stage of life or a period of time. Every Christian has the flesh living in him all the time because every Christian is still human. We are fleshly. This is not the old man that Paul said was crucified, but it is part of our human nature that will not be eliminated until we die and go to heaven. Sin seeks to control us and influences us through our flesh, the part of us that has human feelings, patterns and habits prone to sinful temptations.

The second unexpected statement that Paul makes about Christians is that we are "sold into bondage to sin." This clause explains what it means to be fleshly. We are fleshly because we are sold into sin. How can this describe a Christian? Paul told us back in Romans 6 that we are dead to sin. We are no longer slaves to sin, so how can this speak of a Christian? This particular Greek construction literally means that we had been exported for sale as a slave to sin in the past with continuing results for our lives right now. We have been freed from the bondage in a formal legal manner. We are no longer slaves to sin, but the former slavery still influences us and still has an effect on our lives because of the flesh – the complex set of traits that make up human nature. That is why Paul was careful back in Romans 6 to exhort us to consider ourselves dead to sin and not to surrender to the influences that Christ has freed us from. What was dead comes back to bite us if we let it because the flesh is prone to the directives of sin that once held total sway over our lives.

Jake Thomas was cleaning up the Werris Creek Cemetery when he came across a red-bellied black snake in a vase on a headstone. He cut the snake in half and left it in the vase while he finished cleaning up. He came back 45 minutes later and put his hand in the vase to extract the snake when the snake bit him twice. It was dead but still could bite. Jake was taken to the hospital and spent two days in intensive care recovering from the bite of a dead snake.[5] In the same way, sin can still come back to bite us in our flesh. Sin can influence us who have been freed from bondage to our flesh to slavery again. If we fail to understand the power of the flesh, then we are dangerous to ourselves and others because we are self-deceived!

Some people celebrate the victory over sin by handling real, live snakes as proof that they have been saved from the power of sin.

---

[5] Samantha Townsend, "Jake Thomas thought a long-dead snake couldn't bite. He was wrong," The Daily Telegraph, New South Wales, Australia, January 15, 2014.

Jamie Coots was a snake-handling pastor in Middlesboro, Kentucky who was featured in the National Geographic television show "Snake Salvation." A rattlesnake he was handling bit him and he died shortly after that.[6] The man was dangerous to himself because he was self-deceived. However people who claim to have achieved victory over the flesh spiritually are even more dangerous to others. *The most dangerous person you will meet in your Christian life is the person who thinks that he has gained victory over his flesh.* The man or woman who boasts about his victory over the flesh is the man or woman who is self-deluded and will destroy others with him when he falls into sin. When he falls he falls hard. Watch out. We had better take the power of the flesh seriously in our lives if we want to avoid the sins of the flesh.

WHY THEN DO I SIN?

Wanting to do what is right I end up doing what is wrong, Paul says (vs. 15). Paul is talking about himself as a new man apart from the power of the Holy Spirit throughout this section. He knows that he is a new person in Christ. This new person came to life when he came to Christ. Yet this new person by itself is powerless to control the flesh – his human nature with its willingness to sin. Just because we have a new nature does not mean that we can will ourselves to holiness and control the flesh by the power of our new nature. "I" is the new "me." The "I" in this section is the regenerate believer. The new man is at war with the flesh. This is the normal Christian life. However, if the new man fights this war with the flesh by himself without the power of the Holy Spirit, then the new man will lose the battle. It is like fighting an enemy without any ammunition. When we try to control the flesh by willing ourselves to holiness, we will always fail. It is a losing battle. Paul says, the harder I, in my new nature, try to do what I know I should do the more I

---

[6] "Snake Salvation pastor dies from rattlesnake bite," <u>Portland Press Herald,</u> February 17, 2014, p. A4.

find that I am doing the very things I hate in my new nature. It is all because my flesh – my human nature – is a willing instrument of sin. Sin influences my flesh so much that I follow the patterns ingrained in my human nature to do what I know is wrong to do.

A group of researchers in the Midwest made up of doctors and nurses had become concerned that the nurses in 3 area hospitals were not using their training to protect against blindly following doctor's orders which might endanger patients. They decided to perform an experiment. One of the researchers made a phone call to 22 different nursing stations on various surgical, medical and psychiatric floors of the hospitals. The researcher identified himself as a doctor and ordered the nurse to give 20 milligrams of a drug to a specific patient. There were 4 reasons why the nurse should not administer this drug. 1) Prescriptions were not to be given over the telephone according to hospital rules. 2) The drug itself had not been cleared for use in that unit. It was an unauthorized drug. 3) The dosage was dangerously excessive. The normal dosage was 10 milligrams, and it was clearly marked on the bottle they placed in the cabinet. 4) The order was given by a man the nurse had never met, seen or even talked to before on the phone. However, in 95% of the cases the nurses went immediately to the cabinet and took the ordered dosage to the patient's room. A researcher intervened at this point to stop the nurse and explain what had happened. Why would 95% of the nurses violate the hospital rules designed to protect against such mistakes? The researchers concluded that it was the frightening power of authority at work in human nature. Robert Cialdini, a social scientist who has studied the power of influence on humans concludes that human nature is "programmed" by patterns and social cues which have been ingrained in us to even violate the laws we know to be true. Our natural responses follow predictable patterns.[7] One would hope that hospitals today have even more

---

[7] Robert Cialdini, Influence: The New Psychology of Modern Persuasion, Quill, 1984, p.218.

protections against mistakes, but the reality is that human nature is still human nature.

The truth is that we operate much the same way in our spiritual lives. We know the rules (the law) but we still violate that law because our flesh drives us to do what we know we should not do. Our human nature – that complex set of patterns and desires – influences us to do what the rules tell us not to do. The habits of my flesh often control the choices of my life. Our human nature has been freed from sin's control. We could choose to live differently just as those nurses could have chosen differently, but often it is easier to just follow the habits ingrained in us and that is why we follow the flesh right into sin. The natural instinct of the flesh is to sin. We don't think about what we are doing. We just follow our feelings right into sin. And then wonder why we did it.

There is in every one of us a conflict of desires. Paul says, "I don't understand myself at times. That which I want this I do not practice but that which I hate this I do." What's the matter with me? Our fleshly desire does what our spiritual desire hates. We know this to be our reality all too often. Now this does not mean that we are powerless to avoid sin, that we can't help it if we sin. Sometimes Christians fall into this mental trap. "Poor me, I fell into sin and there was nothing I could do. My needs were too strong and I got caught. The devil made me do it. My passions were too strong for me." NO! NO! Paul will not buy this line of thinking as he will make clear at the end of this section and in chapter of 8 of Romans. Don't fall into the trap of victimization. "Feel sorry for me. I am just a victim here like everyone else." There is no room for a victim mentality in Paul's expression of the Christian life. We are always responsible for our sinful decisions.

Sin happens when the desire to do wrong is stronger than the desire to do right. If you are in a situation where your feelings to do what is wrong become stronger than your feelings to do what is right you will do what is wrong, but it is your choice to do that. Spiritual desires are in conflict with fleshly desires all the time, so don't put yourself in a position to follow your fleshly desires. Fight those desires because you have the power to fight them. You do not have to surrender to the flesh, Paul will argue.

Can Christians cheat, lie, steal, deceive others, succumb to homosexual or heterosexual attractions and still be Christians? Absolutely – all of the above. Does this make them right to do? Absolutely not! You can struggle with homosexual attractions and still be a Christian just as you can struggle with pornography and still be a Christian but – know this – if you give in to those feelings you are sinning. You are letting the flesh gain power over you. Just because you feel something does not make it right to do. Feelings don't determine right and wrong. God does. In fact, even something right in one situation may be wrong in another. Even if you have the legal right to pursue a desire does not make it morally right to do so. G.K Chesterton once put it this way: "To have a right to do a thing is not at all the same as to be right in doing it." What we do with our feelings determines whether the Spirit or the flesh wins out in our lives – whether we soar like an eagle or we wallow like a hippopotamus!

The irony is that when I acknowledge my sin I agree with the law (vs.16). The legalist in all his self-righteousness actually rebels against the law, but the sinner who confesses his sin is the one who truly agrees with the law. You cannot be a Christian by obeying the law but you become a Christian by agreeing with the law about your sin. As long as we excuse our sin and deny our sin we are rebelling against the law, but when we admit our sin and take responsibility for our sin we agree with the law that condemns our sin. The sinner who comes to Christ knows that the law is good, but the sinner who refuses to admit his sin denies the law no matter how scrupulous he is in other areas of his life.

The Apostle John talks about the tests of a true Christian in 1 John. One of the tests of a true Christian is how he responds to this matter of sin. "If we say that we have no sin, we are deceiving ourselves, and the truth is not in us. If we confess our sins, He is faithful and just to forgive us our sins and to cleanse us from all unrighteousness." (1 John 1:8-9) This is how you tell a true Christian from a false Christian. A true Christian constantly – present tense ongoing action – confesses his sins to the Lord and, in so doing, agrees with the law. When I know that I am doing what I should not be doing then I am agreeing with the law that exposes my sin. The response of a Christian is to confess that agreement with the law. In fact, the closer I walk with God the more I see my sin, not the less, and the more I agree with the Law about my sin. A true Christian acknowledges his sinfulness like Paul does in Romans 7 and in so doing he agrees with the law that condemns sin as he opens himself up to receive God's forgiveness. There is no forgiveness for those who deny their sin. If we excuse or explain our sin we are not confessing our sin. We must blame ourselves first. Then forgiveness from God or others can begin. A Christian is one who is constantly in a mode of confession for we recognize the law and our unholiness every day of our lives. We blame ourselves and this frees us to enjoy God's forgiveness.

Who am I anyway?! I am a saint who wrestles with sin. Romans 7 is not a flattering picture of the Christian life. The very fact that you wrestle with sin and you acknowledge your sinfulness is the first proof you are a believer. Saints wrestle with sin. Sinners don't! Sinners apart from Christ are dead spiritually. There is no battle, no struggle. It is only those who have been freed from the slavery to sin and are awakened to what God wants them to be in Christ that feel the struggle of sin in their lives. Saints agree with the law even as they break the law and are frustrated that they cannot live up to the law no matter how hard they try.

11

WHY DO I DO WHAT I DON'T WANT TO DO???

Romans 7:17-20

17 So now, no longer am I the one doing it, but sin which dwells in me. 18 For I know that nothing good dwells in me, that is, in my flesh; for the willing is present in me, but the doing of the good is not. 19 For the good that I want, I do not do, but I practice the very evil that I do not want. 20 But if I am doing the very thing I do not want, I am no longer the one doing it, but sin which dwells in me.

In Romans 6 Paul tells us that we are new people in Christ. We have been set free from slavery to sin to serve a new master. We are freed from slavery to sin to become slaves to righteousness. God calls us to live holy lives. How can we be holy? In Romans 7 Paul explores the ways that Christians try to be holy. The first way is through legalism – keeping the law. The legalist says that I control sin through the law. The moralist is all about enforcing the law both for ourselves and for others. The path to holiness is by keeping the law. Paul tried this and found that he could not be holy by keeping the law because as soon as he was successful in keeping one part of the law he failed in another and stood condemned. The law he thought would make him holy only brought him guilt and judgment, and the harder he tried to live by the law the worse it got. The fault was not in the law. The fault lay inside of him. So … if I can't make myself holy by keeping the law how can I be holy? I must realize that I am a new person by God's grace. Beginning in Romans 7:14, Paul explores the idea that if I am a new person in Christ then the new man can control sin and live a holy life.

I am a new person in Christ, so I can conquer sin by myself. I have been freed from slavery to sin, so I just have to work hard at living right. I may struggle with sin for awhile, but I am a new man made in the image of Christ (Colossians 3:10). I am able to be victorious over sin. Once I have conquered sin in my life, I can help others understand their new life in Christ. I can help others gain victory too. It is the name it and claim it mentality of the Christian life. Believe it and you have it. Fight the devil and you will win. Perfectionism leads to triumphalism. "New Man" triumphalism is the foundation for holy living.

When I graduated from Seminary in 1984 I walked the "sawdust trail" in the Billy Sunday Tabernacle in Winona Lake, Indiana. Billy Sunday was the most popular American evangelist between D.L. Moody and Billy Graham. No one preached to so many and saw so many conversions before Billy Graham began his ministry. Billy Sunday was a professional baseball player who played for the Chicago White Stockings, Pittsburgh Pirates and the Philadelphia Athletics from 1883 – 1890 when he quit baseball to preach the gospel. His crude and earthy preaching style and his energetic antics on the platform attracted much attention. He preached often against the moral evils of his day. No evil was more damnable in his eyes then "Mr. Booze," and his preaching influenced the Prohibition Movement. Along with salvation through Christ's death on the cross, he preached an energetic "New Man" triumphalism. He famously said:

> I'm against sin. I'll kick it as long as I have a foot. I'll fight it as long as I have a fist. I'll butt it as long as I have a head. I'll bite it as long as I've got a tooth. And when I'm old and fistless and footless and toothless,

I'll gum it till I go home to Glory and it goes home to perdition.[1]

"New Man" triumphalism is contrary to Scripture. If we take this approach to the Christian life we will end up in deep trouble. Many Christians do not understand Paul's point in Romans 7:14-25. They understand that legalism doesn't work, but they don't understand that the new man is powerless to win the victory too. We don't become Christians by our power and we can't live the Christian life by our power either. Yes, I am a new man in Christ, and it sounds so exciting to preach that the new "Me" can conquer sin if I will but exercise my "New Me" power, and fight the devil with everything I have in my power. We can look good. We come to church and we can look so holy. We look like we have it all together. We can fool each other into thinking that we are victorious Christians who no longer struggle with sin. After all, God has made us new people – new creations. We have a new capacity for God, a new disposition that orients us toward God. We have a new nature but the problem is that we still have our human nature. The flesh is our human nature controlled and directed by sin. When we become Christians we do not cease to be humans. The new person still has the old capacity for sin as Paul teaches us in these verses.

WHERE IS SIN ANYWAY?

In Romans 7:17-20 Paul is answering the question, why do I do what I don't want to do. Literally, Paul tells us that that the reason we do what we don't want to do is because of the "living in me sin" that we all possess (v. 17). God didn't eradicate sin from our lives when we became Christians. We sin because sin is still inherent in us. Paul is not trying to excuse his behavior here. He is still responsible for his choices because sin living inside of him is part of him. This is

---

[1] "Billy Sunday: Salty Evangelist. August 8, 2008. Christian History & Biography. www.christianitytoday.com/ch/131christians/evangelistsandapologists/sunday.

not a separate entity that he can blame for his sin. When I sin it is because sin is part of me and the sin that is part of me overwhelms me.

The first principle Paul teaches in verse 18 is that the new me lives with the sinful flesh in me. Paul distinguishes in these verses between his "ego" – his "I" – that is the whole person he is in Christ (the New Man) from the flesh that lives in him. Sin lives in the flesh that is part of the new man in Christ, and there is nothing good that lives in the flesh. The flesh is evil but the flesh is not the whole me. The flesh is not all that I am. Rather the flesh is inside of me and is part of who I am as a new person. God left this flesh – this human nature – in us when he regenerated us in Christ. The new me has the flesh, my human nature, still part of me. So "I" – the new person in Christ – want to do what is right and holy but "I" am not able to do what is good because of the flesh living inside the "I." I want to do "good," Paul says, but I actually end up doing evil, which I don't want to do (v.19). Why? I do it because the sin that lives inside of me is the one doing what I don't want to do (v.20). Christ made me a new person, but the new person is helpless to control the flesh that still resides in me as a new person. I am incapable of willing myself to holiness.

We can make several theological deductions from what Paul says here. First, there is absolutely nothing good living in the flesh. The flesh is sinful. Sin lives in my human nature and dominates my human nature. Why didn't God just eliminate my human nature entirely so I could be perfectly good? Because God gets greater glory by taking what is bad in us and remaking it into what is good through the process we call sanctification. He doesn't just dump our human nature. He transforms it into our human nature as He designed us to be. Meanwhile there is nothing good about it, and it still lives in us as Christians.

Second, when we sin it is because the "I" we are in Christ chooses to let the flesh take over. The new "me" gives in to the power of the flesh in me and that is why I sin. But I can't blame the flesh for my sin because the flesh is part of me. It is my personality, my background, my experiences, my genetic makeup, my chemical and hormonal characteristics and my learned behaviors – my habits. It is me but not the whole of me. It is me but I don't have to let it be in charge of me.

Sin isn't out there. Sin is inside of us. Our sin isn't about what our parents did or didn't do to or for us. Even if we clean up our lives, even if we get better jobs and make more money so we can do things we want to do, we will take our same sinful tendencies right along with us. Christians continue to struggle with sin because the flesh continues to be part of their lives no matter how much we paint the barn and put on the Christian mask. Husbands we can put on a good show in church. We can look holy and righteous here but act like selfish jerks at home, treating our wives like dirt when no one is looking. Why? Because we have "jerk" qualities built into us. It is called our flesh. Wives you can look like wonderful Christian ladies here at church while your critical tongues slash like knives at home, slicing and dicing your husbands and children into tiny bits. Why? Because you have something called the flesh living inside of you. The new me lives with the sinful flesh in me. This is my reality as a Christian. So … the new me wants what I cannot achieve by myself.

Only a Christian can make these kinds of statements because living inside of me is my new capacity for God. I now feel a spiritual desire to live for God that I didn't have as a non-Christian. This desire is powerful. I want to do what is right because God has changed me. I am a new person. I wish for new, godly, righteous experiences. Paul gives us his testimony. "I want the good," he says. This wanting to do "good" is present in me as a Christian. The verb translated "to be present" is a word that literally means to lie down beside someone, so the desire to do "good" is right with me all the time as a Christian. The word translated "good" is a word that means "beautiful, noble or honorable." I want what is honorable. I want what is beautiful in life. This is the experience of every Christian. I have yet to meet a genuine Christian who does not want what is pure and noble. No true Christian wants the dirty and the ugly. No true Christian wants to live in the gutter.

However, it is not easy to work this out in our lives, Paul tells us! We desire excellence but the actual doing of what is excellent doesn't happen. We want to be pure and noble, but what we often do is ugly and dirty. No true Christian wants to live in the gutter, but we all do sometimes. We are capable of taking those noble, beautiful desires and turning them into sinful ugly actions. Why? Because nothing that is good lives in my flesh, so when I let my flesh have its way in my life then everything I do turns dirty. It is not that we never do anything good or noble or excellent in our lives. Paul is not making a comprehensive statement here. He is expressing a common experience. We often do good things but we ultimately fail to live up to the desires that we have in Christ. We are always falling short of the ideal that we know God has for us. God has placed that desire for excellence inside of us as new people in Christ. The high ideals are there. We feel them and we want them but we never seem to reach them. I think this is one reason why Christians always have this sense of not quite measuring up. Ladies you want to be the perfect wife, mother and godly Christian, and you never quite get there, so you always have a lingering sense of failure. Men, you want to be the perfect husband, father and godly Christian, but you never quite make it. Just when you think you are doing pretty well – wham – something happens that exposes the rotten flesh in you, and you realize again that you rarely achieve what you want to become.

Matt Starr achieved national notoriety when he belly-flopped over 4-year-old Nick O'Brien to catch a foul ball at a Texas Rangers game on June 13, 2004. Edie O'Brien shouted to him that he should give her son the ball but he refused. Fans were appalled and Ranger TV announcer Tom Grieve administered a scathing commentary about him, but he refused to give up his prize. Players showered the boy with balls and bats after the game. Good Morning America invited Nick and his parents, Jeff and Edie to appear on the show several days later. Matt eventually held a news conference to apologize for his behavior and promised to mail the ball to the boy along with tickets to a future game. He said that he didn't want any more publicity about his actions and complained about the media's hyped coverage. The sad reality was that Matt Starr was a Christian who served in the children's ministry at Sachse Assembly of God Church.[2] What is there inside of us that causes us act like this? It is our flesh. The new "me" does whatever I fail to stop the flesh in me from doing.

AT WAR WITH THE FLESH

Here is an essential principle for understanding the normal Christian life. The new "me" wants to do good but the new me in Christ actually practices evil. I have to stop the flesh from taking control of my life, but I don't have the power by myself to stop it. I am at war with the flesh in me. The new "me" must be active in stopping the flesh because if I passively let the flesh have its way in me I will end up in evil even as a Christian. Yet the Christian while "he can will to do good, is unable to carry out the good he wills."[3] The form of these verbs tells us that this is an ongoing experience of the Christian life not just an event. Victory is moment by moment because I am capable of sinning at any time. The war in me is an ongoing war.

I was an assistant coach for my daughter's softball team for a few years. One week one of the other coaches and I were standing watching a practice when I made a negative comment about another person we both knew had caused some problems. She started to say something and then stopped herself. She put her hand over her mouth and said, "No, I'm not going to say that because then I would be gossiping and we shouldn't do that." I turned to her and said, "Good for you. I was wrong and you are right to stop talking about someone as we were about to do." You see how easy it is, how subtle the flesh is, how quickly it creeps into our lives? The battle

---

[2] Scott Farwell, June 17, 2004 cited by Mike Drago, "Foul Ball faux pax at Rangers game is déjà vu all over again," The Dallas Morning News, April 26, 20012.

[3] C.E.B. Cranfield, A Critical and Exegetical Commentary on The Epistle to the Romans, T. & T. Clark Limited 1975, 1:361.

between the new person I am in Christ and the flesh inside of me is a constant battle.

Why? Because we still have our same personalities, genetic predispositions, interests and past experiences that affect our choices in life. God doesn't change those things in us automatically when we become Christians. If I had a bad temper or was prone to alcoholism before I became a Christian then I still have those qualities inherent in my life as a Christian. If I was judgmental and prone to talk about others inappropriately then I still have those tendencies in my Christian life. If I tended toward negative thinking and depression then I am still prone to depression in my Christian life. If I am manipulative and deceitful then I will still struggle with those tendencies in my Christian life. These are the battles we all face, each one in our own personalities with our own particular flavors of sin. We cannot excuse these traits as personality flaws if they lead us into sin. The same "type A" personality that does great things for God is the personality that can destroy others by grinding them under his feet. Sin is sin no matter what our personality or genetic tendencies toward sin. The flesh is alive and well in us and sometimes we see the flesh come out in horrible ways in our lives. We are all fully capable of doing the most horrible things if we let our flesh have its way in us.

The new me has a new capacity for God along with the old capacity for sin, but the new me cannot control the sin in me by my own power. The only way to understand this battle in Romans 7 is to realize that the Holy Spirit is not mentioned anywhere in this passage. The Holy Spirit is not part of the struggle Paul talks about here. The battle Paul describes is a battle we are fighting without the power of the Spirit to make the right choices. The battle of Romans 7 is between the new me and the old flesh in me. The Romans 7 experience is my attempt to control the sin in me by my own power. I can't do it even as a new person in Christ. The Romans 7 experience is me trying to live right without using the power of the Holy Spirit to make the right choices. We can make the right choices at each intersection in our lives but not by ourselves. We can make the right choices by using the power of the Spirit to control sin, and God in His grace has given us this power to enable us to become holy in Christ. Willing ourselves to holiness will never work. We will end up in the frustrations of Romans 7 as long as we seek to live right by our own willpower. Many Christians rightfully reject legalism as a driving force for holiness, but substitute the power of the Christian will to produce right living. The sentiment is powerful and popular. It is the power of positive thinking over sin. We can do this. We can live like Jesus.

WWJD? What would Jesus do? The slogan was popular and many wore the bracelets as their pledge to do what Jesus would do. As an ideal to which we aspire it is noble. As an expectation that we can will ourselves to live like Jesus, it is unrealistic. We can trace the roots of this question back to Charles Sheldon and his very popular book, *In His Steps: What Would Jesus Do?* It was first published in 1897 to popularize the "Social Gospel" taught by Washington Gladden and Walter Rauschenbusch.[4] The Social Gospel sought to transform society by living out the values of Jesus to love and care for the needs of the hurting in the world. It is a wonderful sentiment doomed to ultimate failure because man cannot will himself to live like Jesus lived. We all inevitably fail.

The story begins on Friday morning as the fictional Rev. Henry Maxwell is trying to finish his sermon for Sunday morning. Henry Maxwell is the pastor of "The First Church of Raymond" somewhere in the eastern United States of America. He was struggling with his text from 2 Peter 2:21. "For hereunto were ye called; because Christ also suffered for you, leaving you an example that ye should follow his steps." He had completed the first two sections of his sermon on the atonement as an example of sacrifice, "giving illustrations from the life and teachings of Jesus to show how faith in the Christ helped to save men because of the pattern or character He displayed for their imitation." He was struggling to

---

[4] Robert Clouse, Richard Pierard, and Edwin Yamauchi, <u>Two Kingdoms: The Church and Culture through the Ages.</u> Moody Press, 1993, p. 487.

come up with suitable applications when he was interrupted by a shabbily dressed man at the door seeking help to find a job. He turned him away with regret and completed his sermon. On Sunday he preached the sermon, but as he concluded the message this same man entered the church and spoke to the people. He told them how his wife died 4 months earlier, and he was out of work. The man commented on how he had listened to the people sing: "All for Jesus, all for Jesus," but observed that if Christians really lived out those words then a lot of the troubles of the world would be eliminated. He asked, "What would Jesus do?" Then he collapsed on the floor of the church.

The next Sunday Rev. Maxwell preached his sermon responding to the man's question. He said:

> What I am going to propose now is something which ought not to appear unusual or at all impossible of execution. Yet I am aware that it will be so regarded by a large number, perhaps, of the members of this church. But in order that we may have a thorough understanding of what we are considering, I will put my proposition very plainly, perhaps bluntly. I want volunteers from the First Church who will pledge themselves, earnestly and honestly for an entire year, not to do anything without first asking the question, 'What would Jesus do?' And after asking that question, each one will follow Jesus as exactly as he knows how, no matter what the result may be. I will of course include myself in this company of volunteers, and shall take for granted that my church here will not be surprised at my future conduct, as based upon this standard of action, and will not oppose whatever is done if they think Christ would do it. ...Our motto will be, 'What would Jesus do?' Our aim will be to act just as he would if he was in our places, regardless of immediate results. In other

words, we propose to follow Jesus' steps as closely and as literally as we believe he taught his disciples to do. And those who volunteer to do this will pledge themselves for an entire year, beginning with to-day, so to act.[5]

The rest of the book tells the story of how the surrounding society was changed by this pledge to live like Jesus lived. The underlying premise of the book is that we can will ourselves to live like Jesus. The hero is the anti-legalist, the new man who can sacrificially love others like Jesus and how, if we followed the ethic of Jesus, our world would be transformed. The sentiment is popular and forms the foundation of many good and ethical churches and organizations but ultimately fails to change the world. Charles Sheldon wrote a wonderful story that never addressed the question Paul raises in Romans 7. Why do I do what I don't want to do? Why do I not do what I want to do? There is simply no room for the "flesh" in social gospel theology. Sadly society isn't changed by doing what Jesus would do because no matter how hard we try we are not capable of living the ethics of Jesus by ourselves. It is fiction not reality!

---

[5] Charles Sheldon, <u>In His Steps: What would Jesus Do?</u> Chicago Advance, 1897 from the Kansas Collection Books, www.kancoll.org/books/sheldon.

12
PRISONER OF WAR!

Romans 7:21-23

21 I find then the principle that evil is present in me, the one who wants to do good. 22 For I joyfully concur with the law of God in the inner man, 23 but I see a different law in the members of my body, waging war against the law of my mind and making me a prisoner of the law of sin which is in my members.

He earned the nickname "Rolaids Robber" because when he robbed a convenience store he would ask the clerk for antacids. Rafiq Abdul Mortland was convicted and sentenced to 8-10 years for robbing 8 local stores in Hennepin County Minnesota. He told police he needed the antacid tablets because of the stress caused by robbing stores.[1] Sin causes stress and Rolaids won't cure it. When we do wrong we feel guilty. Stress develops in those who know what is right but do what is wrong. We are at war so why do we surrender to the enemy so easily? The problem is that sin lurks inside each of us ready to betray us to the enemy. Paul tells us that the law of evil lives in me who loves the noble (v. 21). The law of evil causes stress in us every time we succumb to it.

---

[1] Chuck Shepherd, "News of the Weird," <u>Chicago Reader</u>, January 15, 2004.

Paul continues with his personal testimony here. He says, "I want to do what is noble and beautiful, but I find a law at work in me. Evil is present in my system." What is this law or principle that Paul is talking about? It is not the Law of Moses but rather a principle or rule that exercises authority in our lives even as Christians. In verse 23 Paul will call it the law of sin. This law or principle of sin is active in our lives as Christians. Here is the traitor that would betray us to the enemy whenever temptation rises before us. The sin principle is alive and well in every Christian. No matter how hard we try this sin principle betrays us in the heat of our battle with temptation. There are actually two laws at work in the Christian and Paul will develop this battle between the two laws in verses 22 and 23.

THE INNER AND OUTER MAN

Paul draws a contrast between his inner man and his outer man in these verses. Paul delights in the law of God according to his inner man, but the law of sin is at work in his outer man. I am a new creation in Christ. I am a new me! The new me looks good but struggles with sin. Now Paul is explaining why. The outer man is my physical being along with my personality. Each of us has an outer man. The outer man is our human nature – our personalities, chemical and hormonal characteristics, experiences, habits and lifestyles. The outer man does not automatically change when we become Christians. Paul uses a number of expressions to explain what is going on in our human nature. The outer man is governed by the law of sin. It is our flesh. Not merely our physical flesh but our nature as humans. Evil lurks in our human nature. What we do in life and how we use our bodies is the outer man.

Every Christian has an inner man. The inner man is governed by the law of God and is spiritual not fleshly. The inner man wants what is good, beautiful and noble in life because God has placed in the Christian these desires. The inner man is oriented around the mind not the body with its passions, Paul will argue. What I find most interesting here is that Paul teaches us that the real me is the inner man. This is what I am in my inmost spirit. The inner man is the center of my whole being. These are the deepest desires of my truest self as a Christian. Every Christian in his or her deepest self wants what God wants because God has created this want in us when we became Christians. Paul wrote in 2 Corinthians 4:16: "Therefore, we do not lose heart, but though our outer man is decaying, yet our inner man is being renewed day by day."

So Paul can say, "I rejoice in the law of God according to my inner man" (v. 22). This verb to rejoice is an emotional word – a powerful feeling. It is not just agreeing with God's law but actually loving and taking great emotional pleasure in God's law. The psalmist in Psalm 119 tells us that he delights in the law of God more than riches (14). God's statutes are his great joy. How can someone say that the law is delightful? The Psalmist tells us that he rejoices in the law because God's laws are his counselors (24). They guide him in life. Why can I rejoice in the law of God? I can only say this as a Christian. I rejoice in the law of God because it shows me my sin so I can turn to God to get it corrected. The law is like a magnifying glass to help us see sin for what it is. God's law is an objective standard that reveals our sinfulness. This is a blessing because then we can see sin for what it is and by God's grace correct our behavior.

There is a recurring legend that circulates on the radio and internet which has the ring of truth but cannot be verified.[2] As the story goes a principal of a middle school somewhere is faced with a problem in the girl's bathroom. Some of the girls after applying their lipstick then "kissed" the mirror leaving imprints that were difficult to scrub off not to mention unsanitary for the girls. So the principle gathered the girls with the custodian in the bathroom. The principal explained that it was hard to clean the lipstick off the mirrors every day so he wanted them to see what the custodian had to do to clean the mirrors. The custodian then demonstrated his cleaning process. He took a long handled brush and dipped it in the nearest toilet.

---

[2] www.snopes.com, "Little Print Cesses."

Then he used it to scrub the mirrors. That was the last day they found any lipstick on the mirrors!

The job of the law is to correct sin, and that is a blessing for the Christian who loves God's law. As a Christian I love the law of God in my inner man, but I see the law of sin defeat me in my outer man. Verses 22 and 23 draw a contrast between two laws in opposition to one another that are active in our lives. There is a war going on between these two laws. As Christians we love the law of God according to verse 22, but we also find that another law is operative in us. This law is different than the law of God. Paul calls it the law of sin. The principle of sin is active in us in opposition to the law of God. This law of sin operates in our members. This must refer to the parts of our physical bodies just as Paul talked about back in Romans 6:13 and 19. The sin principle is alive and active in every Christian working in our physical bodies to destroy us.

THE SIN PRINCIPLE

The guinea worm is a round worm parasite called Dracunculus Medenisis. It is found in certain areas of central Africa. People contract guinea worm disease by drinking water contaminated with guinea worm larvae. The larvae enter the human stomach and mate and the female worms grow as long as 3 feet. After about a year of growing the worm will eat its way through the abdomen out to the skin where it forms a painful lesion as it slowly emerges from the body of the host. Often the worm pokes its way out through the foot after working its way through the body. There is no known cure for the disease that incapacitates the person with pain as it winds its way through the body. Once the worm exposes itself there is only one way to extract it. A person must wind the worm slowly around a piece of gauze on a small stick centimeter by centimeter without breaking it off. The painful process can take weeks to complete, and the lesion is susceptible to infection during that time. If the worm cannot be removed the person often dies.[3] Sin is like that. Sin is easy to "get" but hard to eliminate once it takes us captive. Sin destroys us from the inside out unless we deal with the flesh that lives in us. Once sin comes to dominate us, the process of dealing with sin is sometimes a long and painful process. God certainly forgives us for our sin, but, like the guinea worm, we have to slowly clean it out of our system for the flesh comes to control us.

How does the sin principle work in us? The law of sin attacks me through my mind (v. 23). Paul tells us that this "different law" is "waging war against the law of my mind" so the battle takes place in our minds first. God has freed us from the authority or control of sin, but sin takes the field in battle against us to regain what has been lost. The sin principle is at war with us in our minds. If the sin principle can gain a foothold in our minds then the sin principle can regain control over our lives for how we think determines what we do. The sin principle will attack you first in your minds. You will begin to think that maybe the sin you are contemplating is not so bad after all. "Hey, I was overlooked for that promotion and made the scapegoat for a mistake that cost the company some money. Why shouldn't I cheat a little on my expense account or falsify my work log?" "I deserve a few breaks once in awhile so what's wrong with a little lie to make me look better." "The contractor charges too much so I'll just refuse to pay some of the bill that we originally agreed too. He won't mind. He makes enough already." We hired a father and son team to remove some of our trees in the backyard. They had three large orange cones to mark the sides of the road for safety reasons and someone came along in the night and stole one of the cones - just one. They probably thought nobody would miss it but those cones cost him $75 each, and he has lost at least one on the last two jobs. What makes people think this way? Sin. Sin begins in the mind every time. This is where the battle is engaged. Sin always looks good or we wouldn't be tempted in the first place.

---

[3] "Guinea Worm Eradication Program," <u>The Carter Center</u>, 2014.

TEMPTATION'S ANATOMY

This is the anatomy of temptation. Sin engages the mind in battle. The battlefield is the body. As long as we fight back with our minds the battle rages. The irony is that we feel miserable as long as the mind is waging war with the sin principle. We are conflicted. We are at war within! Jill is a hospital nurse working a busy shift. She is so busy that she even misses her break. She fails to give a patient his medication on time and realizes it 3 hours late. She administers the dose but how should she log the medication in his hospital chart? She can post it with the prescribed time or 3 hours late. Her mind struggles with the ethical dilemma. Bill is in the airport on a business trip with a few hours to kill before his next flight. As he walks by the newsstand he notices a magazine with suggestive pictures. He thinks about buying it. Nobody will know. His mind wrestles with a choice he knows is wrong.

Sin engages the mind in battle and when the mind fights back we are at war. When we stop using our minds to battle sin, we become prisoners of war. Sin wins by establishing patterns that control us. We don't see right. We don't think straight and that always leads to disaster in life. What we think looked so good and what we had come to justify in our minds turns deadly and hurtful as the full nature of sin becomes obvious.

The law of sin attacks me through my mind but it doesn't stay there. The law of sin imprisons me through my body. Paul goes on to say, "Making me a prisoner of the law of sin which is in my members." Once the sin principle convinces us to rationalize our choices and justify our behavior then the sin principle has captured us. The law of sin takes us prisoner. We become prisoners of war when the mind gives up. We had been freed from sin, but because we give in to sin it conquers us and we become POW's of the sin principle in our lives. Again, the military image is powerful. We don't belong to the enemy, but we become controlled by the enemy because we chose to let sin regain control in our lives. No longer is this just a matter of fighting temptation, but now it becomes a matter of defeat. No longer is this merely a matter of battle but now it is a matter of surrender to the enemy. The worst part of it is that the enemy is not out there. The enemy is in us. The enemy is the sin principle inside of us that has regained control of our lives and led us back into slavery to sin. If we give in and stop fighting the sin that enslaves us, we will die as prisoners of war.

On a flight back from Germany I read a book called *"Ghost Soldiers"* - the story of a dramatic rescue mission during World War II. When General Douglas MacArthur left the Philippines he abandoned thousands of American soldiers to the Japanese. The infamous Bataan Death March took place when the Japanese marched these soldiers to Camp O'Donnell and later to Cabanatuan. Many were brutally murdered and others died from starvation and malnutrition under horrible conditions in these death traps. The prison camps proved to be incubators for all forms of disease that ravaged the bodies of men, depleted through torture, starvation and vitamin deficiencies. After 3 years, 513 prisoners were rescued by the Army Rangers to tell their story. According to the survivors, many prisoners died in camp from what came to be called "give-up-it is." A prisoner would get this strange look on his face as if he could not bear another moment. His eyes would develop a million-mile stare, and within hours he would die, not from any specific physical infliction but from simply giving up.[4]

When we give up sin becomes evident in our physical lives. Sin does not remain merely a mental issue. Sin eventually becomes evident in our members – that is the members of our bodies. Our eyes begin to look at what we shouldn't look at. Our hands begin to do what they shouldn't do. Our tongues begin to lie to cover our choices. Soon we realize that we are truly captured by sin. We begin to do and say things we would never have dreamed of doing or saying. John Murray writes: "Our captivity to the law of sin is

---

[4] Hampton Sides, Ghost Soldiers: The Forgotten Epic Story of World War II's Most Dramatic Mission, Doubleday, 2001, p. 109.

evidenced by the fact that our physical members are the agents and instruments of the power which sin wields over us."[5]

Suppose that I am frustrated with life. I am unhappy. Life is not going the way I envisioned it. I feel unfulfilled and discouraged. I am ripe for the sin principle to go to work in my mind. After all, even our Constitution guarantees that I have the right to life, liberty and the pursuit of happiness. So, I'm unhappy with what I have, well, the grass is always greener in someone else's yard, isn't it? One of the greatest lies of the law of sin is the lie that we have a right to be happy and fulfilled in our lives right now. I think this is one of the most common excuses I have heard for sinful choices. "I got that divorce because I just wasn't happy in my marriage anymore. I want to find happiness, so I'll just go for what looks like it will provide happiness for me."

AUTONOMIC SPIRITUAL RESPONSES

Sin is addictive because it feels good. Sin anesthetizes the pain we feel, and, for those few minutes, we feel good. We have solved our problem. Sin is the anesthetic that gives us momentary happiness. Sayra Small started with Oxycontin and Oxycodone but graduated to heroin over time. She saw friends die from overdoses but she didn't stop. "What people don't understand is: drugs were not my problem," she said. "Life was my problem. Drugs were my solution."[6] Life is the problem. Sin is the solution. We want happiness but we feel pain. We numb that pain when we succumb to sin. What we don't realize until too late is that sin imprisons us when we surrender. Little by little the sin takes over in our bodies. We stop thinking about it because when we think about it we become unhappy. When we stop fighting sin with our minds then sin takes

---

[5] John Murray, The Epistle to the Romans, Wm. B. Eerdmans Publishing Co., 1965, pp. 267-268.
[6] Eric Russell, "Drug treatment funding in Maine is falling, but demand is greater than ever," Maine Sunday Telegram, February 23, 2014.

us captive. We become prisoners of war. We're chasing after happiness, and we grab what we think will give us happiness; however, when we get it, it doesn't quite deliver.

Robert Cialdini is a researcher in the field of human persuasion. He has spent a lifetime studying how humans influence one another and what makes us do what we do. He tells the story of mother turkeys to illustrate why we do what we do. Mother turkeys are very protective and loving toward their chicks. They warm, clean, feed and protect them very carefully, but researchers have found that virtually all of the mothering is triggered by one thing: the "cheep-cheep" sound that the chicks make. If the chick makes the "cheep-cheep" sound the mother will care for the chick, but if the chick does not make the "cheep-cheep" sound the mother will ignore it and sometimes even kill it. Researchers did an experiment with a stuffed polecat to illustrate this principle. Mother turkeys will fearlessly attack a polecat to protect their young. Even when a stuffed polecat was dragged by a string across the pen the mother turkey would attack it in a rage. But when the stuffed polecat carried a small tape recorder inside that made the sound of turkey chicks going "cheep-cheep," the mother turkey not only didn't attack but actually gathered the cat under her wings and cuddled her greatest enemy. When the tape recorder was turned off the turkey would attack the polecat once again. It is as if the turkey has a little recorder inside of her that has a trigger or switch that activates her mothering instincts. "Click the tape is activated and "whirr" the behavior is implemented. Cialdini believes that humans also have built in tape recorders. These little recorders are developed in us through our experiences, habits, personalities and human emotions. We too have trigger features inside us that activate the behaviors we exhibit. He has studied countless people in countless real life situations and observed that we unthinkingly follow the triggers built in to us. Someone pushes the right button – a husband or wife or child or friend – "click" our personality activates and "whirr" we go into action.[7]

Paul calls this the sin principle in us. It is our flesh, our human nature. As Christians we still struggle with the "click/whirr" triggers built into our personalities, and we must learn by God's grace to overcome those powerful influences if we are to have victory in Christ. Are you chasing after happiness? Just remember that sin takes us prisoner when we stop thinking. We give in to solve our problem in life but the end result is that the members of our bodies become controlled by the sin principle living in us. We want what is good but end up doing what is bad. The law of evil lives in me who loves the noble and that is why I do what I do.

---

[7] Robert Cialdini, Influence: How and Why People Agree to Things, Quill, 1984, p. 17.

13
HOW CAN I WIN MY BATTLE WITHIN?

Romans 7:24-25

24 Wretched man that I am! Who will set me free from the body of this death? 25 Thanks be to God through Jesus Christ our Lord! So then, on the one hand I myself with my mind am serving the law of God, but on the other, with my flesh the law of sin.

P aul has been explaining the conflict that exists between the sin principle living in our flesh and the law of God living in our minds. We know what we should do, but we do what we know we shouldn't do. Wretchedness is the result of the Christian struggling with sin. The word "wretched" means to be miserable and distressed. The Christian living in sin is miserable and wretched inside no matter what he shows to the outside world. Our wretchedness comes from two doctrines in conflict with one another. We believe in the doctrine of human responsibility, but we also believe in the doctrine of human inability.

Who wants to be wretched? We want to be happy and guilt makes us unhappy. Wretchedness cannot be normal, can it? God wants me to be happy so guilt must be bad. Guilt must be avoided or eliminated for me to be healthy and normal. Normal Christians don't struggle with guilt. This is the prevailing approach that I see in much of western Christianity today. We look at others in church and see happy Christians and assume that normal Christians don't struggle with guilt like we do. We must be abnormal. Pastors and counselors work to absolve people of their guilt so they can be free to be happy. The way to free us from our guilt is to deny one side of the dilemma or the other. We either deny human responsibility or we deny human inability. We think this will free us from the shame of our wretchedness.

Imagine Paul telling a modern psychologist his Romans 7 woes. The counselor would work to deny this responsibility/inability dilemma. Paul is not responsible because he is a victim who has been damaged by legalists who controlled him and made him feel guilty for everything. Paul is codependent. He has been hurt by others, let down by those he looked up to. Edward Welch, a licensed Christian psychologist, surveys the literature on codependency and lists the following characteristics of codependent people. Codependents tend to:

- ✓ Feel a sense of low self-esteem as a result of being criticized
- ✓ Feel intimidated by angry people and personal criticism
- ✓ Be either very responsible or very irresponsible
- ✓ Procrastinate
- ✓ Judge themselves and others
- ✓ Suppress their feelings
- ✓ Feel not quite good enough
- ✓ Feel guilty
- ✓ Wish others would like or love them
- ✓ Blame others for the way they feel
- ✓ Get frustrated and angry

✓ Think their lives aren't worth living.[1]

So Paul was a codependent, low self-esteem, guilt ridden victim of his dysfunctional family relationships. He is a victim who is too hard on himself. He should not feel so guilty. He is just needy. He needs some help to live a normal life, but he is fully capable of living a life freed from guilt and shame. It is not his fault. The first step is to stop feeling wretched about himself.

The evangelical church has sadly psychologized spirituality today to the point that the description above would fit almost every person! However, Paul is neither codependent or suffering from low self esteem. Paul is exactly where God wants him to be. Wretchedness is the normal result for Christians who honestly face the responsibility/inability dilemma of the Christian life. C. H. Spurgeon preached a classic sermon entitled "the Fainting Warrior" on this subject.[2] We are war with sin, and we know that we are responsible for our sin. The flesh is us. It is our personalities. It is our choices and our habits. But we also know that we are unable to control the flesh by ourselves. I am responsible for my flesh, my sinful choices, but I cannot get rid of my flesh. These two doctrines will make any man miserable. To know that I am responsible and to be unable to change my behavior is enough to frustrate anyone. No wonder we are wretched people!

Years ago when I was Academic Dean at New England Bible College I received a letter from a former student. The student had graduated many years earlier from Glen Cove Bible College. Glen Cove Bible College had run into financial difficulties and given birth to New England Bible College. New England Bible College was the holder of the official transcripts for Glen Cove Bible College. The

---

[1] Edward Welch, "Codependency and the Cult of Self," in <u>Power Religion: The Selling out of the Evangelical Church?</u> Michael Scott Horton, editor, Moody Press, 1992, p. 224.

[2] C. H. Spurgeon, "The Fainting Warrior," Delivered January 23, 1859 in the music hall of Surrey Gardens.

student wrote to me out of deep guilt. He had cheated his way through school and, although he had graduated, he was consumed by his guilt years later. God would not let him find peace. The Holy Spirit convicted him of his sin and he felt miserable. He asked me to take back his degree – to rescind his graduation. I had no authority to do what he requested, of course. I wrote and encouraged him to accept God's forgiveness for the sin he had committed and stop living under condemnation. His confession to me was sufficient for God to see his heart of repentance and to release him from his sin, and I prayed that he would find peace in his soul.

Guilt is good when it drives us to confess our sins and seek God's forgiveness. We do everything we can to avoid guilt, to deny guilt, to suppress guilt in our quest for happiness. However, guilt will get us whenever we give in to sin. We cry out with Paul, "Wretched man that I am!" This is exactly what should happen in our battle with sin. Guilt should drive us to Jesus who alone can give us victory over sin. He is the only one who can rescue us who live as prisoners of war in this world.

HELPLESS BUT NOT HOPELESS!

I want to be very clear at this point. This is not a cry of hopeless despair. This is a cry of frustration. We are helpless but not hopeless. Paul cries out, "Who will set me free from the body of this death?" He knows there is an answer but the first step is to cry out for help. Paul cries out for a person to help him, not a doctrine. He does not say, "What will set me free." Paul says, "Who will set me free. As Paul writes these words he already knows the answer that he will explain in Romans 8, but first we must see the problem.

The word translated "set free" is a word used of a soldier on the battlefield who runs to rescue his wounded friend crying out for help. God will rescue us who cry for help in our helplessness, but first we must be honest about our situation. We are carrying in our bodies the principle of sin. Sin leads to death, so we are lugging around with us this body of death. It was apparently the custom of some ancient rulers to punish a murderer by tying the dead body to his back, placing the body back to back with the living man. He must drag this rotting, stinking, dead body on his back everywhere he went.[3] This is the image Paul lays out for us in this verse. We are alive but we carry with us the dead body called the flesh, so corrupted by sin. We cannot get rid of it. We live with it for the rest of our lives. We are responsible for it and unable to get rid of it! This is the normal Christian life.

As human beings our physical bodies are damaged by sin. We live with that reality all of our lives. We are not what God intended us to be. As Christians we are not what we used to be, thank God, but we are not what we will become either. We carry in our physical bodies the chemical, hormonal, habitual and experiential aspects of sin. It is still with us. So we want to be good husbands and fathers, but we give in to the selfishness that pursues sin. We want to be good wives and mothers, but we are caught up in our self gratification. We are doing well and then "click/whirr" something triggers in us the flesh that we can never eliminate. We know we are responsible for it, but we are frustrated that we cannot control it.

How can I win my battle with sin? I must understand my own weaknesses – the spots where if someone pushes the "click" I go "whirr" without thinking. The only way for us to win this battle with sin is that we must face this fight honestly. It will do us no good to pretend that we can control our flesh. The person who claims victory over sin in this life is the person who fails to understand the power of the sin principle. The sin principle is so powerful in every one of us that given the right circumstances the "click/whirr" of our flesh will set us off into behavior we hate. The first step to victory is realizing that the flesh is too powerful for us and will drag us under if we try to fight it ourselves.

---

[3] Ibid. See also, Donald Grey Barnhouse, Romans: God's Freedom, Romans 6:1-7:25, Volume 6, Wm. B. Eerdmans Publishing Company, 1961, p. 241. Watchman Nee, The Normal Christian Life, Angus Kinnear, 1961, p. 78.

GOTCHA!

Anthony Wichman hooked into more than he could handle on a fishing trip near Kauai Island in Hawaii on July 19, 2013. He was about 10 miles out to sea when he caught a 280 pound yellow fin tuna. His boat capsized in the struggle leaving him clinging to the boat with the fishing line wrapped around his leg. The tuna dove with Wichman attached and dragged him 50 feet under water. "I had told myself that this was it. If he kept pulling there was nothing I could do," Wichman said. He was running out of air when the fish stopped swimming, and he was able to surface. He called on his waterproof cell phone, and the rescue helicopter arrived to save him. Wichman's friends arrived on the scene shortly after and were able to pull the tuna to their boat. They later sold it for $1400.[4] That is what temptation does to us. It looks great on the surface. Only after we hook into it do we discover its power. We think we have control of the sin, but the sin has us instead.

We had better understand this reality as Christians. We must face our fight honestly, or we will fall into sin. We will be dragged under by our own flesh. Jonathan Edwards was a great puritan preacher who was a leader in the Great Awakening in colonial New England. In his town of Northampton Massachusetts the revival was so incredible that almost everyone in the town became a Christian through the preaching of God's Word. Yet Edwards noted a few years later how the revival had failed to stick with so many. He wrote a classic analysis of true Christianity and false Christianity in which he described the hypocrite as one who claimed the greatest victory.

> The affections of hypocrites are very often after this manner; they are first much affected with some impression on their imagination. ... They are mightily taken with this as a great discovery, and hence arise

---

[4] Neal Karlinsky, "280 – Pound Tuna Capsizes Boat, Drags Fisherman Under Water," ABC News, July 25, 2013.

high affections. And when their affections are raised, then they view those high affections, and call them great and wonderful experiences; and they have a notion that God is greatly pleased with those affections; and this affects them more; and so they are affected with their affections. And their affections rise higher and higher, until they sometimes are perfectly swallowed up: and self-conceit, and a fierce zeal rises withal; and all is built like a castle in the air, on no other foundation but imagination, self-love and pride.[5]

Paul warns us. Beware the person who claims the greatest spiritual victories. He is filled with himself not God. The true Christian is the one who recognizes that he cannot defeat sin by himself. He will always battle the flesh. We must face our fight honestly, and, secondly, we must hope in our future victory. Verse 25 is the answer to the cry of frustration in verse 24. It is a cryptic answer because Paul will fully develop the hope we have in Christ in Romans 8. He just wants us to know at this point that his cry in verse 24 was not a cry of despair but a cry of frustration. The answer lies with the power of God's Spirit to give us victory day by day and moment by moment. When we are honest with ourselves about our sin we can be thankful to God for our future victory in Christ. When we are honest with God about our sin then we can cry out like a wounded soldier on the battlefield for help. We recognize that we cannot help ourselves and we look to God for His help in our dilemma. Paul explains this fully in Romans 8.

Paul is looking ahead to the end of the story in verse 25. While we are in this body that leads to death we will always struggle with sin. The ultimate victory only comes when we rise again with Christ and live forever in our new bodies completely freed from sin.

---

[5] Jonathan Edwards, <u>A Treatise Concerning Religious Affections</u>, 1746, Part III: Showing what are distinguishing signs of truly gracious and holy affections.

This is the end of the story and it is what Paul refers to with thanksgiving. He makes almost the exact same statement over in the great resurrection chapter – 1 Corinthians 15:56-57. Here is the end game that God is working toward in our lives right now. "Death is swallowed up in victory. O death, where is your victory? O death, where is your sting? The sting of death is sin, and the power of sin is the law; but thanks be to God, who gives us the victory through our Lord Jesus Christ." We will never be freed from this battle until we experience the final resurrection in Jesus Christ.

Paul develops this theme in Romans 8. He speaks of the groaning of creation looking for the day when all creation will be set free from "slavery to corruption" (v. 21). We groan along with all of creation for the day when our physical bodies – the battleground for sin – will finally be redeemed. He writes:

> We ourselves, having the first fruits of the Spirit, even we ourselves groan within ourselves, waiting eagerly for our adoption as sons, the redemption of our body. For in hope we have been saved, but hope that is seen is not hope; for who hopes for what he already sees? But if we hope for what we do not see, with perseverance we wait eagerly for it (Rom. 8:23-25).

How does this future hope help us now? We're frustrated now? Knowing our own inability is the first step to victory, and knowing the end of the story is the second step, but there is more to come in Romans 8. For now Paul wants us to understand that we do come out on the winning side of the battle with sin because if there is no hope then we are likely to quit, and the one thing we must not do is quit the race before it is over.

We can easily become frustrated with our inability to win the victory, but we must understand that God is not finished with us yet. The race is not over. That is why Paul goes back to the battle in this verse. He is saying in verse 25 that the victory is won, but meanwhile back on the ground the battle rages. "So then, on the one hand, I myself with my mind am serving the Law of God, but on the other hand, with my flesh the law of sin." This is the battle of every Christian. If you think that others don't fight this battle then you are foolishly mistaken. We all, including our greatest heroes of the faith, struggle for our entire lives with the sin principle living inside of us. How will we fight the battle?

Paul tells us that with his mind he seeks to follow the law of God. We must too. This is our objective every day of our lives. The law is not wrong. The law shows us sin, and we need to correct the sin in our lives as we seek to follow God's law. But we also have to face the reality of our sinfulness. Paul seeks to follow the law of God with his mind while recognizing that his flesh seeks to follow the Law of Sin. Here is the mind/flesh battle once again. We had best be alert to this reality, or sin will sneak up on us and destroy us. We must take the power of sin seriously if we are to win the battle with sin day by day. The mind must engage the flesh with our minds constantly. Mindless Christianity will always lead to failure. The mind must always be alert to the dangers and be prepared to fight the temptations.

In his book *The Unnecessary Pastor*, Eugene Peterson tells about his two sons who are both rock climbers. They carefully plan their climbs. In fact, they spend more time planning then they do climbing. They plot each step of the climb and then they put in what they call their "protection." They hammer pitons into small crevices in the rock face and attach ropes to these pitons so if they fall the pitons will catch them and keep them from crashing on the rocks below. Why? Because they know there is a high probability of falling.[6] We had better have our protection pitons driven into the rock of Christ if we want to avoid crashing in our spiritual lives. We must take sin so seriously that we build into our lives a way out of every potential temptation. If you expect to fall you will take steps to protect against the fall. So it is with sin.

---

[6] Eugene Petersen, The Unnecessary Pastor: Rediscovering the Call, Wm. B. Eerdmans Publishing Co., 2000, p. 12.

THE BATTLE

The normal Christian life is a life-long battle with sin. Some Christians argue that this is such a negative way to look at the Christian life. It is discouraging to look at this battle as a life-long battle. I agree that it can be discouraging to face this daily battle with sin, but we can also look at the frustration as one of the strongest proofs that we are true Christians. The battle with sin is assurance of our salvation. People often give false assurance of salvation based on feeling good about ourselves or having a high self esteem. The real assurance of salvation comes from the battlefield. We know we are with Christ when we are fighting sin that stands against Christ. In C.H. Spurgeon's sermon entitled, "The Fainting Warrior" he said these words:

> There are some here who say, 'I am never disturbed in that fashion.' Then I am sorry for you. I will tell you the reason of your false peace. You have not the grace of God in your hearts. If you had you would surely find this conflict within you. Do not despise the Christian because he is in the conflict, despise yourself because you are out of it. ... You may well be without any pain, for dead men feel no blows. You may well be without the prickings of conscience; for men that are corrupt are not likely to feel wounds, though you stab them from head to foot.[7]

The battle is the proof of a Christian not the opposite. If you are fighting temptation right now, take it from God that you are his, and He wants you to beat the temptation. He will make a way out for you. Take it and run. If you are feeling down because of guilt,

---

[7] C. H. Spurgeon, "The Fainting Warrior," Delivered January 23, 1859 in the music hall of Surrey Gardens.

remember that God offers you forgiveness through confession of sin. Guilt is good when it draws you to Jesus. We must always remember the end of the story as we fight now. This gives us hope, so we don't quit on our families, our marriages, our ministries and our responsibilities before the race is over, and we see the victory that God has planned for us in Christ.

We must face our fight honestly in the hope of our future victory. No man is a saint apart from Christ. Only in Christ do we have the victory, and only by the grace of Christ can we ultimately be freed from sin. We are all the same. There is no place for a holier than thou spirit to permeate Christianity for we are all – from the least to the greatest – sinners saved by grace – doing battle with the flesh by the power of the Spirit. We are all being remade in the image of Christ. We "beholding as in a mirror the glory of the Lord, are being transformed into the same image from glory to glory, just as from the Lord, the Spirit" (2 Corinthians 3:18).

RESTORATION

Our family along with two other families visited Rome in 2005 and enjoyed our tourist tour of the restored Sistine Chapel. I don't know what it looked like before the restoration but it was breathtaking when we saw it on a hot summer day with thousands of other tourists filing through the Chapel. Michelangelo spent four years (1508-1512) painstakingly painting the frescoes on the ceiling. Over the next 500 years candle smoke and burning coal would take their toll on this Vatican artistic treasure. Layers of soot dust and grime covered the masterpiece. The Sistine Chapel has 2 million visitors each year, or 7,000 each day, who carry in outside dirt and breathe out harmful carbon dioxide contaminating the art. Several restorations had been attempted down through the years but with little success. In 1980 a massive restoration was undertaken. It was underwritten by Nippon Television Corporation with a price tag of $3 million. Nippon also received exclusive photographic rights in return for their support – a fact that will be enforced quickly by one of the guards if you dare to pull out a camera! The restorers used a special solvent that was wiped over the surface. After 3 minutes the grime would congeal and could be wiped off carefully with a sponge. It was a time consuming process that was not completed until 1995. It took 14 years for a team of artists to restore the art that Michelangelo painted by himself in 4 years![8]

God is in the spiritual restoration business. He is restoring us to the masterpiece He intended us to be when He created this universe. The process is long and slow, but God will finish His work in us and this world. The Sistine Chapel is a spectacular wonder today. And so it will be with you and me when God gets done with us!

---

[8] Julia Fischer, "The Restoration of the Sistine Chapel," www.fischerarthistory.com.

SECTION THREE:

Living by the Spirit

14
POWER TO WIN

ROMANS 8:1-2

1 Therefore there is now no condemnation for those who are in Christ Jesus. 2 For the law of the Spirit of life in Christ Jesus has set you free from the law of sin and of death.

All those years I struggled to do well but always felt like a failure until that day on my couch in the mobile home studying for a Greek exegesis exam on Romans 6-8. I wanted to be good. I consecrated myself many times over so I could stand on that higher plane of holiness. I worked hard to control my sinful tendencies. From the outside I succeeded. I went to Bible College and Seminary. I won awards in New Testament Greek and Expository Preaching. I served faithfully in the church. I achieved, but, even as I achieved success, I questioned my inner motives. Was I merely achieving "in the flesh" or was "it in the Spirit?" I worked hard at holiness, and, by human standards, I did well. Yet something was missing. I longed to be passionate about the Lord and love people like Jesus. I struggled with pride, selfishness and lust. I read the biographies of Hudson Taylor, Adoniram Judson and many other spiritual giants. They lived on a plane seemingly beyond my reach. I concluded that I was just not cut out to be a spiritual giant so I would wallow along as an average Christian. I was made to be ordinary not extraordinary. I had made peace with my average calling … until that day in Merrywood Trailer Park. That day I saw Romans 8:1 in the light of Romans 7:24 and for the first time it made sense to me. The normal Christian life is both!

I am released from the sentence of sin by the death of Christ. This is my present reality. It is not just that I have been released, but I am right now released. I am released from the sentence of sin (8:1) even as I struggle with the wretchedness of sin (7:24). The first words of Romans 8 in the Greek text are, "Therefore now." Don't gloss over the "now" in this verse. In the light of all that I have just written, Paul says, NOW what is your situation? Right now, in the battle with sin, you need to know what your status is with God. Right now as you struggle with the flesh, as you serve the law of God with your mind but the law of sin with your flesh, you need to know that you are not under God's condemnation even now.

The word translated "condemnation" means literally the punishment that followed the sentence. It was the money paid in a civil suit as the penalty for doing wrong. This word refers to what you face after you are sentenced by the judge for your crimes. The sentence for sin is death. Sinners live in the prison cell of death, but Christ has set us free from the prison of sin. We deserved to die, but Christ died in our place on the cross, so we are released from the death sentence hanging over our heads. All we have to do is accept by faith His pardon, and we are released from our debt. We no longer have to serve our sentence. Before we come to Christ, we stand condemned to die for our sins. We are condemned criminals living on death row. But when we come to Christ, we are released from death row. There is now no condemnation for those who are in Christ Jesus. This is true even as I struggle with sin after becoming a Christian. I have been pardoned for my sins past, present and future. This is my legal status in Christ.

The pardon didn't eliminate my temper or change my personality. The pardon cancelled the penalty for my sin and wiped out the legal record of that sin. Justification declares us righteous. It does not make us righteous. We need to see this point in the context of Paul's argument for how we live holy lives. Let me summarize how Paul has developed his argument in Romans 6-7. The old man or woman that you once were is dead. The old man is you before you became a Christian and that person died and was buried. The old "guy" is gone. He is dead. When you become a Christian a new person comes to life in Christ. You are no longer slaves to sin. You no longer are dominated by sin because the old you is dead and a new you lives in Christ. The new "me" is not under sentence of death any longer. The new "me" has all the potential of living right and doing what God wants me to do. The problem is that the new me still has something of the "me" I once was. It is called the flesh.

A NEW ME WITH AN OLD DISPOSITION

This is Romans 7. I want to be good but I struggle with my human nature which still houses the sin principle. My flesh still wants to sin, but my mind wants to live for God. Just because I have become a Christian does not mean that I do what is right. In fact, I often do what is wrong. Many Christians want to deny this reality. They argue that such thinking is defeatist. God has freed us from the flesh through the power of the new man. John Eldredge is a popular author who has promoted this position. Referring to Romans 7 he writes: "Paul says, 'Hey, I know I struggle with sin. But I also know that my sin is not me – this is not my true heart.' You are not your sin; sin is no longer the truest thing about the man who has come into union with Jesus. Your heart is good. … In the core of your being you are a good man."[1] Eldredge acknowledges the reality of the flesh but minimizes the power of the flesh compared to the goodness of the Christian heart. When we adopt this position we gloss over the power of sin in the Christian's life with "New Man" triumphalism - just claim your good heart in Christ and you will live right. When we minimize sin we set ourselves up for sin. As a pastor, I have seen

---

[1] John Eldredge, Wild at Heart: Discovering the Secret of a Man's Soul, Thomas Nelson Inc., 2006, p. 144. I think there are many inspiring aspects to his book(s) but his terminology needs refining so as not to mislead people.

many (especially men) succumb to sin despite their best intentions. Testosterone Christianity does not control sin. It inflames it. If "my sin is not me" then who is it? Why bother to resist sin if it is not really me? If my heart is good then I don't need to fight evil in me. I am not responsible for my sin since it is not the real me. One man essentially expressed this argument to me in defense of his failure. "What I did was not who I am so you can't hold me responsible for what I did." This is the problem with making the new man into a good man who is not responsible for his fleshly appetites.

The "New Man" is a new person in Christ. This is true. There is no condemnation for that person, and that new person that I am in Christ is no longer a slave to sin. The new man is no longer in bondage. I am a whole new person, but I am a person who still possesses my flesh. I am still responsible for what I allow the flesh to do. The flesh is that sinful disposition in me that entices me to sin. Some call this the "old nature," and, as long as we understand "nature" in the sense of a disposition, I agree.[2] The reality is that we sin because inside of us the flesh is still alive and well. We sin because we want to sin not just because we were tempted to sin. This is the real world of the Christian life. I see it as a pastor and I know it as a person. Paul's testimony was that he still struggled with sin inside of him his entire Christian life because the flesh was still part of who he was even in Christ.

C. H. Spurgeon said in his sermon on the first verse of Romans 8:

> We once heard a friend say, 'I have got out of the seventh of Romans into the eighth.' Nonsense! There is no getting out of one into the other, for they are one. The field is not divided by hedge or ditch. I

---

[2] The two natures or one nature debate is semantically problematic because often the sides define nature in different ways. I would say that we are one person who has a disposition toward sin still living inside of us. This sinful disposition is called the "flesh." It is our human nature as it is inclined toward sin.

thank God with all my heart that since my conversion I have never known what it is to be out of the seventh of Romans, nor out of the eighth of Romans either: the whole passage has been solid truth to my experience, I have struggled against inward sin, and rejoiced in complete justification at the same time.[3]

So how do we deal with this flesh? Paul has outlined two methods Christians have used to deal with this flesh inside of us. First, we try to control the flesh by the law. The legalist, the moralist, tries to apply the law rigorously so as to control sin, but the harder we try to use the law to control sin the more we struggle with sin. The law exposes our sin, and we are miserable for no man can control the flesh through legalism as Paul demonstrates in Romans 7:1-13. The second method is to control the flesh through our new man. Some try to control sin by simply believing with our minds that we are freed from its power. We are new people with good hearts who can simply choose to live as God wants us to live. Paul tried live by the power of his new man in Romans 7 and it didn't work. He failed miserably and became frustrated by his inability to control the flesh. Yes, we are new people in Christ, but we are not strong enough in ourselves to control sin. We need a power that is stronger than the flesh and that is not our new man in Christ. This power is the Holy Spirit of God. The battle is a supernatural battle and requires a supernatural power to win.

A CAPACITY FOR HOLY LIVING

We now have a capacity for holiness living inside of us that we never had before. God the Holy Spirit gives us the power to live as God wants us to live. This is Romans 8. It is wonderful to realize that we are no longer under a death sentence. We no longer have to

---

[3] C. H. Spurgeon, "In Christ No Condemnation" preached on August 29, 1886 at the Metropolitan Tabernacle in Newington. Spurgeon's Sermons: Volume 32 (electronic edition), Logos Library System; Spurgeon's Sermons, Ages Software; Albany OR.

serve sin, but it is even more important to understand that we are no longer under the power of sin either – not merely because we are new people, but because the Spirit of God releases us from that power. C. H. Spurgeon said it well. "If He gives you the grace to make you believe, He will give you the grace to live a holy life afterward."[4]

Paul goes in verse 2 to tell me that: I have been released from the power of sin by the Spirit of life. The key word here is "Spirit." Paul uses the word "Spirit" only 5 times in chapters 1-7 of Romans and only 8 times in chapters 9-16. However, Paul uses the word "Spirit" 21 times in Romans 8 alone![5] As many have pointed out, there is no mention of the Holy Spirit in Paul's struggle in Romans 7:14-25. Paul's frustration, and our frustration, is living the Christian life apart from the supernatural power of the Holy Spirit. As soon as we leave behind our attempts to live the Christian life by the power of the new man, then we can learn to live the Christian life by the power of the Holy Spirit.

Paul calls the Holy Spirit the Spirit of Life because He gives life to all of us who were dead. We were like a desert before the Holy Spirit came to live in us. We were dry and barren spiritually. The Spirit of God brings life to our dead souls but this life must be cultivated and developed so that it does not grow dry and barren again. The new life we have comes from our justification. We are no longer condemned to die, but the cultivation of that new life refers to sanctification. Sanctification is the process of living as God intended us to live, of becoming what God intended us to become. Verse 1 is about justification. We are declared righteous. We are no longer under any condemnation for sin. This is a legal act. Verse 2 is about initial sanctification. Initial sanctification takes place simultaneous

---

[4] C. H. Spurgeon, The New Park Street Pulpit, "Justification by Grace," Sermon No. 126, delivered on the Sabbath morning, April 5, 1857 at the Music Hall, Royal Surrey Gardens.

[5] C. E. B. Cranfield, A Critical and Exegetical Commentary on the Epistle to the Romans, in The International Critical Commentary, T. & T. Clark, 1975, Vol. 1, p. 371.

with justification. It is the starting point for the new life in Christ. The Holy Spirit does something very real in us. He changes our status not just with God but with sin and death.

Sanctification requires the control of the Spirit. Paul tells us that the Law of the Spirit of Life has set us free. We are released from the law of sin and death by the law of the Spirit of life. How does this work? Paul is using the word "law" in an interesting way here. The law of the Spirit of life is not something written down in a legal document somewhere. It is not a legislated code of conduct. The word law must be used in the same way for both sides of this contrast. The law of sin and the law of the Spirit are opposites. So the word law is used here as an active force or power that is operating to control our lives. It is a law like the "law of gravity" – a force that controls us. A better word for the law here might be control. Which law controls your life? Is it the law of the Spirit of Life or the Law of Sin and Death? Paul is arguing in Romans 8 that sanctification requires the controlling power of the Holy Spirit to be active in our lives because we are not righteous just because God declared us righteous. We are righteous because God the Holy Spirit sets us free from the control of sin and death. The work of sanctification is a supernatural work.

The verb that Paul uses here is a past tense verb. The Spirit of God has already set us free. The verb means to exempt from liability or release a debtor from his obligation. Here we have initial sanctification. There are three phases of sanctification for every Christian. There is initial sanctification. There is progressive sanctification and there is final or ultimate sanctification. Initial sanctification is the beginning point of God's supernatural work to change us by the power of the Spirit. The Holy Spirit set us free from the control of sin when God justified us by the blood of Christ. This is not merely a forensic act like justification. Initial sanctification actually takes place in us the moment we are justified. Something real changes in us. We are set free from the control of sin. We are no longer in slavery to sin. We no longer have to sin.

Donald Barnhouse tells the story of a United States Marine who came to him to confess his sins and find forgiveness from God. The young Marine had been a Christian from his youth, but he had been caught up in the whirlpool of sin as a young adult, and now sought to experience the cleansing grace of God. They turned to 1 John 1:9, and he confessed his sins and found the forgiveness he sought. Afterward the man said he knew that he was forgiven but what was to stop him from returning to his sinful life? He didn't want to keep confessing the same sins over and over again because of his sinful weaknesses that had come to control his body. Barnhouse took him to Romans 8:2 and they read the verse together. He pointed out that the verse was in the past tense. God had set him free from the controlling power of sin in his life. Barnhouse said that it "was like money in the bank that had been deposited long ago to his credit. If he had been living in poverty while the credit was there, it was not the fault of the Holy Spirit who had provided the credit. It was there, as it is for every believer, living assets of life in Christ Jesus available now."[6]

USING THE POWER

God has set us free from the law of sin and death by the power of the Holy Spirit, but if we do not use that power to live then it is our fault not God's. We need to understand that even as Christians we struggle with sin, and God calls us to do battle with the flesh by the power of the Spirit as we shall see in Romans 8. This doctrine was precisely what the Higher Life Movement denied. Keswick teaching stressed non-exertion in the battle. A favorite term of Keswick teachers was "resting" by faith in what Christ has done for us. He has already won the victory over the flesh so rest in His victory. In fact, to fight with our flesh was to try to win the battle by the flesh. Watchman Nee taught that God places no demands on us at all. The sooner we give up trying to be better the sooner we will learn how to live the victorious life because our trying gets in the way of the Holy Spirit doing His work in us. The trouble with most of us

---

[6] Donald Grey Barnhouse, Romans: God's Heirs, Romans 8:1-39, Wm. B. Eerdmans Publishing Company, 1963, vol. 7, p. 12.

is we are not weak enough. Until our resources are exhausted we are not ready to let the Holy Spirit take over. "As long as we are trying to do anything, He can do nothing. It is because of our trying that we fail and fail and fail. God wants to demonstrate to us that we can do nothing at all, and until that is fully recognized our disappointments and disillusionments will never cease."[7]

In Keswick teaching you could be doing right but doing it "in the flesh" and so be wrong in doing right! The key to the victorious Christian life was to trust completely in the work of Christ and stop our striving with sin in this world. Consecration meant emptying self of self so that we could trust Christ to do His work. Hannah Whitall Smith wrote these words in 1867 under the heading "Willing to be Holy:"

> The whole thing seems so simple to me now, that I am perfectly astounded at my old darkness and am overwhelmed with astonishment that every Christian does not know all about it. It is just trusting Jesus that is all that can be said about it. It is to consecrate – a 'willingness to be holy.' That is what is really meant, because to be willing to give up sin is after all the only dedication we can possibly make, and even that willingness must be the work of Jesus and we must trust Him for it, just as much as for anything else." The only necessary steps are, first, being brought to see our own utter inability to help ourselves in the slightest degree, even to dedicate ourselves, and second, being enabled to exercise faith in Christ to do the whole work for us.[8]

The power of the Spirit has broken the control of sin but if that leads to passive spiritual lives then we are in big trouble for Paul

---

[7] Watchman Nee, <u>The Normal Christian Life</u>, Angus Kinnear, 1961, p.76.

[8] H. W. Smith, and M. E. Dieter, <u>The Christian's Secret of a Holy Life: The Unpublished Personal Writings of Hannah Whitall Smith</u>, Oak Harbor: Logos Research Systems, Inc. 1997.

does not teach passivity in Romans 8 as we shall see. Verse 2 is Paul's introduction to how we can have victory over sin in our lives. Christ didn't die just so we could be legally pardoned but left in our sin. God didn't save us to continue sinning. God has set us free from sin's control through the Spirit, but He has not guaranteed that we should be free from the battle with our flesh. Notice that the word "flesh" is not used here since we still have the flesh resident in us. In our initial sanctification God has set us free from the power of sin and death, but we will do battle with the flesh. Paul will go on in Romans 8 to talk about this battle with the flesh even though we are set free from the power of sin. However, now the battle is between the flesh and the Spirit, and this is where the victory will be won in our lives. God intended that we have victory so He broke the power of sin. He provides the power to defeat the flesh and break the control of sin our lives. God wants to set us free from whatever sin is controlling our lives today. God came to free us not just from the penalty of sin but from the power of sin as well.

God wants us to be free! He wants us to soar in Christ not wallow in sin, but it takes the power of the Spirit of Life activated daily in our lives to find that freedom. P.T. Forsyth was a well known theologian a century ago. He wrote: "Unless there is within us that which is over us, we shall soon yield to that which is about us."[9] He summarizes well Paul's introduction to the Spirit of Life in Christ Jesus that sets us free from sin and death. The Spirit of Life has set us free from the power of sin and will give us victory in the battle with our flesh. This is the supernatural power we need to win the war within.

The Trevi Fountain in Rome is the most famous modern fountain in the city. The fountain stands in front of three statues dedicated to the gods of this world. The Roman god, Neptune, is in the center and at each side is Health and Abundance. Isn't this life in our world? We want health and abundance. We want to be free to live successfully, but we will never find that true freedom apart from

---

[9] www.goodreads.com

Christ. We need God within us in control of what we are by human nature if we are to avoid giving in to the health and abundance drives of this world we live in as Christians. Apart from the Spirit of God we will never be able to truly find spiritual health and abundant life.

NEEDHAM AND THE CRABAPPLE TREE

David Needham's classic illustration of the crabapple tree helps us understand Romans 8.[10] The fruit of the crabapple tree is bitter and useless but if you cut the crabapple tree back to its trunk then you can graft new branches into the trunk. The new branches will produce the fruit of whatever strain of apples the branch came from originally. My father-in-law loved to graft new strains of apple tree branches on to old apple trees and developed a little orchard where he experimented with the grafting process. He would take a crabapple tree and splice in a shoot from a Macintosh Apple tree. He would carefully bandage the splice to protect it until it grew strong. The sap would begin to flow from the crabapple trunk into the Macintosh branch and as the sap began to flow the branch would live. Eventually the branch would produce fruit, but it was no longer the fruit of the crabapple tree. It was now a Macintosh apple, sweet and tasty. He would actually graft different kinds of branches to the same trunk. Each branch received the sap of the crabapple but produced the fruit of the branch. The tree might produce Red Delicious or Granny Smith apples depending on the branches. The tree had to be cultivated, or it would revert to its original crabapple status. He explained to me how the grafts had to be protected. He showed me how suckers would grow below the grafts. If those suckers were allowed to grow then the sucker branches would produce crabapples and would take the life away from the new branches that he had grafted in to produce good fruit. So he would carefully tend the tree. He would lovingly protect the grafts so they remained alive. He would carefully prune the suckers so they would

---

[10] David Needham, <u>Birthright: Christian, Do You Know Who You Are?</u>, Multnomah Books, 1999.

not return the life of the tree to a crabapple. It was an ongoing process of cultivation that started with a cutting back of the original tree.

Initial sanctification is a supernatural act of God in our lives. We are set free from the control of sin and death. The crabapple tree was cut back to its trunk. The Spirit of Life has cut back the crabapple tree the moment we came to Christ. God grafted in new branches that take the human life we each possess and turn it into the fruit He intends us to produce. The sap flows into new branches grafted into the tree, and those branches produce new fruit. Unfortunately, the crabapple trunk is still there. Our flesh was not eradicated. We were set free and the sap of human nature that flows through us is transformed by the Spirit into the branches we have become in Christ. These grafts have to be nurtured and protected so that the flow of life is not impeded and the branches dry up and stop producing fruit. Our flesh is still our human nature. The connection to the Spirit of Life must be maintained, or we will revert to our fleshly lives. The suckers that grow must be pruned regularly, or we will become crabapple Christians once again. The flesh will take the life away from the fruit we want to produce. Human nature (the flesh) takes over if the life of the Spirit is not cultivated carefully.

The next verses of Romans 8 are all about the cultivation of the life we have been given in Christ. It is an active, not passive, process. We must keep the Spirit's life giving power flowing freely to the fruit. We must constantly trim the suckers away from our fleshly human nature. All of this takes the supernatural power of the Holy Spirit to succeed. Without the Spirit we are doomed to live like Romans 7. With the Spirit we can enjoy the life of Romans 8.

15

SATISFYING GOD'S REQUIREMENTS

Romans 8:3-4

3 For what the Law could not do, weak as it was through the flesh, God did: sending His own Son in the likeness of sinful flesh and as an offering for sin, He condemned sin in the flesh, 4 so that the requirement of the Law might be fulfilled in us, who do not walk according to the flesh but according to the Spirit.

American author James Thurber gave this advice. "All human beings should try to learn, before they die, what they are running from, and to, and why."[1] What are you running away from in life? What are you running to? And do you know why? Everyone is running away from something and running to something else. Most people don't know why they are running, or where they are going. Psychologists devote their lives to these questions, and they offer many useful insights for people. The

---

[1] James Thurber. BrainyQuote.com, Xplore Inc, 2014.
http://www.brainyquote.com/quotes/quotes/j/jamesthurb153737.html, accessed February 28, 2014.

Bible gives us the ultimate answers to those questions because ultimately the answers are spiritual not psychological. Many people are running away from God to pursue sin. That is the wrong direction to be running. The Christian is a person who is running away from whatever particular flavor of sin dominates his human nature and running to the call of God on his life. This is what it means to be a follower of Jesus Christ. This is what sanctification is all about.

Paul tells us in Romans 8:3-4 that God sentenced sin in our flesh to satisfy His call on our lives. The flesh is what we are running away from, and the call of God is what we are running to. Why? Because God is at work transforming us into the people He wants us to become. If you boil down Paul's statement in these two verses it would be this one. God condemned sin in the flesh in order that the righteousness of the law might be performed in us. There you have it. That is what we are running away from and to and why! Do you want to be righteous? Here is how you actually perform as God wants you to perform. The first principle we must understand in that process is that the law is powerless to make us perfect.

FLESH AND LAW

Paul writes: "For what the law could not do, weak as it was through the flesh." Paul has stressed this principle again and again. Here we have it once more. *The law cannot change our hearts. The law cannot eliminate our flesh.* The moralist never understands this cardinal doctrine of the faith. Many try very hard to be good people, to keep the law but in the end all fail. The law is powerless to change us. The law is incapable of changing us inside where it counts. It is impossible to change our hearts by imposing an outside force like the law on ourselves. The law itself is not bad. It serves an important purpose and it accomplishes that purpose well. The law's job is to expose our sin, not change our natures.

Why? The law is rendered powerless through the flesh. The flesh is our human nature controlled by sin. The flesh nullifies any power the law might have in our lives. There are at least two reasons why the flesh renders the law powerless. First, because we are humans we will always selectively apply the law in our favor. This is human nature. It is human nature to paint the other person's sin black as night while we color ours a dull grey! That is why Jesus said; don't try to take the speck out of someone else's eye before you take the beam out of your own eye. It is simply too easy in our self-righteous pride to paint the other person as bad when we compare our sins. This is the flesh. It is human nature, and that is why the law is powerless to change us.

The second reason is similar. Because we are human we will always struggle with sinful defects in our own personalities. The flesh is still with us as Christians. We may be able to make ourselves look good to others. We may be able to justify our choices to satisfy ourselves, but we will never satisfy God this way. Deep down inside, where only God can see, lurks sin living in our flesh and influencing our choices. Billy Graham illustrated how God sees our sin by telling this story.

> Cliff Barrows and I were in Atlantic City many years ago with our wives. We had had a service, and we were walking down the boardwalk. A man was auctioning diamonds and other jewelry. We decided to go in. When we got married, I had given my wife a diamond that was so small, you couldn't see it with a microscope. So I decided to get her a better diamond. I had $65 in my pocket. I eventually bid it all and bought the diamond. It was a perfect diamond, I thought. The next day, I went to a jeweler, and I said, "Can you look at this diamond and tell me how much it is worth?" He looked at it through his glass and said, "Oh, maybe $35 or $40." "What?" I said. "This is supposed to be two carats!" "Look at it," he said and gave the glass to me. I looked at it, and even I could see it was full of defects. And that's the way God looks at us. We go to church and pray. We are good, moral people. But he looks at us through his

own righteousness, and he sees in all of us the defects our sin.[2]

And that's the way God looks at us. We go to church and pray. We are good, moral people. But God looks at us through his law and he sees in all of us our defects called sin. The law is powerless to make us perfect … but God does what the law cannot.

Christ came in the flesh to defeat the flesh. God condemned sin in the flesh. Doesn't the law already condemn sin? How is this condemnation different then what the law already does? Excellent question! The answer gives us the clue to our sanctification. The job of the law was to condemn sin meaning to point out our sinfulness, so Christ's condemnation of sin must mean more than just telling us sin is wrong here. The law already does that. The word "condemn" can mean pronounce a sentence of death or it can mean to execute that sentence – to carry it out. Here the word must mean to carry out the sentence of death on sin. God did that on the cross. He carried out the sentence of death for sin in this world. How does this relate to our lives today? What remains in us has already been judged – not just condemned but defeated. The law cannot destroy the power of sin, but Christ did on the cross. We are capable of defeating sin, not in our power of course, but in God's power because God has already defeated sin on the cross.

On March 19, 2003, the United States attacked Iraq and very quickly defeated Saddam Hussein. He was found hiding in a hole near Tikrit on December 13, 2003. Saddam Hussein was defeated. His power was removed and the people liberated but he was not tried and executed until December 30, 2006. Messy skirmishes continued for years and it was not until August 18, 2010 that the last American brigade left Iraq for Kuwait. So it is in our lives. The power of sin has been defeated, but we must still fight sin daily in our lives by God's power.

---

[2] Billy Graham, "The Meaning of the Cross," <u>Decision</u>, January 2005.

How and when did God defeat sin? Paul tells us. God did it when He sent His son "in the likeness of sinful flesh and about sin" (literally). God sentenced sin to death in the flesh because Christ, His son, came in the flesh. Paul has already told us in Romans 7:18-21 that the sin principle lives in our flesh. So Christ had to come in the flesh to defeat the sin principle living in the flesh. But Paul is very careful here. He chooses his words very carefully. Christ came in the likeness of sinful flesh. Paul is guarding the sinlessness of Christ by this expression. He came in the flesh but not in the sinfulness of human flesh. The word "likeness" means that which is made like something else. Jesus' flesh was very real. He was completely human but he was not sinful. This is a key verse in the doctrine called the "hypostatic union" of Christ's two natures in one person. It is simply the doctrine that Jesus Christ was fully man and fully God at the same time, and, as fully man and fully God, he suffered all that man feels, but he lived by all the power that God is. So Jesus was a sinless man. In fact, he could not sin and still be God.

STRAW AND STEEL

Jesus is fully God and fully man at the same time. Imagine that you have a steel beam to be used in construction. It will carry the weight of the building to be constructed. It is strong and unbreakable. This is the nature of God in Jesus Christ. Now suppose that you have a flimsy plant – straw or wheat! This plant can be easily broken. It will not carry the weight of the building being constructed or even the weight of two hands breaking it. This wheat is the human nature in Jesus Christ. If you keep these natures separate, as some have taught, then Jesus in his human nature could sin. He could be broken even though He would never sin in His divine nature. Many have taught this concept down through the centuries. The debate raged in the first few centuries of the Christian church over the union of God and man in Jesus Christ. The key is to understand that the Bible never separates Christ's "God nature" from His "man nature." The church has taught that such separation is heresy for then Jesus becomes less than God, and, as less than God, he could not destroy sin in the flesh for he would have been weak in the flesh. The answer is to understand that Jesus was God and man united in one person.

If you take that steel beam and you attach the straw to it in such a way that the straw could not be separated from the steel then you could not break the straw because of the steel. So Christ's human nature was united indissolubly to His divine nature and He could not sin. Paul is carefully guarding this doctrine here. Jesus is the God/Man. He came in the likeness of sinful flesh, but He was the only man who ever lived who never sinned. Thus He could defeat sin in the flesh because He was more powerful than the flesh. Jesus is like us in our human nature, but He is unlike us in that He was still God. God was wedded to man in one person in order to be our savior from the sin that controls us.

Christ was sent in the likeness of the flesh in which sin lived, but He also came, Paul says, to deal with the issue of sin in this world. Most translations supply some words here and refer to Christ's death as a sin offering. Literally, the verse reads simply that Christ was sent "about sin" or "concerning sin." This expression in the OT, however, often was translated as the sin offering or the sin bearer. Perhaps Paul intended that point here, but I'm not really sure that he did. Paul's point is fairly simple. We have issues and the issues are related to sin that lives in our human nature. Christ was sent to deal with those sin issues living in our human nature. He came to defeat the power of sinful flesh over us. He has destroyed that power, and we can live in victory in our battles with our sinful human flesh because there is a power available to us that is God's power.

WALKING IT OUT

This leads to the third principle in verse 4. We become perfect by walking in the Spirit. Here we find God's purpose in condemning sin in the flesh. This is the reason that God did what the law could not do. God condemned sin in the flesh so that we could become perfect. I use the term intentionally. Yes, perfect.

This verse is experiential not positional. We have been declared righteous positionally but we will become perfectly righteous experientially. We will become all that the law demands because God has condemned sin in the flesh.

The word "fulfilled" means completed or performed. God sentenced sin so that all the righteousness of the law could be performed or completed in us. This is God's goal, but the growth is a life-long process. All that God wants us to become is implanted as a seed in our souls at conversion, but the seed must grow and develop until we become all that God wants us to become in Christ. The law cannot produce this kind of fruit. You cannot command a tomato plant to produce tomatoes by passing a law that the plant must produce tomatoes. You can cultivate the soil, fertilize and water the plants, but the fruit is in the seed. The seed is what produces the fruit. So it is with God's righteousness. *God has implanted His Spirit in us when we become Christians. The seed of all that God requires is implanted in our souls.* It must grow and develop, but it is all there inside you right now.

Jesus taught this principle in Matthew 13:31-32. "The kingdom of heaven is like a mustard seed, which a man took and sowed in his field; and this is smaller than all other seeds; but when it is full grown, it is larger than the garden plants, and becomes a tree, so that the birds of the air come and nest in its branches." The power is in the seed, not in the sower. Perfection has been planted in you though it takes a lifetime to grow. Godliness lives in each of us in seed form the moment we put our faith in Jesus Christ. Why? Because the Spirit of God takes up residence in us in order to carry out the sentence God has pronounced on our sinful flesh and to fulfill all the requirements of the law.

We are called to produce the fruit of the Spirit but the fruit is in the seed. "The fruit of the Spirit is love, joy, peace, patience, kindness, goodness, faithfulness, gentleness, self-control; against such things there is no law" (Galatians 5:22-23). If we try to produce the fruit of the Spirit in our own energy and by our own abilities, it is like trying to command the tomato plant to produce tomatoes. The fruit is the work of the Spirit of God in us, not our own will power accomplishing these objectives. Sometimes we try to focus on one at a time. OK today I'm going to be faithful. No matter what someone does to me I will be loyal to them and to the Lord. Tomorrow I will work on gentleness and Tuesday will be self-control day! It doesn't work that way. It is all or nothing, and the fruit is produced by the power of the Spirit not my abilities.

Having said all that we would be wrong if we just sat back and waited for the fruit to come popping out in its full glory. Keswick teachers liked to use the term "counteraction" to describe the power of Christ to control sin. The Spirit was the agent of "counteracting grace" in our lives as long as we didn't resist Him. Charles Trumbull, one of the popular Keswick teachers liked to use the slogan, "Let go and let God." Christ was within us, and so, by faith, we were to let go and let God take over, and He would counteract the flesh in our lives.[3] Keswick teachers pictured the Christian life like a balloon that was not inflated attached to a cart. The cart was the flesh. Christ would fill the balloon with the Spirit, and the balloon of the Spirit would counteract the weight of sin in our lives so that we could soar in Christ. The filling of the Spirit of Christ counteracted our tendency to sin, although we were still liable to sin without His filling our lives. The balloon must be constantly filled again and again so that we could overcome the flesh.[4] The role of the Christian was to wait on the Lord in faith for Him to fill our lives with His Spirit. If we tried to fill the balloon ourselves, we would simply be blowing the hot air of the flesh into the balloon. We might achieve some success but the end result was always spiritual failure. The key to victory in our spiritual lives was to "let go and let God." We must sit back and wait for God to fill our balloons.

Paul is clear that this will not work. The righteousness of the law is fulfilled in us who walk according to the Spirit and not according to the flesh. Walking is an active process. Walking is not passive. Walking is not sitting. Walking is movement on our part. We are going somewhere. We are taking steps in the direction we need to

---

[3] George Marsden, <u>Fundamentalism and American Culture</u>, p. 98.
[4] Marsden, <u>Fundamentalism</u>, p.78.

go. Walking is not sitting in the recliner of the Spirit waiting for God to lift us up to holiness. Walking is not resting it is participating. We must participate in this process of producing the fruit just as the gardener works with the soil and the seeds. Paul uses the word "walk" to tell us that this is an active not a passive process. The verbal construction used here teaches us that our walking is an ongoing, continuous process of walking. All the righteousness of God is produced in us who walk not according to the flesh but according to the Spirit. We must be walking and our walking must be in tune with the Spirit of God, or we cannot live righteously. We will not be producing the fruit of righteousness. Paul will spend most of the rest of Romans 8 telling us what it means to actively walk according to the Spirit and not according to the flesh because if we are not walking in the Spirit we will not be living right.

One day I was in an airport rushing from one terminal to another to make my connecting flight on time. I was sweating and puffing pretty hard when I noticed a man nearby walking half as fast I was walking but going quickly past me. He was walking on one of those moving sidewalks. I am sure you have all had similar experiences. I can walk on the moving sidewalk without working half as hard but moving twice as fast. This is what it means to walk in the Spirit. When we walk in the Spirit, he carries us along. We're still walking, but we walk dependent on him. That is a good analogy as far as it goes but there is more to it than just carrying us along. We must actively obey what the Spirit commands. We must follow what the Spirit says to do. We must be walking in the direction He commands. I often hear people say that they know it is the Spirit of God directing them because they feel peace about their choice. I do not deny that peace is an element in the process, but walking in the Spirit is not determined by feeling peace. This is far too subjective and, in fact, not the emphasis of the Bible at all. The emphasis of the Bible is on obedience.

Christians can justify almost any decision by using the phrase, "I feel peace about this decision" or "God gave me peace about what I am doing." If the choice violates what the Bible commands then all the peace in the world cannot justify disobeying God. You are walking in the flesh no matter how much peace you say that you feel.

Many years ago a fellow seminary student was faced with a crisis. His wife had suddenly left him in the middle of the semester to move back to live with her parents. He told me his story. They had been married for a couple of years. He had a good job and they lived in a nice apartment near her family home. She enjoyed her job and they both attended a good church and were active in ministry at the church. He came home one night and announced to his wife that he had quit his job. He had decided to go to seminary. God had called him to be a pastor and had given him peace about this decision. There was no prior discussion with his wife. He had never even prayed about it with her. He made the decision and within weeks they moved halfway across the country to go to seminary. He started school soon after and was happy in his studies and doing well. He had peace about his decision, but she had to pick up the pieces of her life. She couldn't do it, so she left him. We prayed about it together and, to his credit, he withdrew and returned to rebuild his marriage. He may have felt peace about his choice, but he had been walking in the flesh even though it sounded so spiritual. This is not how God operates in our lives. He had a God-given responsibility to his wife that he totally ignored. This is not how we walk in the Spirit.

Obedience, not peace, is the primary mark of walking in the Spirit as we shall see. A recovering alcoholic once told me that he was leaving his wife because if he stayed in the marriage she would drive him back to drinking. He had to make a choice, he said, and it was more important for him to stay sober then to stay married. He felt peace about his decision! No. He needed to stay sober and stay married! If you are acting sinfully, you are walking according to the flesh. If you want to walk according to the Spirit, you have to walk on out of that sin. God won't do the walking for you. If you want to walk according to the Spirit, you must stay away from those places that cater to your flesh. If you are walking on the right paths, you won't be standing in the wrong place.

Walking is our choice. The power to produce righteousness is His choice. *Don't worry about being perfect. Worry about being obedient, and God will take care of the perfecting.* His purpose in condemning sin in the flesh is to fulfill the righteousness of the law in us who walk according to the Spirit and not according to the flesh. God is more interested in the quality of your walk with Him than the quantity of your talk about Him. Walking according to the Spirit means listening to what God says and doing what God wants.

One of my favorite movies is the movie "Hoosiers," perhaps because I have an appreciation for Indiana basketball. In the state of Indiana teams from both big and small schools battle in one state tournament instead of being separated into divisions by school size. The movie is based on the true story of a tiny school and their amazing march to the state basketball championship. The Hickory Huskers led by Coach Norman Dale had only a handful of players. One of the players was a backup forward named Strap who was very religious. Early in the season as the Huskers leave the locker room for the season opener, Coach Dale noticed Strap kneeling in prayer. He wasn't moving at all so Dale asked one of the players, "How long is he going to be like that?" The player shrugged and said, "Until he gets ready."

The season plays out and near the end of the regular season the team is playing an important game. Everett, one of the starters, gets injured near the end of the fourth quarter. The team only has a couple of substitutes so Coach Dale looks down his bench and yells, "Strap, you're going in for Everett." The Huskers break the huddle and jog on to the court but Strap doesn't budge. He is kneeling on the floor near the bench with his head bowed. Everyone is screaming. The referee blows his whistle for the game to start but Strap doesn't budge. Dale yells, "Let's go, Strap." He still kneels in prayer. Dale yells again, "Let's go!" Strap doesn't move. Dale walks down the sideline until he is next to Strap, still kneeling on the floor. Coach Dale kneels down and says quietly but firmly, "Strap, God wants you on the floor." Strap looks up, and with a huge grin he rushes on to the court. Strap scores two baskets and the Huskers win the game.[5]

---

[5] "Hoosiers," Hemdale Film Corporation, 1986, written by Angelo Pizzo and directed by David Anspaugh.

Are you listening to God's voice in your ear? The Spirit of God speaks to us through the Word of God. The Bible functions like the guard rails on a mountain highway. To walk in the Spirit means to stay inside the guard rails. If we wander outside the boundaries of the Bible then we are walking in the flesh. We are not listening to God's voice in our ears. We must be obedient to God's Word first, and only then are we listening as He leads us step by step on His path to holiness. We must be willing to listen and obey – to stop or to move – as He directs our steps within the guard rails of the Bible.

16

WHAT ARE YOU THINKING?

Romans 8:5-8

5 For those who are according to the flesh set their minds on the things of the flesh, but those who are according to the Spirit, the things of the Spirit. 6 For the mind set on the flesh is death, but the mind set on the Spirit is life and peace, 7 because the mind set on the flesh is hostile toward God; for it does not subject itself to the law of God, for it is not even able to do so, 8 and those who are in the flesh cannot please God.

Romans chapter 8 is not so much a manual on how to live the normal Christian life as a description of what it looks like. Paul is describing the key elements that demonstrate a normal Christian life. We can tell what a normal Christian looks like and lives like by examining these verses, and the most important factor for living a normal Christian life is the mind. The mind is the key to life, Paul tells us. How we think controls who we are. The mindset of a normal Christian is different from the mindset of the world. If our minds are dominated by the interests of this world then we are not living a normal Christian life. Whatever concerns dominate our minds, control our lives. The mind is the continental divide for life. We are what we think.

Paul has just finished teaching that there are two paths we can walk in verse 4. We can live according to the pattern of the flesh, or we can live according to the pattern of the Spirit. Those who walk according to the Spirit find out that God completes or fulfills all the requirements of the law in them. Those who walk by the flesh carry out the works of the flesh. They sin. We can walk in one path or the other, but we can't walk in both at the same time because how we think demonstrates who we follow.

George Barna published a book entitled, "The Seven Faith Tribes: Who They Are, What they Believe, and Why they Matter." He discussed the book in an interview published on his website in 2009. According to Barna "Casual Christians" make up 66% of the adult population in America. On the other hand, "Captive Christians" make up only 16% of the adult population followed by the other 5 tribes (Jews 2%, Mormons 2%, Pantheists 2%, Muslims .5% and Skeptics 11%). He was asked in the interview, "What are the primary differences between the Casual and Captive tribes. Barna said:

> The lives of Captive Christians are defined by their faith; their worldview is built around their core spiritual beliefs and resultant values. Casual Christians are defined by the desire to please God, family, and other people while extracting as much enjoyment and comfort from the world as possible. The big difference between these two tribes is how they define a successful life. For Captives, success is obedience to God, as demonstrated by consistently serving Christ and carrying out His commands and principles. For Casuals, success is balancing everything just right so that they are able to maximize their opportunities and joys in life without undermining their perceived relationship with God

and others. Stated differently, Casuals are about moderation in all things while Captives are about extreme devotion to their God regardless of worldly consequences.[1]

Casual Christians choose happiness over holiness in life. They want both the pleasures of this world and the security blanket of faith when they need it. To use Paul's descriptions in Romans 8, Casuals walk according to the flesh while Captives walk according to the Spirit. Casual Christians are not normal Christians and may not be Christians at all. They are merely cultural Christians. Captive Christians are normal Christians because they are walking by the Spirit not the flesh.

If we act according to the pattern of the flesh that means that we are thinking about the things of the flesh. If we act according to the pattern of the Spirit it is because we are thinking about the things that matter to the Spirit of God. So the spiritual battle we face as Christians – and Paul is addressing Christians here – is first of all a mental fight. We must fight the battle with sin in our minds first. This is where the battle is engaged. The reason we sin as Christians is because we let the flesh dominate our minds. We sin because we allow the flesh to shape what we think about and how we establish our values. To mind the things of the flesh is to set our affections and our interests on the matters of the flesh. We establish fleshly things as our purpose in life. We pursue and desire the things of the flesh. We want what the flesh wants and this is why we sin. Every Christian who sins is sinning because he or she is doing what he most wants to do at that moment. We sin because we follow the flesh and not the Spirit.

What is the flesh? John Murray gives us a good working definition of the flesh. "The flesh is human nature as corrupted, directed and controlled by sin."[2] The flesh is our personality, our

---

[1] George Barna, "Casual Christians and the Future of America," www.barna.org, May 22, 2009.

[2] John Murray, The Epistle to the Romans, Wm. B. Eerdmans Publishing Co., One Volume Edition, 1968, p. 244.

nature, our disposition as human beings. This disposition, as we saw in Romans 7, is not eliminated when we become Christians. God doesn't zap us and change our personalities. God doesn't alter our genetic makeup, our chemical and hormonal drives, our learned habits and characteristics just because he justifies us by the blood of Christ. We are Christians, but we still have our fleshly characteristics so the man who struggles with a bad temper will still need to deal with his bad temper. The woman who struggles with pride must still deal with pride. The habits that dominate us are not automatically eliminated by conversion. You might say that the flesh is our default mode of operation. It is who we are when we revert to what we were before Christ. If we do not consciously and continuously shape our thinking by the values and priorities of the Spirit of God, we will simply fall back into the thinking of the flesh. We will slip into default mode.

HABITS OF HOLINESS

"But the ones living according to the Spirit think the things of the Spirit," (v. 5). The normal Christian focuses his/her mind on the ideas of the Spirit of God. We must allow the Spirit of God to shape and control our thinking. This takes effort on our part. There is nothing casual about this process. The Holy Spirit works out His power in us through the everyday habits we develop in life. What we do, say, think and feel on a daily basis become the habits of our lives. These habits carve channels in our minds so that we gradually learn a new default mode of operation for life. If thinking according to the flesh is the habit of our minds, then thinking according to the Spirit must become the new habit of our minds. This takes practice just like any other habit. *Habits happen only through practice.*

J. I. Packer put it this way;

Holiness teaching that skips over disciplined persistence in the well-doing that forms holy habits is thus weak; habit forming is the Spirit's ordinary way of leading us on in holiness. The fruit of the Spirit itself is, from one standpoint, a series of habits of action and reaction: love, joy, peace, patience, kindness, goodness faithfulness, gentleness self-control are all of them habitual dispositions, that is accustomed ways of thinking, feeling, and behaving. Habits are all-important in holy life, particularly those biblically prescribed habits that we find it difficult and even painful to form.[3]

Habits don't just happen. Habits are practiced until we do those practices by habit! Years ago the law did not require people to wear seat belts so I hardly ever wore my seat belt. Then I was rear-ended by a truck while stopped at an intersection on Route #30 in Warsaw, Indiana. The whiplash I experienced for weeks brought about a change in my behavior. At first, I had to consciously choose to put on my seat belt, but, as I did that consistently, putting on my seat belt became a routine. Now I hardly even remember putting on my seat belt when I get in a car because it has become a habit. On the other hand I am trying to get into the habit of going to the gym 3 times a week. Something always comes up and my gym time lacks consistency. The result is that I have to make it a duty until it becomes a habit. My daughter played two sports in college. Training was all year long. She talked about developing "muscle memory" by doing the same skill over and over again until the muscles remember and do it instinctively. The game skills are instinctive because they are habits developed through practice. We develop spiritual habits in the same way. Our spiritual muscles develop spiritual muscle memory through practice. Habits come from routine practice.

I know from personal experience and from pastoral observation that *holiness doesn't happen by chance. Thinking patterns are developed through discipline. The Holy Spirit must change us but He changes us*

---

[3] J. I. Packer, <u>Keep in Step with the Spirit</u>, Fleming H. Revell Company, 1984, p. 109.

through the habits of our lives. Prayer and the study of Scripture are vital habits to develop if want to think according to the Spirit. Private and corporate worship are essential habits through which the Holy Spirit works in our minds. Gathering regularly with other believers in a local church is a vital habit to cultivate because through church the Spirit changes our thinking. One man told me recently that he notices more struggles during the week when he misses church on Sunday, not because the preaching or the music is so inspirational or exciting, but because the reminders from the Word and Worship are necessary to keep him on track during the week. Believers rub on each other and that rubbing is important for our spiritual lives. If we only associate with those people that we like and are like us, then we will not grow spiritually.

Church is messy sometimes, but we need that messiness to shape our sanctification. The habits we develop at home are just as important. We practice patience, gentleness, self-control and kindness first at home. These become habitual dispositions when we are habitually practicing them with our families. I know that I will not learn the habits of love apart from the challenges of loving people in the daily experiences of family, work and church. These are the settings where the habits of holiness are practiced and this is why "hermit" Christianity will never work to produce holiness. Spiritual habits are developed in community. Holiness is worked out through relationships.

FLESH VERSUS SPIRIT

The fundamental battle in the Christian life is between the flesh and the Spirit. When we sin it is because we are thinking according to the flesh. We wail that God doesn't talk loud enough, but all we hear are the voices of the flesh talking in our heads. The devil simply appeals to what is already inside us to get our attention. We sin because we let our thinking become fleshly thinking, and we no longer hear God's warning. If we fill the hours of our days with television and romance novels, why should we be surprised if we become dissatisfied with our marriages and look for fulfillment elsewhere? If we focus our attention on boats, ATV's, nice homes and cars, is it any wonder that we become materialistic. Every sin starts in our minds. We didn't suddenly wake up addicted to drugs. We were enticed into the lifestyle by our thoughts. We become discontented with what we have so we lust for what we don't have, and as those thoughts come to shape our desires we slide into sin. What we are reading, watching and thinking about all week long will come to influence our choices to sin. We need a power beyond ourselves to refocus our thinking on God's values and interests. The Holy Spirit is our guide in this battle with sinful flesh. We need to learn the ways of God, and let the mind of the Spirit shape our wants if we are to enjoy victory over temptation.

Paul goes on to teach (v. 6) that how we think produces what we receive. What we think about produces what we get paid. The mind of the flesh results in death. Remember what Paul said in Romans 6:23 – the wages that sin pays is death. The mind of flesh is working for its employer sin and sin always pays deathly wages. Ultimately, of course, this death is eternal separation from God. The Christian does not have to worry about that for we have been justified by the blood of Christ, but the Christian still deals with the flesh, and the flesh still pays back deathly wages when we sin. The mind of the flesh leads to death. When we get caught up in the fleshly mindset we usually don't realize that we are working out death in our lives. We think that what we are doing feels good, but the flesh is working death in our lives, even while we pursue the sin. It comes as a shock when the flesh pays us back in death wages. The essence of death is separation. Sin leads to alienation from God. When we mind the things of the flesh, we will find that God seems very distant from us. This separation from God is deathly. When we mind the things of the flesh, we usually find ourselves creating distance from other believers. We begin to feel alone, and we withdraw even more from fellowship. The fleshly mindset leads to alienation, separation and loneliness.

However, the mind of the Spirit, Paul writes, leads to life and peace. We find closeness with God when we are thinking in tune with the Spirit of God. Life here on earth is a spiritual life. It is fellowship with God (Jn. 17:3). We also find peace. Notice that the next verse defines the mind of the flesh in terms of being God's enemy. So, to be at peace with God is to be a friend of God. To be at peace with God is to be in agreement with God. When we are in tune with the Spirit of God, and we are thinking the thoughts of God, we will live in harmony with God. So real, lasting peace comes from obedience. Life and peace are the results of thinking and acting in accord with the Spirit of God. We submit and obey, and it is in that obedience that we can be at peace. We may not feel tranquil. We may face great obstacles. We may struggle with feelings of failure, but, if we are obeying God, then we are at peace with God, and we can find closeness with God by being content with His call on our lives.

The thought product is either life or death. The issue is how are we thinking? What are we filling our minds with and what are we focusing our attention on? What we fill our minds with, what we think about will pay our wages in the end. What we produce in life comes directly from what we are in our inner man. Jesus said, in Matthew 7 that: "You will know them by their fruits. ... Every good tree bears good fruit; but the bad tree bears bad fruit. A good tree cannot produce bad fruit, nor can a bad tree produce good fruit." (Matthew 7:16-18) It is the basic spiritual principle of "garbage in/garbage out." Paul wrote in Galatians 6:7, "Do not be deceived, God is not mocked; for whatever a man sows, this he will also reap." What we think about and where we focus our attention will come back to pay us wages of life and peace or wages of sin and death. Count on it.

Nicholas Carr, author of the book entitled, *The Shallows: What the Internet is Doing to our Brains,"* said in an interview with CNN that the way we think is being shaped by the tools we use to think. The internet is changing the way we think.

> The net encourages the mental skills associated with the rapid gathering of small bits of information from many sources, but it discourages the kind of deeply

attentive thinking that leads to building of knowledge, conceptual thinking, reflection and contemplativeness. So, as with earlier intellectual technologies, the net strengthens certain cognitive functions but weakens others. And because the neural pathways in our brain adapt readily to experience, the changes occur in the actual cellular wiring of our brains.[4]

The irony is that in a matter of five minutes online I located this article in a search for information on how the internet influences our minds! Of course, this proves his point. The internet is extremely useful for "the rapid gathering of small bits of information." I, like most of you, use it all the time. I can access libraries of information sitting in my study through my finger tips tapping a keyboard. However, thinking – real thinking – is much more than gathering information. Real thinking is conceptual and contemplative. We have become good information gatherers but weak thinkers. We have the illusion of knowledge without the reality of knowledge. We need deep thinking to understand the mind of the Spirit. The mind of the Spirit will not produce life and peace through the gathering of bits of information no matter how useful those tidbits might be. The mind is our central command for life, and the mind of the Spirit is only developed through the disciplines of the Spirit. The disciplines of the Spirit are contemplation, Scripture, prayer and worship. As these disciplines shape our thinking, we will find real life and true peace.

WORLDLINESS IS A MINDSET

Finally, how we think determines how we live (vss. 7-8). Martin Luther famously said: "Temptations, of course, cannot be avoided, but because we cannot prevent the birds from flying over our heads, there is no need that we should let them nest in our hair."[5] When we listen to the mind of the flesh, we are letting the birds nest

---

[4] Matt Ford, "Mind Control: Is the Internet Changing How We Think?" 2013 Cable News Network, Turner Broadcasting System.
[5] www.quotationspage.com 1994-2013, Michael Moncur.

in our hair. There is no sin in being tempted. We are tempted all the time. What happens is that we begin to nurse that grudge or let our minds dwell on that picture, then the flesh begins to take control of our minds. When we are tempted we have about 5 seconds before we better start fighting back, or the flesh will take over. Alexander Whyte, the great 19th century Scottish preacher pierced the hot-air balloon of those who think that we can reach a point in life where we are above temptation when he said, "Aye, it's a sair fecht [sore fight – fierce battle] all the way."[6] There is no getting beyond our battle with the flesh in this life. If you find yourself playing around with sinful thoughts in your mind, then you know the birds are starting to nest in your hair. Watch out.

Worldliness was often defined in the past by what we did. Certain deeds were worldly, so the Christian was defined by what he did and how he looked because these were easily measurable standards. We must not drink, dance, and watch movies, smoke, attend the horse races, play cards or pool or even bowl depending on the Christian sub-culture. Certain activities were acceptable on every day but Sunday with some Christians. So playing cards was fine on Saturday but sinful on Sunday. Or perhaps it was the deck of cards that was used so playing "Rook" was acceptable but playing with face cards was sinful. The list was endless but the common denominator was what we did or how we looked. Holiness had a look. Worldliness was easily defined. It was simple to define worldliness by our outward deeds. There was a security in knowing what was worldly and what was not, and we could be comfortable in our spiritual lives once we defined the check list we would use for worldliness. We could feel safe in our holiness because we did not practice worldliness as defined by our check list.

The Bible does not treat worldliness so simplistically. *Worldliness is not what we do but how we think.* The Bible does not define worldliness by what we do unless what we do violates God's moral code in Scripture. Worldliness is not having a beer at a backyard

---

[6] Quoted by J. I. Packer in <u>Keep in Step with the Spirit</u>, p. 111.

barbecue or drinking champagne at a wedding. Whether I drink a beer or I don't drink a beer does not define whether I am worldly or not. This is far too simplistic a test of worldliness. The test is not whether we drink or not, but what the drinking demonstrates concerning how we think about life. Worldliness is how we think. What we do is worldly if we do it because of a fleshly mindset. This is a much harder concept to follow, but it is biblical. Why we do what we do is much more important than what we do provided what we do is not a violation of the moral code of God.

Years ago when I was in Ireland teaching some seminars my hosts would take me out to dinner in the evening. We enjoyed eating at the local pubs with the live – and lively - Irish music playing and the good food. It was a wonderfully pleasant experience filled with laughter and good friends. The pub life was a part of the culture, and drinking was a part of the pub life. I could not help but notice that whole families regularly ate at the pubs. Children grew up eating at pubs and, while the children did not drink, drinking was part of their culture. I noticed also that the pubs would have stacks of beer kegs on the sidewalk every morning, and my hosts told me that these were consumed every day so as to require a new delivery. Ireland has one of the highest rates of alcoholism in the world, and I think the culture has much to do with it. Alcoholism, of course, is a complex matter but one factor surely is a way of thinking about alcohol that starts at a young age. Alcohol is associated in the minds with good times, good food and good friends. This is a mindset – a way of thinking – that can be, but is not necessarily, worldly. It becomes worldly if it takes us away from God in our thinking. The critical concern is not what we do but why we do it. Young people in America commonly go to a bar on their 21st birthday to celebrate their rite of passage into adulthood by having a beer with friends. Is this worldly? Not necessarily but it could be. Do you feel compelled to have a beer because of social pressure and cultural values – because it is expected in our world? If this is the reason then it is worldly because you are succumbing to the world's way of thinking about alcohol. Worldliness is a mindset that is focused on the world's values. Such thinking will draw you away from God and can even become a form of rebellion. But if not, then it is not worldly for you can do it without surrendering to the mindset of the world. You see, this is a much more difficult and subtle test of worldliness.

Worldliness is not what we do but how we think about what we do. Worldliness is in the mind. The mind of the world is the mind of the flesh, and Paul describes the mind of flesh with 4 clauses (vss. 7-8). First, the fleshly mind hates God. This is why the fleshly mind leads to death. We will have no peace with God as long as the mind of flesh has control of us. The word means to be in a feud with God – to be God's enemy. We become hostile towards God so, of course, there is no peace. Even Christians can nurse a feud with God. We can begin to blame God for what He did or didn't do for us in our time of need. We can blame God for how others have mistreated us. We can blame God because we feel we missed out on the pleasures of this world. We can actually start to feud with God and the person who is feuding with God turns away from Him. This is the fleshly mind at work in us. God will always be drawing us back to His love and grace through the mind of the Spirit. Don't feud with God. It leads to misery and death.

The fleshly mind rebels against God's law. The mind of flesh does not subject itself to the law of God. The word means literally to arrange under or assign. The mind of flesh does not submit to the Law of God. The Law of God is the moral code prescribed in the Bible so violating this moral code is, by definition, fleshly or worldly. The Law of God reveals the character of God so it is natural that the flesh would not want to surrender to the Law of God. Here again we see that we can fight God by refusing to submit to what He tells us, and, if we are fighting God in our minds even if we do the right things before other people, we will find no peace with God. We are rebelling against God even in church.

Paul goes on to say that the fleshly mind cannot obey God. The mind set on the flesh is not capable of surrendering to God. It is impossible for the flesh to submit in obedience to God. It is a moral and psychological impossibility for the one who is focused on the flesh to submit to God. This is why when someone pursues sin they will always work to justify that sin in some way because they simply cannot accept the fact that God tells them that it is sin. They are unable to submit. It is the mind of the Spirit that surrenders to God and is capable of obeying God. So a person who is not a Christian and does not have the mind of the Spirit cannot obey God and a Christian who has given his mind over to the flesh cannot obey God until He lets the Spirit of God take control of his life through repentance from sin.

PATTERNS OF THE FLESH

Finally, Paul summarizes the fleshly mind with his fourth description. The fleshly mind cannot please God. If we are living in the flesh, we cannot even please God no matter what we do. A Christian, who is working hard and doing lots of good things where other people can see him, but living in sin in his private life, cannot please God at all. God is not pleased with all those wonderful things we do for others to see, if we are living in sin in private. We can preach great sermons. We can lead great worship services, but if we pursue sin in private, none of it pleases God. The ancient Israelites thought that they could perform the sacrifices and do the externals of the law while pursuing their sinful ways, and God would be pleased. God told them that He didn't even hear their prayers. We cannot please God while living in sin. It is impossible.

Now the flesh is our default position in life. It is what we fall back into whenever we do not have the mind of the Spirit. I like this quote attributed to Eli Stanley Jones, missionary to India: "If you don't make up your mind, your unmade mind will unmake you."[7] To use Paul's terms, if you don't stay in tune with the Spirit of God your fleshly mind will destroy you because the flesh is our default position as human beings apart from God. *Sanctification is the process of learning to think according to the Spirit and not according to the flesh.* This means that we must develop the habits and patterns of the Spirit otherwise we will default to the habits and patterns of the flesh. Sin is habit forming. A pattern develops in us as we practice sin that is hard to

---

[7] www.dailychristianquote.com

break. The flesh triggers our learned response and we mindlessly "fall" into sin because the pattern has become habitual. To learn to think according to the Spirit requires the breaking of the fleshly patterns and the practicing of new patterns that will lead to holy behaviors.

Earl Wilson is a Christian therapist and author whose secret sexual addiction eventually was exposed. He went through a biblical discipline and restoration process with a Spiritual Care Team. The process took seven years to complete and included the loss of his ministry during that time. He was eventually restored to ministry but the process was long and difficult. Earl and his wife Sandy tell their story along with Paul and Virginia Friesen and Larry and Nancy Paulson, the members of the Care Team. Together they tell the story in the book, *"Restoring the Fallen: A Team Approach to Caring, Confronting & Reconciling."* Dealing with habitual sin is a bit like peeling an onion. The team had to carefully peel back each layer to expose the patterns so that repentance leading to real change could take place. Several years into that process Earl made a very important discovery. The deceitful patterns that had become ingrained in his life over ten years of lies had become autonomic to him. He saw it for the first time when he had an appointment to meet his friend Nate at his home. Nate was not there when he arrived, and Nate's wife said he would be back soon so Earl was free to wait in the living room. Earl realized that Nate was already fifteen minutes late so he responded that he should leave. As he was leaving, it struck him for the first time that this was the method he had used to cover up his sexual sins in the past.

> When I was stood up for a social or business engagement or finished the engagement early, I'd use the extra time to feed my sexual sin. I would call the woman with whom I was having the affair, or I'd go to a XXX-rated movie on my way back to the office. I would then justify my time to others by telling how long I had waited for an appointment that did not

show, or I'd leave the time of my meeting vague. No one would question my statements. ...

So when I became aware of the pattern while at Nate's house, I reversed my decision and decided to wait for Nate's return. A new pattern was being formed. I reinforced this new pattern by sharing the experience with Nate as we had a late lunch. I also shared the experience with Sandy, then with Larry and later with the entire Spiritual Care Team. The process of honest disclosure is one step toward ruling out sin.[8]

Patterns of sin become hard-wired into our mind so that we develop automatic responses to situations that lead to mindless sin. We do what comes naturally without thinking about the choices. These habits are hard to break. We must learn a new pattern of behavior which means practicing a new response to a situation, and asking others to hold us accountable until the new response becomes hard-wired into our minds, and we start living according to the Spirit.

---

[8] Earl and Sandy Wilson, Paul and Virginia Friesen, and Larry and Nancy Paulson, <u>Restoring the Fallen: A Team Approach to Caring, Confronting & Reconciling,</u> InterVarsity Press, 1997, p. 70.

17
OUR SOURCE OF LIFE

Romans 8:9-11

9 However, you are not in the flesh but in the Spirit, if indeed the Spirit of God dwells in you. But if anyone does not have the Spirit of Christ, he does not belong to Him. 10 If Christ is in you, though the body is dead because of sin, yet the spirit is alive because of righteousness. 11 But if the Spirit of Him who raised Jesus from the dead dwells in you, He who raised Christ Jesus from the dead will also give life to your mortal bodies through His Spirit who dwells in you.

In *The Lord of the Rings,* Aragorn faces a decision regarding the battle with the Dark Lord who is trying to conquer the world. Aragorn's forefather, King Isildor, won a great battle against the Dark Lord, but he refused to destroy the Ring of Power out of pride. King Isildor wanted to keep the ring for himself, but the ring ultimately led to his destruction. Now Aragorn, King Isildor's only direct heir, faces another battle with the Dark Lord. Aragorn is filled with shame regarding the past, and doubts whether he should emerge to fight the Dark Lord. He knows that he has the same pride in him that was the downfall of his forefather thousands of years earlier. The lovely Arwen comes to him to help him make up his mind about the battle. Arwen asks, "Why do you fear the past? You are Isildor's heir, not Isildor himself. You are not bound by his fate." Choked with fear, Aragon explains, "The same blood flows in my veins - the same weakness." "Your time will come. You will face the same evil," Arwen affirms. "And you will defeat it."[1]

In the same way, the flesh – the human nature of our forefather Adam - lives on in each of us. Yet we are new creations in Christ, and the Spirit gives us the power to defeat sin. Paul tells us in Romans 8 how we can win this war even though we still have the blood of Adam flowing through our veins. The key is to understand the power of the Holy Spirit who lives inside us. Paul teaches us in Romans 8:9-11 that success in life comes from the Spirit of life. Someone might say, "My past is not very pretty. I know I have the blood of Adam running in me. I've failed in the past. I'm afraid that I will fail in the future." God knows all that and calls you to follow Him anyway. What is more He gives you the power to be successful if you will walk in step with His Spirit. *If we have a responsibility to be holy combined with an inability to control the flesh, then the solution is conscious dependence on the Spirit who lives in us.*

Paul tells us in verse 9. We are in the Spirit because the Spirit is in us. He has just finished telling us in verse 8 that anyone living "in the flesh cannot please God." The flesh can never do anything to please God. Now Paul quickly moves on to point out that the Christian does not live in flesh but in Spirit. I think it is important to understand that the definite article, "the," is not used here. When the definite article is not used, then the writer is referring to a state or quality of life. "In flesh" means the state or quality of life that is fleshly. "In Spirit" means the state or quality of life that is spiritual. Paul is talking about our state if life. If the Spirit of God lives in us, then we are not in flesh as a state of life or quality of life.

Does this mean that we cannot sin? Obviously not! Does this mean that we do not slip into fleshly living? Of course not or else

---

[1] <u>Lord of the Ring: Fellowship of the Ring</u>, New Line Cinemas, 2001, directed by Frances Walsh based on the book by J. R. Tolkien.

Paul would not have exhorted us to walk according to the Spirit and not according to the pattern of the flesh in verses 5 and 6. I like the way Donald Grey Barnhouse, the famous pastor of Tenth Presbyterian Church in Philadelphia, explained it years ago. He pointed out that a Christian is not in the flesh, but the flesh is still in the Christian. There is a great deal of difference, he said, between being in the flesh and having the flesh in you. I am not in the flesh but the flesh is in me. The non-Christian is in the flesh as a state of being, but the Christian is not in the flesh as a state of being. Our state or position is in the Spirit of God. We may revert to living in a fleshly way. When this happens we are turning back to living the way we lived before we became a Christian. We are slipping into the patterns of behavior and thinking that dominated our egos before we became Christians, but we do not have to go back to the way we were. We are in Spirit not in flesh as a state of existence, and so we can live as God wants us to live. We can please God.[2]

Paul goes on to qualify the statement. We are in the Spirit if the Spirit lives in us. The word translated "dwells" means to colonize or settle in somewhere. When we become Christians, the Spirit of God establishes a colony in us. He settles into our lives. He makes His home in us. The classical writers called this the "mystical union" of God living in man. We don't fully understand this mystical union but we know it is true. God takes up residence inside our bodies when we become Christians. These are holy carcasses that we walk around in every day! This mystical union is the secret to controlling the flesh which still lives inside us too. But Paul quickly adds an explanation in verse 9 that is also a warning.

WARNING!

We have the Spirit or Christ does not have us. Paul continues in verse 9 by saying, "But if anyone does not have the Spirit of Christ, he does not belong to Him." The Spirit of Christ and the Holy Spirit

---

[2] Donald Grey Barnhouse, <u>Romans: God's Heirs, Romans 8:1-39</u>, Wm. B. Eerdmans Publishing Company, 1963, p. 41.

are the same person, so if we do not possess the Holy Spirit then Christ does not possess us. Literally we are not "of Him." We are not of Christ at all, if we do have the Spirit of Christ living in us. This is a very important warning. There are those who would argue that you become a Christian. You accept Christ but you get the Holy Spirit later at some point in time when you are fully consecrated to God. This special event sets you up to live in the power of the Spirit but until then you are still living in the flesh. You can see how this kind of thinking quickly sets up two levels of Christians.

According to this viewpoint, Romans 7 is talking about a carnal Christian – one who has not yet experienced the controlling power of the Spirit of God in his life. Some have taught that when you become a Christian you are a baby Christian who lives in the struggle of Romans 7 until you experience the power of the Spirit in Romans 8. If a person backslides into Romans 7, then they need a new infusion of the power of the Spirit to live in Romans 8. Romans 8 is a description of the victorious Christian after he has received the second blessing of the Holy Spirit. Then the Christian experiences what some called "entire sanctification" meaning that we reach a level of perfection in the Spirit that allows us to be free from known or conscious sin in our lives.

The two stages doctrine led to perfectionism where a person aspired to achieve a level of the Christian life where he or she was freed from all known sin. This perfectionism was celebrated as entire sanctification, and became the basis of many Christian communities that sprang up across the country, and focused on living the perfect or holy life. It also led to triumphalism because the superior Christians were living above the inferior Christians, and the sense was that if you could just experience this second blessing you would be up here with us too. Abuses took place with this doctrine and many lives were ruined by perfectionism. Others who were touched with this doctrine have lived their entire lives feeling like they never could get to Romans 8, and that they were somehow lesser Christians than those who claimed such experiences of holiness. Sadly and perhaps unintentionally Christian perfectionism inevitably leads to "holier-than-thou" attitudes within the church as those who have achieved look down their noses at those who have not yet arrived at entire sanctification or have not yet experienced this "second blessing." I, as a pastor, have talked to far too many Christians who struggle with feelings of failure spawned by this theology. They live with constant and excessive guilt that is unhealthy and debilitating.

Verse 9 flatly contradicts such a theology. All Christians, not just some Christians, have the Spirit of God. You are not a Christian at all if you do not have the Holy Spirit. Furthermore, you cannot divide the Spirit up. *All Christians have all the Spirit the minute they become Christians. We have the Spirit or Christ does not have us.* Romans 7 and 8 are not talking about two levels of the Christian life. We will always, like Paul, struggle with the flesh. Romans 7 is talking about the wrong way to fight the battle with the flesh, and Romans 8 is talking about the right way to fight this battle with the flesh. We will never fully arrive at entire sanctification until we are with Christ in heaven for all of eternity. Until then we must fight this battle by the power of the Holy Spirit who lives equally in all of us as Christians.

TWO METHODS

Paul is talking about the right method and the wrong method that we use in trying to achieve holiness in our lives. Romans 7 is man's method. We try to be holy through legalism. We enforce the law and its consequences so people won't sin. This approach is ingrained in us often in our families and in our churches by well-meaning parents and pastors. You mess up so you must pay up - or else. There is little grace and all law, but it never works. So, we then try to have enough faith in the new people we are in Christ. Claim who I am and believe it because I can beat this thing called sin. It becomes a spiritualized self help concept. Have faith in who you are as a Christian because you can live right. Just think positive!! But this doesn't work either as Paul told us in Romans 7.

Romans 8 is God's method. We must walk in step with God's Spirit at work in our lives. This leads to discipline and obedience. We must surrender to God's directions for living. Paul is in the midst of talking about this concept in the first part of Romans 8. But

237

then he will move on in the middle of Romans 8 to teach us that God's Spirit shapes us through our sufferings and our struggles. There is no room for triumphalism in the Christian life. We don't arrive at some special level of the Christian life where we are free from struggle while on this earth. In fact, Paul will tell us, it is in the struggles and in the suffering that God actually is able to shape us into holy people. Pain is God's method of purification. Pain is God's refining fire that changes and shapes our lives to be more like Him. Paul closes the chapter by pointing out that God's Spirit leads us to victory when He glorifies us. He will do His job in us. We will be victorious but not until heaven. This is the great hope we have in Christ.

The wonderful truth is that we all have the Spirit right now if Christ has us. I like the illustration that James Emery White uses for the filling of the Holy Spirit. He would set up two glasses of water. Then he would drop one sealed packet of Alka-Seltzer into one glass and he would plop an unsealed packet into the second glass. The second glass would immediately begin to fizz as the Alka-Seltzer spread in the water. Then he would make his point with the students. "Both glasses have the Alka-Seltzer, just as all Christians have the Holy Spirit. But notice how you can have the Holy Spirit and not his filling."[3] Our goal is to live in such a way as to unwrap the packaging around the presence and power of the Holy Spirit within us. We must not stifle the Holy Spirit with our choices. We must not grieve the Holy Spirit by rebelling against His work of conviction in our lives. We can live in Romans 8 instead of Romans 7, but it is a matter of daily, moment by moment walking in step with the Spirit of God who lives inside of each of us. If we don't use the resources of the Spirit, then we will not be living in Romans 8, but in Romans 7.

---

[3] James Emery White, Long Night's Journey Into the Day, Waterbrook, 2002.

REALITY

We face the consequences of sin by the life of the Spirit (v. 10). If you have the Spirit of Christ, then you belong to Christ, and if the Spirit lives in you, then Christ lives in you. This is the mystical union. There is one God in three persons but both the person of the Spirit and the person of the Son take up residence inside the "New Man" that we are as Christians. Paul then sets up a contrast between the dead body and the living Spirit in us. The body in this verse must be the human body. Our physical bodies are in view because the next verse talks about our mortal bodies being raised from the dead. This body that I live in is dead because of sin. This carcass I walk around in already carries death in it. Death is built into our bodies. Paul said in Romans 6:12, "Do not let sin reign in your mortal body that you should obey its lusts." Our bodies are dying bodies. They are decaying as we live. D. Martyn Lloyd-Jones called it the "seed of death" that is sown in our bodies because of sin.[4] Paul wrote in Romans 7:24, "wretched man that I am who will set me free from this body of death?" Our physical bodies are characterized by death and they are the instruments of sin. Our dying bodies are the battleground for sin in our lives. There are many results of sin in our physical lives. We get sick. We feel pain. We ache. We struggle. God didn't create us this way. This is the result of sin. But we also struggle with sin in our bodies. The battle with sin takes place in our bodies with our bodily passions. This is where the flesh lives. The seed of death is in our bodies, and that is why Paul tells us later in this chapter that we groan in our bodies waiting for the final redemption of our bodies (8:23) when we will be freed finally from this body of death.

Yet there is hope. The Spirit of God is life. The seed of life has been implanted into us when the Holy Spirit took up residence in us. I take it that this reference is to the Holy Spirit and not our human spirit here. When the Holy Spirit comes to live in us the seed

---

[4] D. Martyn Lloyd-Jones, Romans: An Exposition of Chapter 8:5-17, The Sons of God, Zondervan Publishing House, 1974, p. 69.

of life is implanted. We call this regeneration. We have new life in Christ. All the wonder of God's perfect holy character is in that seed of life. *All that we will become in Christ in heaven is already there in the seed that lives inside of us right now.* What an incredible concept?!! We are in seed form what we will become in fruit when the process of growth has been completed. The moment we become Christians, God gives us everything we need for godliness. Peter wrote: "Seeing that His divine power has granted to us everything pertaining to life and godliness through the true knowledge of Him who called us by His own glory and excellence" (2 Peter 1:3). God did this so that we might "become partakers of the divine nature having escaped the corruption that is in the world by lust" (2 Peter 1:4). We have the seeds of holiness from the moment of our new life in Christ, but that does not mean we can neglect to apply ourselves to developing holiness by His power. Peter writes: "Applying all diligence in your faith supply moral excellence" (1:5) followed by a list of character traits that we are to be supplying in our lives. "For if these are yours and are increasing they render you neither useless nor unfruitful in the true knowledge of our Lord Jesus Christ" (1:8). If we lack these qualities it is because we have "forgotten His purification from our (his) former sins" (1:9). So we are to be diligent to be holy because we have been given all we need to be holy. Normal Christians are actively pursuing holiness in their daily lives. Holiness is not reserved for the spiritual giants – the special Christians. Holiness is for normal Christians, but the power for holiness comes from the Spirit who gives us life.

The Spirit is life because of righteousness. Paul ties the life we have in the Spirit of God directly back to the doctrine of justification he taught in Romans 5. Justification is a bookkeeping or accounting term. The best way to understand it is to see it in this light. When God looks at us apart from Christ our sin column is filled up and our righteousness column is empty. We are sinners. Christ's righteousness column is full but His sin column is empty because Christ never sinned. Justification means that God transferred his assets and our sins. When you accept Christ as your Savior then your sins are transferred to His sin column. He becomes sin for you. And His righteousness is transferred to your righteousness column. So when God looks at you in Christ, He sees all white in your sin column. Your sins are gone. The slate is wiped clean, and, instead, God sees all righteousness in your righteousness column. So Paul says in Romans 8, the Spirit is life in us because of righteousness. We have life because we are righteous before God, not because of our good deeds, but because His righteousness has been transferred to us by His grace. We are clean and pure in Him, so we can be alive in His Spirit. Justification is initial sanctification. The result is hope.

HOPE

We expect the resurrection through the power of the Spirit (v. 11). Paul is telling us that our salvation is not complete until the resurrection of our bodies. The Holy Spirit is the Spirit of the one who raised Christ from the dead, and the Holy Spirit lives in each one of us as Christians. God will enliven our mortal bodies one day. Our bodies that are right now subject to death will be literally brought to life by God the Father by means of the Spirit who lives in us. Even though we are subject to death right now, even though we have many flaws, we are under warranty. The Holy Spirit guarantees our future resurrection. We will one day be freed from sin and all the effects of sin in our lives because what God starts He finishes.

Relief in our war with sin comes in the resurrection. This gives us hope. We know that whatever we face today as a result of sin in this world we will finally be victorious over sin in the end. This also gives us pause to remember that until the resurrection we cannot claim perfection. *We are under construction until the resurrection. God is shaping us now for eternity.* He is making us into the people we will become forever but we are not there yet. This frees us from the seduction of perfectionism and the pride of triumphalism. We must keep walking in step with the Spirit all the way to the end of the path. Walking in step with the Spirit means that we must be practicing the habits of holiness through active participation with the Spirit. J. I. Packer writes: "All our attempts to get our lives in shape need to be soaked in constant prayer that acknowledges our inability to change ourselves… Holiness by habit forming is not self-sanctification by self-effort, but is simply a matter of understanding the Spirit's method and then keeping in step with Him."[5] Sanctification is a supernatural process that we cannot do by natural means. This process will not be completed until the resurrection. We will not see the final product until after we die.

No matter how rich or powerful we are, we all die. The tomb of Caesar Augustus was a grand monument to the greatness of Rome's first emperor. The circular mound was 287 feet in diameter and contained the remains of his family and every succeeding emperor until the end of the first century. The barbarians who sacked Rome took the urns containing the remains of the emperors and their family members, emptied the ashes on to the floor and carried off their treasures. It was later used as a fortress, for cock fights and bear baiting until not much of the marble mausoleum remained. It was home to a colony of cats and a shanty town in the 1980s. Today it is being excavated and protected but remains a sad, visual commentary on the legacy of Augustus. Men try so hard to leave a legacy, a monument to their greatness, but it never lasts. How we live is all we have. As the saying goes, "Only one life, 'twill soon be past, only what's done for Christ will last." God has given us the resources to live victoriously. We have the power of Almighty God living inside of us ready to make us into the people God calls us to become. What are we doing with this power?

THE RESURRECTION LIFE

Christians are people destined for the resurrection while living out their lives here on earth. *Those who will be resurrected possess the resurrected life now.* We are becoming now what we will be then. We died with Christ to what we once were, and we rose again with Christ to what we are now. Our lives are His life, and we can only

---

[5] J. I. Packer, <u>Keep in Step with the Spirit</u>, Fleming H. Revell Company, 1984, pp. 109-110.

live them by His power. It is not us but Him. Paul wrote in Galatians 2:20, "I have been crucified with Christ; and it is no longer I who live, but Christ lives in me; and the life which I now live in the flesh I live by faith in the Son of God, who loved me, and delivered Himself up for me." The normal Christian life is Christ living in us who actively live by faith in Him.

George Barna published a book in 2005 that was provocatively titled, *"Revolution: Worn out on Church? Finding Vibrant Faith Beyond the Walls of the Sanctuary."* He wrote that this Christian revolution was "on track to become the most significant recalibration of the American Christian body in more than a century."[6] Barna pointed to research that indicated the movement was over 20 million strong and growing as revolutionary Christians were leaving the church to live out their revolutionary faith in the world. Nearly a decade later the revolution appears to have fizzled as new churches have sprouted all over the landscape of Christianity, and established churches manage to keep going despite the dire predictions. It turns out that the hyperbolically labeled "revolutionary" is really just a description of a normal Christian.

Barna defines a "revolutionary" as "someone who lives only to love, obey, and serve God, rejecting and overcoming every obstacle that emerges to prevent such a life."[7] He argues that a revolutionary is characterized by seven core passions that reflect the passions of the first century Christians. The core passions are; 1) Intimate worship; 2) Faith-based conversations; 3) Intentional spiritual growth; 4) Servanthood; 5) Resource investment; 6) Spiritual friendships; 7) Family faith.[8] "Revolutionaries are Christ-followers who refuse to make excuses for their failings; instead they address and overcome their inadequacies."[9]

I call these normal Christians and this is the normal Christian life. These are the core people in the church where I pastor and I see

---

[6] George Barna, "Revolution: Worn out on Church? Finding Vibrant Faith Beyond the Walls of the Sanctuary," Tyndale, 2005, p. ix.

[7] Barna, p. 17.

[8] Barna, pp. 22-24.

[9] Barna, pp. 25-26.

them in virtually every church that is alive in Christ. Not everyone who attends church is a normal Christian, alias revolutionary, but every Christian who is actively involved in ministry desires to live out these passions. These are the people who serve faithfully in our children's ministries and small groups. I meet these people every week as they study their Bibles and ask the questions of faith seeking to know all they can about life in Christ. Normal Christians in our churches are working hard to live out their faith on the job and leading their families to love Jesus at home. They struggle to balance their time and invest their resources for eternity. Normal Christians struggle with sin and confess when they fail seeking forgiveness from the Lord. They serve on mission teams helping Christians rebuild cities like New Orleans and doing work projects in Haiti or the Dominican Republic. They help in local soup kitchens or in food distribution ministries for the poverty stricken. Normal Christians give to support missionaries who are serving Christ around the world. I see them all the time in our growing contemporary churches where young people are getting excited about living out their faith in fresh ways. I see them in the people I counsel as they struggle with suffering, failure, loneliness and heartache, but who work through those struggles by the power of Christ living in them. I weep with them and laugh with them as we worship together in church. Call them revolutionaries if you want. I call them normal Christians!

18
LIFE AND DEATH

Romans 8:12-14

12 So then, brethren, we are under obligation, not to the flesh, to live according to the flesh—13 for if you are living according to the flesh, you must die; but if by the Spirit you are putting to death the deeds of the body, you will live. 14 For all who are being led by the Spirit of God, these are sons of God.

We are the sum of our choices. We become what we decide to become. The Apostle Paul has been teaching us in Romans 7 and 8 that our default position in life apart from God is the flesh - our human nature, disposition or personality. Paul exhorts us not to walk according to the pattern of this human nature but to walk by the pattern of the Spirit. God the Holy Spirit is the only one who can overcome our human nature with its sinful habits. Does this mean that we sit back and wait for God to fix us? Do we just "let go and let God?" No. We are active participants in this process of spiritual growth. What is our role? We have already seen that we, in our own power, cannot overcome the flesh in us, so how do we participate in this process of spiritual growth? Paul tells us that we live in the Spirit by executing our habits of sin. We cannot eliminate the flesh, but we can live in the Spirit, and so execute the sinful habits that rise from our flesh.

I think that these 3 verses may be the most important verses in the Bible outlining our responsibility in the process of growing spiritually – the actual practice of sanctification. D. Martyn Lloyd-Jones states it well.

> It is here for the first time, in this chapter, that we come to the realm of practical application. All we have had up to this point has been a general description of the Christian – his character, his position. But now the Apostle has really come explicitly to the doctrine of sanctification. Here we are told exactly how, in practice, the Christian becomes sanctified. Or, to state it differently, here we are told in detail and in practice how the Christian is to wage the battle against sin, and especially as it tends to come to him, and to defeat him through his body. This is one of the chief problems of the Christian life.[1]

As we shall see in these important verses, our job is to put to death – to execute – the practices of our physical bodies. These actions or practices are the habits of the flesh that we must execute, but we can only do so by the power of the Spirit. Spiritual growth can be painful and executions are not pretty. We must actively participate in the process by making specific choices about our lives. These choices are life and death choices. The choices we make are choices that lead to life or to death.

Living by our sinful habits leads to death (v. 12). When Paul writes that "we are under obligation, not to the flesh, to live according to the flesh" he literally says that we are not "debtors" to the flesh. The flesh is that complex set of characteristics that is our nature governed by sin. It is our personality as directed by sin. We are not debtors to

---

[1] D. Martyn Lloyd-Jones, <u>Romans: The Sons of God,</u> Zondervan Publishing House, 1974, p.92.

this personality. We do not owe our human nature anything at all. We have been freed from that obligation. We do not have to do what our human nature tells us to do. When that temper wells up within us, we can say "no" to our human nature. We owe it nothing and do not have to indulge the temper at all. We were in slavery to sin before we became Christians. We were not free. Christ set us free from that slavery but if we choose to act according the flesh then we are living on the path to death. Paul goes on verse 13 to tell us that, if we are living according to the flesh, we are destined to die, for the flesh always leads to death. The verb translated "destined" indicates a strong probability in the present or future. It is not destined as in fatalism but in likelihood. Living according to the flesh is the pathway to death, not eternal damnation but deathly results in life. Sinful habits always destroy our relationships and our opportunities. Sin kills.

Paul laid out an important principle back in Romans 6:16 regarding what takes place in our lives as we make choices. We become slaves to whatever we want the most in life. Whatever or whoever we present ourselves to becomes our master in life. If we give ourselves to money, then money becomes our master. If we give ourselves to another person, then that person becomes our master. If we give ourselves to drugs or alcohol, then drugs or alcohol become our master. We think that we are in control, but really we have become slaves of what we want. If it is sin, then we become slaves to that sin. If it is obedience to God, then we become slaves of God. We make the choice, but the results are clear – death or life.

We grow in righteousness or we descend into death. Death is the result of choosing to follow our sinful habits in life. The ironic truth is that what we think will bring us life only brings us death instead. Modern morality tells us that we should follow our feelings. Be what you want to be and do what you want to do. Assert yourself and grab for what you want in life. Modern morality tells us that you only really live when you grab for all that you can get. God says that what we think will give us life – if I could just have that person, job or experience then I would be really living it up – will actually bring us death in the end. When we open the doors to our sinful feelings, then we are really opening the doors to our own destruction.

After a final stop for fuel at St. Paul, a tiny island in the Bering Sea, Dave Rundall piloted his 92 foot fishing trawler "Arctic Rose" into the remote Zhemchung Flats in pursuit of more fish. She was last seen by her sister ship, "Alaskan Rose," at 10 p.m. on April 1 before she moved out of sight. The fishing trawler sank at 3:30 a.m. on April 2, 2001 in heavy seas. No distress call was ever sent. An orbiting satellite recorded a ping from the locator designed to transmit when submerged, and the Alaskan Rose quickly moved to assist. By the time they arrived on the scene there was no sight of the boat. They found the body of Captain Dave Rundall floating in his red survival suit but no other person was visible. Fifteen people died in the tragedy making it the worst U.S. fishing accident in 50 years. Four months after the sinking the Coast Guard used a remote controlled underwater camera to view the Arctic Rose sitting perfectly upright on the ocean floor 400 feet below. Everything was intact. The only sign of a problem was a water tight door that was left open. The Marine Casualty Board spent 2 ½ years investigating the accident and concluded that the boat capsized in less than 3 minutes, and flooding began in less than 8 minutes. The Marine Board determined that the cause was a left rear hatch which had been left open allowing seawater to flood the boat. They speculate that the inexperienced crew had probably opened the hatch for air as they worked in the hold below deck. The open door led to death for all of them in a matter of minutes.[2] Not all open doors are positive opportunities. Some open doors lead to death. When you follow your sinful feelings, you follow them into disaster.

---

[2] Mike Carter, "Arctic Rose report may have lasting impact on fishing," The Seattle Times; "The Mystery of the Arctic Rose, Crew's Letter tell of Fishing Boat's Final Voyage,"www.abcnews.com, June 27, 2013, original story aired on Feb. 7, 2002, ABC News Internet Ventures.

LOT AND THE SLIPPERY SLOPE

Choices can be a slippery slope. What starts out innocently enough can quickly turn deadly as we slide down that slope. Alcoholism starts out with one drink. The affair begins with a friendship. Compromising our values begins with a profitable business partnership. Lot in the Old Testament is a great illustration of the slippery slope. Abram and Lot came to a parting of the ways in Genesis 13. Lot "lifted up his eyes and saw" all the riches of the valley of Jordan life (Gen. 13:10). He saw the prosperity of cities like Sodom and Gomorrah. He did not see the wickedness that God saw because he did not see with God's eyes. Now observe the slippery slope. Lot pitched his tent near Sodom (13:12). He was not in it. He was near it. Yet in the next chapter Lot was living in Sodom (14:12). Finally, by the time we get to God's judgment of Sodom we read that Lot was sitting in the gate of Sodom (19:1). He was a leading citizen of the city that God would judge. He was enmeshed in the politics and the prosperity of Sodom. The choice that started out as a good business proposition ended up in destruction. Lot will lose everything (except his two daughters) including his wife who couldn't leave the lifestyle she loved. Lot didn't start out to pursue sin but ended up in disaster.

I watch Christians today follow the same path to worldliness. It is easy for all of us to follow that path. We start down the path innocently enough. I have seen families get caught up in careers and possessions and lose their love for the Lord. What do you expect when you pitch your tent near Sodom? I have seen parents focus on the material success of their children instead of church and then the children don't go to church any more. What do you expect when you pitch your tent near Sodom? I have watched young people grow up in church but like what they see out there in the world so much that they slowly walk away from the Lord. What do you expect when you pitch your tent near Sodom? Many Christians want to have their faith but get close to the world too. It is a slippery slope. How close is too close? We may not realize the danger until it is too late, and we wake up to spiritual disaster. What we think brings life actually brings death, and what we think brings death actually brings life.

Killing our sinful habits leads to life (v. 13b). It is vital to understand that we are responsible as Christians to put our sinful habits to death. We can't do it by ourselves, but we can do it by the power of the Spirit living in us. God doesn't do it for us. We have to do it. This is our responsibility. The word translated "putting to death" is used in the ancient literature especially of the work done by a public executioner. We are to execute the sinful habits in our lives. The old English used the word "mortify" so preachers in the past often talked about the "mortification of the flesh." John Owen, the great Puritan preacher, said, "Mortification abates [sin's] force, but doth not change its nature. Grace changeth the nature of man, but nothing can change the nature of sin...Do you mortify: do you make it your daily work; be always at it whilst you live; cease not a day from this work; be killing sin or it will be killing you."[3] This is a biblical concept, but it is a doctrine that has been so misused and abused that many avoid talking about it today. Yet, I believe mortification of the flesh is the key to spiritual victory in our lives. Before I explain how we kill our sinful habits biblically, let me briefly address some of the false teaching that has developed in church history about the mortification of the flesh. I want you to understand what mortification of the flesh is not so we can understand and apply what it is.

WHAT MORTIFICATION IS NOT!

Mortification is not legalism. Legalism does not work as we have already seen in Romans 7. Legalism in its fullest form leads to a joyless, fear filled Christianity. It is morbid. Legalism produces Christians who develop martyr complexes – "look at poor me, I'm

---

[3] John Owen, "The Works of John Owen," 16 volumes, 1967 reprint; Edinburgh: Banner of Truth, 1853, 6:177, 6:9. Cited by John MacArthur Jr., "Mortification of Sin," The Master's Journal, 1998, Vol. 5, No. 1, Spring 1994, p. 4.

doing God's will and you know I'm doing God's will because of how miserable I look when I'm doing it." Everything is duty and obligation. Happiness is the enemy of holiness. All fun is sin. Whatever makes me miserable must be God's will. Legalism is three words – control, control, control!! I must control my flesh by the rigid application of duty and obligation. We have not the power in ourselves to control sin by the application of rules to our lives.

Mortification is not monasticism. There have always been those down through church history that have tended toward monasticism. Monasticism says that since the world is evil then we must renounce the world and everything in it. If we want to be spiritual, then we must separate from the world. We must avoid all contact and give up all the comforts and material possessions in this world. Monastics took vows of abstinence from money, possessions, marriage and many other worldly comforts in order to be spiritual. They falsely taught that this was what it meant to mortify the flesh. Be holy by avoiding all contact with outside temptations.

Mortification is not dualism. The third form of false teaching on this subject rose out of the philosophy of dualism. Dualism taught that the spirit is good but the body is evil so anything spiritual must avoid all the pleasures of the physical. They advocated starving the body through fasting and other vows of abstinence. Discipline the body through "flagellations." In the extreme forms of dualism the people would beat or whip their bodies seeking to control the flesh and its sinful habits. The body is bad. The body is full of lust. It is our spirits that are good so drive out the lusts of our bodies through deprivation. Deprive the body of any enjoyment, pleasure or comfort so as to live the spiritual life.

These are abusive false doctrines, and Paul is not teaching us to mortify the flesh in these ways. Paul tells us that we will live if we are executing the practices of the body by the power of the Spirit. First we must note that we can only do this by the power of the Spirit. That is why Paul made it very clear that every Christian has the full power of the Spirit available to him for defeating the flesh. We have no excuse. We can kill the habits of the flesh. Paul is very clear that we are to kill the practices or actions of the body. The word "practices" is a word that is often used with bad things such as deceit of treachery. We must kill these sinful habits in our bodies. Why the body? We don't want to fall into dualism here so we must be clear about Paul's point. The body in and of itself is not evil but Paul is very clear that the body has not yet been redeemed. He tells us later in Romans 8:23 that the body will not be redeemed until the resurrection so until then our bodies are the places where sin is lived out. That is why the battle with sin takes place in our bodies and why we must kill the practices of the body. We don't kill the body, but we kill the sinful cravings, habits and activities that use the body for their ends.

WHAT MORTIFICATION IS!

What does this mean? How does this work? Mortification means an execution of whatever (or whoever) is leading us to sin. The residual sin that still lives in our bodies must be executed. This is our job. Jesus made a powerful statement of this same doctrine in Matthew 5:29. He said: "If your right eye makes you stumble, tear it out, and throw it from you; for it is better for you that one of the parts of your body perish, than for your whole body to be thrown into hell. And if your right hand makes you stumble, cut it off, and throw it from you; for it is better for you that one of the parts of your body perish, than for your whole body to go into hell." Do you want to live? You must kill whatever would lead you to death. You must execute it. Now Jesus is not talking literally here. This is figurative language that is deliberately brutal and bold. His point is not to mutilate your physical body. His point is to execute whatever in us leads us to sin. Sin becomes addictive. It begins to control our bodies. We come to crave the sin in our lives. If we are to gain victory over that sin, then we must brutally kill all parts of us that would crave the sin. If we like to gossip about our spouses or other people, then we must be brutal in eliminating that from our lives. If we have problems with lust, then we must cut out of our lives anything that would lead us to lust.

We are experts at rationalizing our sins. Our favorite tactics for dealing with sin are hiding, repressing or substituting. I see this many times in my responsibility as a pastor, but I see it also in myself. Sin is not executed in us by covering it up. Our fleshly inclination is to cover up our sin. We fear exposure and want to hide the sin from others. This will never do. Exposure of sin is the one weapon that works to kill sin. This does not necessarily mean public exposure, which is more like shaming then correcting in most cases. Exposure to a few mature Christians who will hold us accountable for the sin is one of the best weapons we can use to kill the habits of sin in our lives. Repressing sin is not killing sin either. Repressing sin is simply burying it deep inside of us until it rears its ugly head again in our lives. Legalism is mostly about repressing sin, but burying sin does not kill it. Sin is not executed by substituting one form of sin for another. Sometimes Christians faced with a specific sin stop that sin but substitute another less heinous form of sin in its place. This happens most often when we are caught in some sin. It is exposed and the sin goes "underground" in our lives to be replaced by something else. We can end up rationalizing sin away but fail to kill those sinful practices in our lives. The result is that they simply lie dormant for awhile only to rise up and bite us again later. Sin is never killed by hiding, repressing or substituting.

Sometimes I hear people pray something like this: "God I can't control this sin in my life. I've tried so hard to get rid of it. Please God take this sin out of my life. Remove this craving from me." Do you understand that the Bible never teaches us to pray that prayer? God can remove such sinful cravings and habits but he rarely does. Most often God tells us: "Look, I've already given you the power to remove that sinful habit from your life. You kill it." We, as Christians, have no right to say, "I am so weak. The temptation is just too powerful for me. Poor, poor me. I'm such a victim."

The Bible's answer is: STOP IT! If you have a problem with dirty jokes and crude talk, the Bible tells you to stop doing it. If you have a problem with alcohol or drug addiction, the Bible tells you to stop it. Cut it out of your life. If you have a problem with pornography, the Bible tells you to kill it. The pornographer must take steps to kill the sinful habit by removing the computer from the house or giving his/her spouse the password control. He must not go near any place that sells pornography. Don't even go down the same street if you can avoid it. The alcoholic must stay out of bars and remove all alcohol from his home. He must join AA or some other 12 step program and get straightened out. We are not cured from these sinful cravings, but we must kill them by the steps we take. An execution is not pretty. It is brutal and harsh. An execution is painful, but we must cut out of our lives the sinful habit. Don't go near that person or place of sin. Eliminate that from your life.

We kill the sinful habits in our lives if we stay away from dangerous people. Paul wrote: "And do not participate in the unfruitful deeds of darkness, but instead even reprove them; for it is disgraceful even to speak of the things which are done by them (sons of disobedience) in secret." (Eph. 5:11-12) Peer pressure is powerful, and it is not just for young people. The friends we hang around with will influence us for better or for worse. We are not to leave this world because we are to be witnesses, but we will encounter in our lives people and situations that are dangerous to us. Get away from them. Cut them out of your life. Period!

We kill the sinful habits in our lives if we discipline our bodies for good. "Therefore I run in such a way, as not without aim; I box in such a way, as not beating the air; but I buffet my body and make it my slave, lest possibly, after I have preached to others, I myself should be disqualified." (1 Corinthians 9:26-27) We don't literally abuse our bodies. Paul is talking figuratively here of how we need to discipline our desires so that we don't live our lives seeking to indulge our bodily passions which disqualifies us from serving God.

We kill the sinful habits in our lives if we don't give opportunity to the flesh. "Let us behave properly as in the day, not in carousing and drunkenness, not in sexual promiscuity and sensuality, not in strife and jealousy. But put on the Lord Jesus Christ, and make no

254

provision for the flesh in regard to its lusts." (Romans 13:13-14) Make no provision for the flesh. Don't set yourself up with opportunities to fall. Don't put yourself in places and situations where you will be prone to sin. We are told to "flee immorality" (1 Cor. 6:18). Each of us has different issues with sin so my temptations are different than yours. What will be a problem for me may not be a problem for you and vice versa. You must not make any provision for those places where you are weak. If you do you are setting yourself up for sin. Stay away. Stop going there. A Danish proverb says: "No one can be caught in a place he does not visit."

HOW DO I KNOW I AM A NORMAL CHRISTIAN?

How do I know that I am a son God? We could ask the same question another way. How can I know that I am a normal Christian? Paul lays out the sequence in reverse order in verse 14. I know I am a Son of God – a normal Christian - because I am led by His Spirit. "For all who are being led by the Spirit of God, these are the sons of God." The verb translated "being led" is in a form that indicates this leading is ongoing and continuous in our lives. We are developing new habits as we follow the Spirit of God. The habits of holiness gradually replace the habits of the flesh as the Spirit of God convicts us of sin, and we choose to obey Him in cutting those sinful habits out of our lives. The only way to be led by the Spirit is to obey the Spirit. A child is led by the father when he obeys the father. This is no mystical "second blessing" experience but an ongoing daily process of following what the Spirit of God tells us to do.

The Bible commands us, "Do not be drunk with wine for that is dissipation but be filled with the Spirit" (Eph. 5:18). The Higher Life Movement spoke often of the filling of the Spirit as a repeated and repeatable experience. I picked one of many books on my shelf written by Keswick teachers who all write in a similar fashion about this experience of filling. Ruth Paxson, a well known teacher in her day, wrote:

> My friends, to be filled with the Spirit is God's standard for every Christian here these afternoon. Are you filled? The only normal Christians here are those who are filled with the Holy Spirit. We sometimes think this is such an extraordinary spiritual experience that the person, who is so filled, is abnormal. It is the exact contrary. I put it to you today, is it normal for one who is in Christ and has Christ in him and who is indwelt by the same Spirit that indwelled Christ, to be constantly defeated?[4]

The answer is "no" of course. The normal Christian life is lived in the Spirit. Unfortunately, the Keswick teachers like Ruth Paxson described the filling of the Spirit in almost mystical terms. We need to prepare for the filling of the Spirit through total consecration of our spirits to His Spirit. We need to clean out unconfessed sin and yield every part of our inner being to Him. We need to "thirst" after the Spirit, and, finally, we need to accept Him into our lives by "drinking" deeply of the Holy Spirit.[5] This teaching led, perhaps unwittingly at times, to a quest for a spiritual experience of the higher life that was almost mystical. How do I know when I have yielded enough to receive the Spirit? How do I know when I am thirsty enough? How do I know when I have drunk deeply of Him? Such a mystical passive experience of receiving or drinking deeply is not what Paul describes in Romans 8:13-14.

Paul does not even mention the "filling of the Spirit" in these important verses regarding sanctification, not because it is not important, but because he is describing the same experience in a different way. Being led by the Spirit is the same as being filled with the Spirit. Far from a passive mystical experience, it is simply the process of obeying what the Spirit tells us. We can be led no other way than through obedience to Him who leads. We are commanded

---

[4] Ruth Paxson, <u>Called Unto Holiness</u>, Moody Press, 1936, p. 70.
[5] Paxson, p. 95.

to be filled with the Spirit which means it is our responsibility to be filled. We are to obey the Spirit of God, and that is how we are filled on a moment by moment basis. We are being led by the Spirit as we are obeying the Spirit. John Owen wrote:

> He doth not so work our mortification in us as not to keep it still an act of our obedience. The Holy Ghost works in us and upon us, as we are fit to be wrought in and upon; that is, so as to preserve our own liberty and free obedience. He works upon our understandings, wills, consciences, and affections, agreeably to their own natures; he works in us and with us, not against us or without us; so that his assistance is an encouragement as to the facilitating of the work, and no occasion of neglect as to the work itself.[6]

How do I know I am led by the Spirit of God? I am continuously killing my sinful habits by His power. I am choosing to obey Him. A biblical principle is to starve the wrong feelings and feed the right ones. Cut out of your life the wrong activities and habits. Be brutal about it, if you have to, but cut it out. Then fill your life with the good and righteous things of God. We become slaves of what we give ourselves to serve. The Spirit helps us kill the old habits and create new habits, but the process of forming habits is an ongoing daily process of making choices.

Years ago we visited Rome with our girls and two other families. We walked around the ruins of a great civilization on a very hot day. We admired the glory of what once was the greatest city in our western world. Rome was once the most powerful nation on earth, but she fell from the inside out. Now only the symbols of past glory remain to remind us of her power. The same is true for us spiritually. We too can fall from the inside out, destroyed by our own

---

[6] John Owen, "Works," 6:20, cited by MacArthur, "Mortification of Sin," p. 19.

lusts. I read the stories in the Bible and I am struck by how often our great heroes of the faith fell into sin later in life. David, Solomon, Uzziah, Hezekiah, and Josiah – to name but a few of the kings – all started well and did much good for God but failed in the second halves of their lives. The warning is important for all of us. We are all, no matter how high we climb for God, capable of the worst sins imaginable because the flesh lives on in each of us. None of us are exempt from the fall if we give in to the sin within. We must always remain on alert and seek to obey the Spirit's leading by killing the sinful habits that can develop in our lives. We must all work with the Spirit to put into practice new habits throughout our lives or we too can fall from within.

On April 20, 2010, the Macondo well in the Gulf of Mexico exploded and sank to the bottom of the ocean killing 11 of the 126 workers on the oil platform and causing an oil spill that took 87 days to get under control. The oil spill was an environmental and economic disaster of epic proportions for the entire Gulf Coast region. A joint task force of the Bureau of Energy Management, Regulation and Enforcement and the Coast Guard released their 500 page report in the fall of 2011 detailing the problems they had found. They concluded that British Petroleum took many shortcuts because they were weeks behind schedule and tens of millions of dollars over budget. The Deepwater Horizon drilling rig failed because of weak cement at the base of the 18,000 foot well. The cement casing failed to contain the oil and gas which led to human and mechanical failures causing the giant eruption and resulting explosion. "The loss of life at the Macondo site on April 10, 2010, and the subsequent pollution of the Gulf of Mexico through the summer of 2010 were the result of poor risk management, last-minute changes to plans, failure to observe and respond to critical indicators, inadequate well control response and insufficient emergency bridge response training by companies and individuals responsible for drilling at the Macondo well and for the operation of the Deepwater Horizon," the report concluded.[7]

The reason for failure in our spiritual lives is the same. If we take shortcuts in our spiritual lives, we will face disaster. If we don't prepare by getting the proper training in God's Word, we will face spiritual disaster. If we are not vigilant and alert to the warning signs of sin, we will face spiritual disaster. If we do not take the flesh seriously so as to maintain healthy risk management procedures in our lives, we will face spiritual disaster. If we minimize the power of sin in our lives and pretend that we can overcome anything, we will face spiritual disaster. We need to take spiritual threats seriously if we are to be victorious in our lives.

---

[7] John Broder, "BP Shortcuts Led to Gulf Oil Spill, Report Says," The New York Times, September 14, 2011.

19
ABUNDANT LIFE IN THE SPIRIT

Romans 8:15-17

15 For you have not received a spirit of slavery leading to fear again, but you have received a spirit of adoption as sons by which we cry out, "Abba! Father!" 16 The Spirit Himself testifies with our spirit that we are children of God, 17 and if children, heirs also, heirs of God and fellow heirs with Christ, if indeed we suffer with Him so that we may also be glorified with Him.

Shawn waited patiently to talk with me between sessions at one of the seminars I was teaching in Ireland. He introduced himself, and we made arrangements to talk together at lunch. I would guess that Shawn was around 50 with a pleasant smile and a solid knowledge of God's Word that he had demonstrated in our sessions. Shawn told me his story. He was married and his children were now mostly grown up. Years earlier he had responded to God's call on his life and went to a Bible school with plans to serve as a missionary. He and his wife raised their support and left Ireland for a church planting ministry in another country. They had served for many years with great success. The church grew both in numbers and quality. He proved to be a very effective evangelist and pastor. Then the ministry began to unravel. Sin infiltrated the church and the ripple effects undermined his ministry. The more he tried to deal with issues the worse it got. He said that for years he seemed to have the "Midas" touch in ministry. Every decision he made worked out great. Suddenly he lost that "Midas" touch. It seemed like everything he did was wrong. He went from a rousing success in ministry to total failure almost overnight. Conflict developed both in the church and with his agency back home, so he left the mission field and returned with his family to Ireland. He was a failure. His financial support quickly dried up, and he was left trying to support his family in a bad economy. There were few jobs that he was qualified to do in Ireland, and the jobs he could get didn't pay enough to support his family. The government would pay him more money not to work, but, since his family needed the money, he took the government income. He was allowed to work a couple of days a week as an apprentice, so he had apprenticed himself to a stone mason. He was frustrated. He had ministry skills and biblical training, but nobody wanted him. He felt like a complete failure in his Christian life. He wondered, "Has God abandoned me? Am I doomed to be a "second class citizen of the kingdom" for the rest of my life?" It was bad enough that other Christians viewed him as a failure, but he felt like God considered him a failure too. He knew that his spiritual life had crashed in the pit of discouragement, and he didn't know where to turn. He wasn't even sure about his faith anymore.

As Christians we need a sense of security – assurance – after all, it is tough to face a life time of struggle with sin and suffering if we have no assurance of God's acceptance. It is discouraging to face our failures in service without assurance that God accepts us, and we are not doomed to be "second class citizens" forever. Paul continues in Romans 8:15-17 to give us God's assurance. *Life in the Spirit brings assurance of salvation.* Have you ever doubted your salvation? I have. Have you ever struggled with failure and the despair that God might cast you away because of your sin? King David felt the same way. If this is to be a life long struggle, what sustains us in the fight? How do we keep going in life? Paul has just said in verse 14 that all who are being led by the Spirit of God are the sons of God. Now he teaches us that our sonship guarantees eternal life.

ADOPTION: THE CRY OF A CHILD

The first principle Paul lays out in verse 15 is that *our spirit cries out in our need.* The very fact that you cry out to God in your time of need is the first proof of your salvation. Like a father with his little child, God's heart is turned by our cries. God does not ignore your cries for help. He hears and He cares. You can trust His heart even if you can't understand His plan. Sometimes God has to strip us of our false security so that we will trust Him for our true security. Sometimes God has to humble us through failure in order to teach us to walk dependently on Him. But always, God is at work to draw us to Himself and to embrace us with His love like a father with His little son.

Verse 15 has been understood in several ways over the years. Some have said that the "spirit of slavery" or "bondage" is our human spirit, but the "spirit of adoption" is the Holy Spirit. Others have tried to make both refer to the Holy Spirit by adding some explanatory ideas to the text. The best way to understand it is the way the New American Standard Bible translates it. The translators use the small "s" for both "spirits." This is our human attitude or disposition. The verse contains a parallelism. If one is the human spirit then the other must be too, and, since the Holy Spirit is never a spirit of slavery, then He is not the spirit of adoption either. He is the Spirit of freedom for where the Spirit is there is liberty Paul tells us in 2 Corinthians 3:17. The spirit of slavery and the spirit of adoption are two opposite responses, feelings or attitudes that humans experience. Shawn felt the spirit of slavery very deeply and he needed to feel the spirit of adoption once again. When we experience the spirit of slavery we fall into fear – fear that God has abandoned us or rejected us. We are enslaved to the fears of defeat.

However we need to feel the spirit of adoption as sons adopted by a Father who loves us. We need to cry out to God as little children when we are defeated so we can once again feel His love lifting us up.

This is the subjective side of our assurance. Our feelings, our inner attitudes, our spirits testify to our salvation. There is a mystical side to Christianity. It is a feeling side, an emotional side and it is very important. We don't want to reduce Christianity to merely a set of rational propositions. Christianity is a relationship with God, and relationships between two people involve feelings. The first witness to our salvation is how we feel toward God when we are in trouble. Paul tells us that we have not received a spirit of slavery or bondage. This is not how God works with us. Religions may induce feelings of bondage. Legalism breeds feelings of slavery, and that leads to fear. The word means "panic" or "dread." Many Christians relate to God in a sort of panic mode. When they sin they feel like God is done with them. He will cast them aside for their sins. The message of God according to the legalist is that when I mess up God says I must pay up! So I am doomed. I will pay big time for my failure. The result is that the Christian runs away from God for fear that God will make him pay for what he has done. "I feel guilty. God must be mad at me so I will stay away from God."

But this feeling did not come from God, Paul tells us. We have received a spirit of adoption, not of slavery. This is something that has already happened to us as Christians. God gave us a spirit of adoption when we became Christians. Adoption was a Roman legal term. Biological children were little more than slaves until they were officially adopted in a legal process that conferred the full rights of sonship on the child. Adoption meant the child was a full heir to all the father had and was legally a son. Paul tells us that as Christians we are both children of God and sons of God. We are legally heirs of God. We have the spirit of adoption in our souls. This spirit of adoption leads to our cry of "Abba, Father." The word "Abba" is an Aramaic term that was used by small children. It was term of endearment sort of like our "papa" or "daddy." "Father" was the

Greek word that spoke of a more formal relationship, a legal relationship. We are both little children and legal sons of God.

Thomas Goodwin, a Puritan preacher, says that this verse pictures a father with his little son walking hand in hand down a forest path. The child might feel afraid and cry out, "daddy" and hold out his arms to his father. The father picks him up and embraces him in love. The child was no less the child of God when he was walking and he is no more the child of God when God hugs him but the hug brings reassurance of his relationship. So it is with us. Our cries produce God's hugs.[1] But what if that child lets go of his father's hand and runs into the woods. He disobeys his father, and then he feels afraid. He is still no less a child of the father, but now he fears his father's rebuke. So he does not cry out for help because of his fear. This child does not feel the hugs of God because of the spirit of slavery that has overwhelmed him. Or perhaps we become like a toddler going through separation anxiety from his mother who simultaneously wants the hug of the babysitter while pushing away that embrace. We feel terrified that God has abandoned us so we cry out to God. We reach out for his embrace only to push it away when it comes because we feel conflicted. Our sense of unworthiness leads us to push away God's hug of reassurance. We don't receive what He has given to us so we continue in a spirit of slavery to our panic. What happens when our own feelings of worthlessness hinder us from receiving God's hugs of reassurance, love and intimacy?

Dan Allender is a Christian counselor who has spent his life helping victims of sexual abuse recover from the trauma of deeply wounded hearts that cannot accept intimacy with God or with others. He writes: "The abused woman has plenty of reasons to despise her own passion. Hating her longings (for intimacy) starts a self-annihilating civil war that kills the soul." The abuse produces in the victim deep shame and contempt so that the victim of abuse cannot

---

[1] D. M. Lloyd-Jones, <u>Romans: The Sons of God, An Exposition of Chapter 8:5-17</u>, Zondervan Publishing House, 1974, p. 280.

accept even the love of God. He says that the real enemy is neither her longings nor the abuser, but sin in her own heart that is keeping her from intimacy with God.

> The enemy is the internal reality that will not cry out to God in humble, broken dependence. It is the victim's subtle or blatant determination to make life work on her own by refusing to acknowledge or let God fulfill her deepest longings. The enemy is the same for the abused person as it is for those who have not been sexually abused: a determined, reliable inclination to pursue false gods, to find life apart from dynamic, moment-by-moment relationship with the Lord of life.[2]

Allender tells the story of an abused friend who hated herself "for being uncomfortable in the presence of people (especially men)." He asked this friend what she would do if his 9 year old daughter pulled away from her when she tried to love her. Would his friend ignore the little girl's rejection and pursue her in love? If she saw the little girl cry would she be angry with her or would she hold her and love her tenderly? His friend responded that, of course, she would love the little girl and would never treat her with anger like that. She would love her tenderly. He then pointed out that she was that little girl, and God wanted to love her. It was a breakthrough in her life as she wept over her own sin of contempt for herself and rejection of God. She learned to accept the love of God and, after that, the love of others. Allender says that abuse victims need to repent not of anything they did wrong in the original situation but of their choice to live in contempt for themselves and to reject God's love for them.[3] He writes: "Repentance is a process that ... awakens

---

[2] Dan B. Allender, <u>The Wounded Heart: Hope for Adult Victims of Childhood Sexual Abuse</u>, Navpress, revised edition, 1995, p. 59.
[3] Allender, pp. 225-226.

266

our hunger for our Father's embrace and deepens our awareness of His kind involvement."[4]

Abuse victims have been horribly traumatized in ways that many of us have not, but the process of restoration is the same for all of us. The key here is the word "receive." We received the spirit of adoption when we trusted Christ, but, sadly, we often return to the spirit of slavery bringing fear to our souls. We must cry out to God to receive the spirit of adoption. This is a subjective matter. If you are running away from God, then you will feel empty. You will not feel God's hugs because the spirit of bondage has gripped you. God is waiting to love you, but you are not ready to receive that love because of your guilt and your fear. This is the way it is in any relationship. You must be ready to receive love if you are to feel loved. God wants you to know that all you have to do is cry out "daddy," and He will reach out to hug you, but as long as you refuse to receive His love, you will never feel his hug. The first step in assurance is to cry out to God in our need.

ADOPTION: ASSURANCE OF HIS LOVE

When we cry out to God in our need it brings us to God's response in verse 16. *His Spirit assures of His love.* This is the Holy Spirit. The Holy Spirit joins with our human spirit to witness to our salvation. The verb means "to witness together with" our spirits. The two witnesses go hand in hand. Our human spirit witnesses to our relationship when we cry out "daddy." The verb "cries out" in verse 15 means to scream or shriek for help. When we cry out for help we feel God's hugs, and God's hugs are His witness to go along with our cry. This too is a subjective experience. It is a mystical element of our faith. Reassurance, when we are afraid, is not so much a rational thing as an emotional thing. Paul is still talking about our feelings as children of God, and how those feelings can reassure us of God's love. We signal our readiness to receive God's love by crying out for

---

[4] Allender, pp. 232-233.

help. God responds by reassuring us with His love. There are two sides to any love relationship. It is wonderful to tell someone you love them, but it is even more wonderful to be told by that person that he or she loves you. This is the heart cry of every lover. It is the need of every little child. To feel love for someone is great. To feel loved by someone is even greater.

Let us return to Thomas Goodwin's illustration of the father and the son. When the child holds out his arms and says, "Daddy" he is speaking his love for the father. When his father picks him up and hugs him he is feeling the father's love. Thomas Goodwin said, the first aspect is verse 15 and the second is verse 16. In verse 15, we tell God that we love him. In verse 16, God tells us that He loves us. In verse 15, we reach out our arms to hug God. In verse 16, God reaches down to hug us. He doesn't say, "That is silly. Why do you need reassurance from me? You shouldn't need to be reassured. Look at all I do for you." God doesn't tell us, "I'm too busy doing good things for you or I don't feel like hugging you right now." No God hugs us anyway whenever we signal our need to receive His love. God is always ready to respond in love when we cry out in need.

Erwin Lutzer tells the story of Mary who was outgoing, beautiful and successful. She was a committed Christian, and nobody in church would have ever suspected the emotions she experienced underneath the Christian mask she wore. Mary struggled with feelings of bitterness and resentment that led her at times to even contemplate suicide. She had it all, so it seemed, but inside her life was in constant despair. She prayed much to God for deliverance, but she remained in emotional bondage. Mary had grown up with a stepfather who treated her harshly. Whenever Mary, who was 3 or 4 years old at the time, would come to him for affection he would push her away. He told her, "I'd like to throw you out! You should be pushed into a ditch." Mary grew up with that deep sense of rejection, and it resulted in contempt for herself. She could not believe that any man could truly love her. She was worthless. She did get married to a decent husband but settled for duty rather than love in her marriage.

They had 4 children together and 20 years of marriage when she came to Erwin Lutzer for counsel. She felt worthless and rejected despite her beauty and success. Lutzer knew that just telling her she was wrong about her feelings would never help her accept herself. She had to learn to accept God's love and see herself through God's eyes to feel whole again, and that would take time. It is the same with all of us who have been hurt or fail in life. We may fail at a job or ministry. We may fail in marriage. It may take years to overcome our feelings of failure, but there is hope in God. We have to accept how God made us; see ourselves in God's eyes and receive His love despite our failures. We can be free from the slavery of self-contempt.[5]

I have had people say to me, "You don't understand what I have done. I am like the little boy who has run off into the woods and disobeyed his father. I have sinned. I have failed. God will never accept me. I'll just keep the walls up and stay in my own little world of fear and loss because God could never want me now." Here is God's truth. You do not understand the first thing about God if that is your spirit. You have the spirit of bondage not the spirit of adoption. God waits in true love to embrace you. God waits with open arms to hug you. You are His child. You are not defined by your failure. You are not the sum of your sin. You are who you are – a normal Christian. You are not perfect. The battle rages inside of you and you sometimes lose the battle. You must accept yourself in Christ. I do not say you should accept the sin but you must accept yourself as a person who sins. You must accept yourself as a Christian who fails, but you are loved by God. You are not perfect and you never will be short of heaven. You may be dirty and shattered by sin but He loves you. You may be marked by failure but He wants you. He waits for you to accept His hug. He pursues you in love until you accept His embrace.

David Seamands tells this moving story in his book, *Redeeming the Past*. John Everingham was a journalist working in Laos in August

---

[5] Erwin W. Lutzer, Failure: The Back Door to Success, Moody Press, 1975, p. 70.

1977. He was expelled by the communists, but he was engaged to be married to a Laotian young lady named Keo Sirisomhone. He had to leave the country without her and for 10 months he worked on rescuing Keo. On May 27, 1978 he set out to rescue his bride. John used scuba gear to swim through the Mekong River that separated Laos from Thailand, and he carried gear for his bride. The waters were so muddy that he could not see so he was equipped with a compass attached to his facemask. The current was so powerful that he had to grope along the muddy bottom to make progress. He surfaced only to find that he was hundreds of feet from shore and being carried downstream fast. He could see Keo, disguised as a fishing woman on the shore, but he could not get to her. Exhausted he swam back to Thailand. He tried again later, but this time entered the river farther upstream to compensate for the current. He made it to the shore and as he crawled up on the bank he could see Keo walking away in despair. He yelled as loud as he could yell, and she turned to see him. She came running to him and they embraced in the mud. Keo could not swim so he gave her a life vest and put a regulator in her mouth from the oxygen tank. He bound them together with a quick-release strap and swam out into the river. Swimming hard for both them, he finally made it to Thailand and safety. The story illustrates the love of our Lord. He goes to incredible effort to love us who are helpless to achieve victory by ourselves.[6]

ADOPTION: THE SEAL OF SECURITY

Our spirit cries out in our need. His Spirit assures us of His love and *God's promise seals our security* (v. 17). God tells us in this verse, that since we have testified to the reality of our relationship with God by crying out for help, and since we have received the love of God as He witnesses to us that He wants us forever, then we know that we

---

[6] David A. Seamands, Redeeming the Past: Recovering from the Memories that Cause our Pain, Victor Books, 2002, pp. 47-48.

are God's children. We know we have been adopted. We feel reassurance as we receive His love by His Spirit with our spirits. Now we understand that God's promise is for us. We are heirs of God the Father and joint heirs with Christ the son. We inherit all that God has for us in Jesus Christ. We can now risk our lives, our hopes, and our dreams for Him even as we struggle in this life because we know He has already guaranteed our future with Him.

God promises an inheritance that is being kept in heaven for us until we get there. The Apostle Peter writes that we were born again: "to an inheritance which is imperishable and undefiled and will not fade away, reserved in heaven for you, who are protected by the power of God through faith for a salvation ready to be revealed in the last time." (1 Peter 1:4-5) Here is God's guarantee. He wants us so bad that He adopts us into His family by the blood of Christ. He cleans us up and makes us whole. He gives us hope and reassures us with His hugs. God guarantees that we have an inheritance that is reserved for us in heaven. We are protected by Almighty God for a salvation that will be completed when we receive our inheritance.

This too is the work of the Holy Spirit. The Apostle Paul tells us in Ephesians 1:13-14 that: "having also believed, you were sealed in Him with the Holy Spirit of promise, who is given as a pledge of our inheritance, with a view to the redemption of God's own possession" (that is us!). Later Paul exhorts us in Ephesians 4:30, "Do not grieve the Holy Spirit of God, by whom you were sealed for the day of redemption." We can grieve and hurt the Holy Spirit but we cannot lose the Holy Spirit. We can bring God tears but we cannot lose God's love. We can fail God but His promise will never fail us. We are sealed by the Spirit for the day of redemption. God never gives up on us. This is God's promise to us and this promise seals our security. God guarantees our destiny.

Yet, Romans 8 brings us back to reality at the end of the verse. We must suffer with Him in order to experience the glory with Him. Just as Jesus experienced suffering first and cried out in His agony, "Abba Father, if it is your will let this cup pass from me" and only afterwards experienced the glory, so we must suffer and cry out in our own pain if we are to fully experience the joy of His great reward. It is certainly true that we do not face the troubles that Christians in other parts of the world face or that our forefathers in the faith faced, but we still face trouble, and it is through those troubles that God shapes our lives for eternity. Some time ago I read Elisabeth Elliot's book, *A Path Through Suffering*, and she made this comment.

> We may well wonder how our particular kind of trouble (especially trivial ones) can in any sense be said to be for Christ's sake. We are not in prison for speaking the truth. We are not persecuted for our faith. … Yet it seems to me that having something we don't want or wanting something we don't have, no matter how insignificant, is like learning the scales on the piano. They're a far cry from a fugue, but you can't play the fugue if you haven't mastered the scales. Our Heavenly Father sets the lessons suited to our progress. All are of His grace.[7]

I was 11 when war broke out between India and Pakistan in August of 1965 when Pakistan attempted to take the disputed state of Kashmir by force. The Pakistani commandoes who infiltrated the region were Special Forces trained at military camps in Murree not far from Murree Christian School, where I attended. The Indian army responded quickly with a major offensive against the state of Punjab in central Pakistan leading to the largest tank battles since World War II. Pakistan had a much smaller military but defended itself very well against the much more powerful Indian military. The heroes for Pakistan were the small contingent of Air Force pilots flying American jets who fought back very effectively while outnumbered two to one. The war did not last long. The United

---

[7] Elisabeth Elliot, <u>A Path through Suffering: Discovering the Relationship Between God's Mercy and our Pain</u>, Servant Publications, 1990, p. 106.

States and Great Britain moved to cut off arms supplies to both India and Pakistan which brought about a cease fire on September 22. The decision to cut off arms supplies to Pakistan with its much smaller military resulted in significant anti-American sentiment for not supporting the country in its dispute with India.[8]

Dad was in Lahore, hundreds of miles south of Murree, the day war broke out. He rushed to catch the last north bound train leaving the station before all traffic was halted. The police yelled for him to stop, but he ignored their cries and jumped on the moving train to get back to the family. My youngest sister, Dorothy, was less than a month old, having been born in Abbottabad just before Dad made his trip south to Lahore, and he was determined to get back to Mom. My parents stayed in Murree along with the other missionaries until the cease fire was signed.

The missionaries had a tough choice to make once the cease fire was signed. It was past time to leave the children in boarding school and return to the mission stations in the south. My brother had joined me in boarding school and my parents knew they would be 600 miles away from us with little chance of getting back if war broke out again. The decision was to trust God for the children in boarding school and return to the work in the Sindh. The trip to Sindh in the aftermath of war was a tension filled trip. Dad took the back roads down from the mountains to avoid the main highways near the war zones, stopping at police checkpoints along the way. All the way they prayed for the safety of their three children traveling with them and the safety of the two they had left behind.

Murree Christian School was located just outside of Murree near a little village called Jhika Gali. The road from Murree passed Kashmir Point and wound through the mountains past the school on its way to Muzzaffarabad and the border with Kashmir only a short distance through the mountains. I can remember convoys of soldiers

---

[8] For additional explanation and similar experiences see Jonathan Addleton, Some Far and Distant Place: Muslim-Christian encounters through the eyes of a child, University of Georgia Press, 1997, pp. 118-119.

passing by the school shooting guns in the air to flex their military muscles. Air Force jets regularly flew overhead as they patrolled the skies. Windows were blacked out at night so no light would shine through and we were not allowed to wander off site at any time. Every child maintained an evacuation kit. These were small bags that contained our passports, some cans of fruit, clean underwear, and toiletry items like toothpaste and soap. They were regularly inspected by staff to make sure we were ready in case the American Embassy called for an evacuation. The entire school would evacuate through the mountains into Afghanistan making our way to Kabul. A charter plane would fly us from Kabul to either Beirut or Tehran – both considered safe havens in those days! Our parents, meanwhile would evacuate south through Karachi and the families would be reunited in Beirut or Tehran. The evacuation never became necessary but the choice that my parents and other missionary parents made was a difficult faith choice. These were exciting days for me as an 11-year-old boy watching the sounds of battle all around me but they had to be agonizing times for my parents.

What motivates Christians to risk the security of their children to carry out God's call to missionary work? They were heirs of the king of heaven and earth. Our final destination is not affected by what happens to us along the way. Our security in Him allows us to risk our lives on earth. My parents were not famous. They were just like many other missionary parents who had to make tough choices in order to fulfill God's call. They were normal Christians who invested their lives for eternity. I think there are many normal Christians all over this world that we do not even realize are doing amazing things for God. Normal Christians are living out the values of heaven on earth, and heaven is where we will one day find out what normal Christians have been doing for Him throughout history.

The Roman emperor, Hadrian, built a cylindrical tomb for his ashes and the ashes of his wife. The mausoleum was later used for several other Roman emperors. Then it was used as prison and finally as a castle to defend the city from enemies. Today it is part of the Vatican property and attached to St. Peter's Basilica by a fortified hall. It is also known as the Castel Sant'Angelo because it celebrates the legend about the angel Michael sheathing his sword to end the plague of A.D. 590. The Popes also used Sant'Angelo as a prison. On top of the castle is the statue of Michael the Archangel sheathing his sword as the symbol of the one who protects God's people. Of course, no statue or castle can defend us, but God can and does. Our security comes from His Spirit living inside of us. Run to God in your time of need. He will love you and protect you as His child.

Sanctification is a process of growth in Christ. We will not achieve perfection in this life, but we can progressively grow in holiness throughout life. Whenever we struggle and fail, we can turn to the Lord for forgiveness and experience the confirming work of the Spirit collaborating with our spirits to let us know His love and grace. We can run into His arms and find love any time the struggle becomes overwhelming. The process of change is never easy and never over. We cannot emphasize that truth enough. The normal Christian life is a life of change as we grow to be like Christ. It involves our daily choice to trust God with our love. Dan Allender raises a fundamental question we all must ask as we wrestle with sin in our striving for holiness; experience the hurts of sinful people, and face the discouragement of failure as we progress through life.

> The question is this: Do I believe that God is a loving Father who is committed to my deepest well-being, that He has the right to use everything that is me for whatever purposes He deems best, and that surrendering my will and my life entirely to Him will bring me the deepest joy and fulfillment I can know this side of heaven?[9]

---

[9] Allender, p. 191.

LIFE IN THE SOUK

The air was oppressively hot although it was nearing midnight as we walked into the Djemaa-El-Fnaa (Central Square) at Marrakech in Morocco. The place was alive with people and little stalls selling many items. This was the cool time of the day in a city where temperatures regularly reach 120 degrees so people nap during the day and shop at night. A festival was going on which made the square even livelier than normal. We wound our way through henna artists, palm readers, dancers, tea stalls and crude tables spread with various delicacies sampling a few on the way. We were headed toward the famous Souk of Marrakech, a labyrinth of shops reached through narrow old stone streets and covered with canopies for shade during the day. As we plunged into one of the streets, my nose was assaulted with pungent odors, and my eyes were mesmerized by the colorful sights. Vendors called out for our attention. You can buy most anything you want inside this souk, and you can get lost in the winding streets faster than I could say, "Where am I." I was glad for my guide through the maze that night.

We were looking for the shop of a Christian leatherworker. We found him, and, after the warm hugs and introductions were completed, we sat down for some tea and fellowship. The shop was tiny – maybe 10 feet by 15 feet at best. It was filled with various leather goods for sale. A circular stair went up to a room above the store. This was where the young man lived as well as worked. It was stifling even at midnight. I purchased some beautiful leather Bible covers from the man, and he shared his life with me. It was a hard life for a Christian. He was open about his faith which meant that many Moroccans wouldn't buy anything in his store even though the workmanship was exquisite, but he would not let that hinder his witness for Christ. He pointed to a large picture behind him. The cultural law of the land was that each shop owner had to display a picture of King Hassan II who was nearing the end of his reign at that time. This was expected by his world, but he did not display a picture of King Hassan II behind his work bench. He displayed a picture of Jesus. He explained to me that Jesus was his king. He was heir to all that Jesus owned. He was a child of the king. He wanted everyone who entered his little shop to see who he followed in life. His eyes twinkled with life and his laugh was infectious. Joy filled his life though he had little of this world's comforts to enjoy. Reluctantly we took our leave from this man whose ordinary life was filled with the joy of Jesus. I will never forget his laugh. I had come to Morocco to help others but I left inspired by the abundant life I witnessed in this simple brother from the souk in Marrakech – a normal Christian who lived as a child of the king, transformed by adoption.

We live in the souk of this world as heirs of the new world!

EPILOGUE SUMMARY

Our church is a normal church. We are not too big, but we are not small either. I have served as the teaching pastor of our church for nearly a quarter century, as I write these words. Together we have seen our share of successes and struggled with our share of failures. Together we have seen people come and go. We have cried together and laughed together, worked together and walked together, prayed together and sang together. They have stood with me in my failures as I have stood with them in their struggles. We have eaten more church suppers together then I can remember. We have shared 24 Christmas Eve candlelight services and 24 Easter celebrations together. If you were to visit our church on any given Sunday you would consider us to be a normal church filled with normal Christians doing normal things.

I was overwhelmed by God's grace as I stood with our congregation singing His praises in worship one Sunday morning. It happens to me from time to time. I sit and stand with the congregation rather than on the platform until it is time to preach. I have always done that over the years, and I love worshiping with our church in this way. As I looked around that Sunday, I was overwhelmed by God's grace. I know the "back stories" of many of those who gather each week. We are not a mega church so I know the tragedies and triumphs of those around me. I see the widows who suffer through the loneliness that never ends. I see the husbands who tenderly care for their wives with minds shuttered by Alzheimer's. I see the wives who patiently care for husbands incapacitated by Parkinson's. I see the weariness of one struggling with cancer and the tears of parents whose child has succumbed to drugs … again. I see the victims of abuse long past but always near and the hurting marriages struggling to survive. I also see the once broken marriages rebuilt by His grace. I see those who struggle with pornography, and those who have gained victory over it. I see the woman who once struggled with constant guilt transformed into an exquisite expression of joy. I see the man who once wrestled with materialism generously giving to God's work. I see the broken hearts mended and the proud hearts humbled. They are normal Christians just like me and I love them. Sometimes I am overwhelmed by God's grace as I see all these people lifting their hearts and voices together in praise to Him. It is the true worship of normal Christians at once flawed, yet flawless, by the grace of God.

WHAT IS A NORMAL CHRISTIAN?

THINKING STRAIGHT ABOUT HOLINESS

1. A normal Christian believes that he is no longer the person he was before Christ (Romans 6:1-7).

2. A normal Christian counts on the fact that he is a new person in Christ who has been freed from sin (Romans 6:8-11).

3. A normal Christian knows that he must fight sin so that he does not become enslaved again by sin (Romans 6:12-14).
4. A normal Christian understands that he has been freed from sin to be a slave to righteousness (Romans 6:15-19).

5. A normal Christian recognizes that sin always pays the wages of death (Romans 6:20-23).

WILLING OURSELVES TO HOLINESS

6. A normal Christian realizes he will always fail whenever he uses rules to control human nature (Romans 7:1-6).

7. A normal Christian sees that the purpose of the law is to show us our sin (Romans 7:7-13).

8. A normal Christian grasps that the new person he is in Christ cannot control his human nature (Romans 7:14-20).

9. A normal Christian accepts the reality that the battle with the flesh always rages inside him throughout life (Romans 7:21-25).

LIVING IN THE SPIRIT

10. A normal Christian rejoices that God condemned sin in the flesh so that he no longer stands condemned for sin in life (Romans 8:1-4).

11. A normal Christian chooses daily to practice the habits of the Spirit instead of the habits of the flesh (Romans 8:5-8).

12. A normal Christian depends on the life of the Spirit to develop the habits of the Spirit (Romans 8:9-11).

13. A normal Christian uses the power of the Spirit to execute the habits of the flesh in the practice of daily life (Romans 8:12-14).

14. A normal Christian runs to the Father whenever he fails to receive the reassuring love that never fails (Romans 8:15-17).

A normal Christian is a spiritual orphan transformed by adoption into the Father's family.

Made in the USA
Charleston, SC
03 July 2014